Negotiating NAFTA

Explaining the Outcome in Culture, Textiles, Autos, and Pharmaceuticals

MARYSE ROBERT

UNIVERSITY OF TORONTO PRESS
Toronto Buffalo London

© University of Toronto Press Incorporated 2000
Toronto Buffalo London

Printed in Canada

ISBN: 0-8020-4348-8 (cloth)
ISBN: 0-8020-8170-3 (paper)

Printed on acid-free paper

Canadian Cataloguing in Publication Data

Robert, Maryse
Negotiating NAFTA: explaining the outcome in culture, textiles, autos,
and pharmaceuticals

Includes bibliographical references and index.
ISBN 0-8020-4348-8 (bound)   ISBN 0-8020-8170-3 (pbk.)

1. Canada. Treaties, etc. 1992 Oct. 7.   2. Free trade – North America.
3. Canada – Commercial policy.   I. Title.

HF1746.R62 2000   382'.917   C00-930486-X

University of Toronto Press acknowledges the financial assistance to
its publishing program of the Canada Council for the Arts and
the Ontario Arts Council.

University of Toronto Press acknowledges the financial support
for its publishing activities of the Government of Canada through
the Book Publishing Industry Development Program (BPIDP).

NEGOTIATING NAFTA

International negotiations have become an important feature of the world trading system, but very few scholars have attempted to analyse this process. Using case studies in four areas – culture, textiles and apparel, autos, and pharmaceuticals – negotiated in the North American Free Trade Agreement (NAFTA), Maryse Robert uses a theoretical framework to help explain the outcome of such negotiations in terms of structure and process. Structure is made up of the resources a state brings to the table in a given issue area. Process, in contrast, refers to the state's behaviour as expressed by its tactics during negotiation. The key message of this book is that it is the right mix of resources and tactics that determines the outcome of negotiation.

Among the questions the author raises are: What counts as winning and losing in a given issue area? What are a state's resources in a trade negotiation? Are all resources equally important? Is the utility of some tactics linked to certain resources? Robert presents a cogent analysis of the structure and tactics of Canada, the United States, and Mexico in the four areas being considered, and provides fascinating insights into the negotiations that led to NAFTA.

MARYSE ROBERT is a senior trade specialist in the Trade Unit of the Organization of American States.

Contents

Preface

The publication of this book ends a long journey, which began in August 1992 when I first started doing research on the North American Free Trade Agreement (NAFTA). Canada, the United States, and Mexico built on the success of the Canada–U.S. Free Trade Agreement (FTA) to negotiate between 12 June 1991 and 12 August 1992 a free trade agreement that has laid the foundation for a stronger, more competitive North American economy. NAFTA has improved access for goods, services, and investment within a market of over 360 million consumers. It provides a rules-based framework on which trade among the three partner countries can grow.

Since its inception, NAFTA has been the subject of numerous books and studies, conferences, seminars, and workshops. Scholars, journalists, representatives of the business community, and members of non-governmental organizations have either provided an overall economic assessment of the agreement or expressed their views on the substance and implications of this deal. This book takes a different approach. It is a first attempt at proposing a framework to help explain trade negotiations and the process by which outcomes are reached in these negotiations. The book focuses on the objectives of the negotiators and on their resources and tactics during the NAFTA negotiations. Four sectors are analysed here: culture, textiles and apparel, autos, and pharmaceuticals.

I wrote this volume while completing my doctoral studies at

the Fletcher School of Law and Diplomacy (Tufts University) in 1993–4. George H. Mitchell, Jr, now of Howard University, deserves my deepest thanks. He, along with Jeswald Salacuse and Alan K. Henrikson, guided my research. I am also extremely grateful to the many individuals who have offered suggestions and useful comments after reading the manuscript. Other people and organizations have also been very generous. First, and foremost, I am indebted to the NAFTA negotiators and members of their private sector advisory groups with whom I conducted over 100 interviews on a not-for-attribution basis in the autumn of 1993 and spring of 1994. Librarians at the Fletcher School, Harvard University, at the Department of Foreign Affairs and International Trade in Ottawa, and at the Canadian embassies in Washington, DC, and Mexico City were a precious resource. A special note of thanks is also due to Virgil Duff and the staff of the University of Toronto Press for their assistance and patience in facilitating the publication of this book. I also want to acknowledge the financial support of the Social Sciences and Humanities Research Council of Canada and the Fondation Desjardins.

Last, but not least, I wish to extend my sincere thanks to my family, in particular to my parents, to whom I dedicate this book, and to my colleagues at the Organization of American States for their support and encouragement. I also want to stress that the views expressed in this book are my own and should not be attributed to the Fletcher School or to the Organization of American States and its member states. The responsibility for any errors or omissions lies with the author.

PART ONE

Theory and History

CHAPTER ONE

Explaining Negotiation Outcomes

International negotiations are an increasingly important fixture of the world trading system. Economic reforms recently implemented by developing countries have led to a substantial increase in the number of free trade agreements negotiated at the bilateral and regional levels. Issues ranging from tariffs and non-tariff barriers to services, intellectual property, investment, and dispute settlement are now covered by these agreements. Markets are, in fact, becoming more integrated throughout the world. As Gilbert Winham observes, 'Nations are negotiating more and more today, but they are doing so less and less to resolve conflicts. The focus instead is on the management of economic interdependence.'[1] In North America, where the economies of Canada and Mexico are closely linked to the U.S. market, continental integration has taken place in several phases. Corporate strategies, government policies, and sectoral agreements such as the Auto Pact of 1965 between the United States and Canada have enabled producers to rationalize their operations and become more efficient. In the recent past, the North American Free Trade Agreement (NAFTA), the first comprehensive free trade agreement ever negotiated between developed countries and a developing nation, has also been fostering closer economic ties among the three partners since it entered into force on 1 January 1994.

Students of international relations have long attempted to explain outcomes in asymmetrical negotiations. How do countries with fewer resources such as Canada and Mexico 'win' in negotiations with countries, such as the United States, that have more such resources? The usual answer has been that aggregate structural power – a state's total resources vis-à-vis the rest of the world – explains little about the power structure in given issue areas. Frederick Frey mentions that 'there are as many power structures as there are issues fruitfully distinguished.'[2] Therefore the key variable is not aggregate structural power but issue-specific power – an actor's resources in different issue areas. According to this approach, as a country's resources vary from one area to another, negotiation outcomes will also vary in the same direction. If a state has more resources than its negotiating counterpart in one area, it will 'win' in that area, even if overall it has fewer resources.

However, scholars have noted that issue-specific power *alone* is not sufficient to explain outcomes.[3] David Baldwin summarizes their views: 'failure to translate "potential power" (or power "resources") into actual power [outcomes] may be explained in terms of malfunctioning conversion processes.' The negotiator 'is described as lacking in skill and/or the "will" to use his power resources effectively.'[4] Yet skilful tactics *alone* are also not sufficient to explain outcomes. William Mark Habeeb emphasizes that it is the state's behaviour, as revealed by its tactics and the process by which it uses its resources, that causes outcomes.[5] Tactics must be combined with power resources in order to produce a 'win.'

Although trade negotiations have become a major feature of international economic relations, negotiation theorists have traditionally focused their attention on Cold War–era issues – arms control and nuclear weapons – and on the Middle East. Very few scholars have sought to analyse trade negotiations or, more specifically, asymmetrical trade negotiations such as NAFTA, which embraces a geographical area with an annual gross domestic product (GDP) totalling over U.S.$6 trillion, 85 per cent of which comes from one country, the United States.

This book is an attempt at proposing a theoretical framework to help explain trade negotiations, using as cases four areas – culture, textiles and apparel, the automotive sector, and pharmaceuticals – discussed in the NAFTA negotiations. The key question that this book is concerned with is how to explain negotiation outcomes. We can divide this central idea into five questions:

- What counts as winning and as losing in a negotiation?
- How does one define 'resources' in a trade negotiation? What are the resources available to a negotiator? Are some more valuable than others?
- What tactics can produce a 'win'? Is the utility of some tactics linked to some resources?
- How does one take advantage of contextual factors?
- Are there any 'linkages' among issues in a trade negotiation?

Before part II analyses the four cases, this chapter examines in greater detail the theoretical turning points that have led scholars to identify the determinants of negotiation outcomes. Following this brief review of the literature, the chapter explains the main argument of the book, the methodology, and the case selection. Chapter 2 describes how NAFTA came into being by providing a historical perspective on how the idea of a free trade agreement in a North American context has evolved over the years. It also presents a broader perspective on the structure and the process of the negotiations leading to NAFTA.

Part II (chapters 3–7) deals with the four cases – culture, textiles and apparel, the automotive sector, and pharmaceuticals. It considers each in terms of objectives, outcomes, structure – resources (industry and government) and issue-specific power – and process, or tactics. The conclusion summarizes the findings from the case studies, points to implications for negotiation theory, and draws lessons for policy-makers.

STRUCTURE: POWER AND RESOURCES

Defining Power

To explain 'negotiation outcomes' between power asymmetric countries, a number of writers have first sought a definition of 'power.' However, defining 'power' has proven difficult. 'We may say about it ... what St. Augustine said about time, that we all know perfectly well what it is – until someone asks us.'[6] Baldwin mentions that power has been defined as a causation by several authors, including Herbert Simon, James March, Robert Dahl, and Jack Nagel.[7] As Nagel writes, 'A power relation ... is an actual or potential causal relation between the preferences of an actor regarding an outcome and the outcome itself,' while Habeeb notes that 'a causal definition of power focuses attention on the process of change, and the end result of change (the outcome).'[8] William Zartman warns that 'to be complete an explanation must not merely correlate effects or assert a causative relation, but also must, in its chosen terms, tell what it is in one element that causes another.' Power will be present in a negotiation when one actor causes another to move towards his or her positions.[9]

The causal conception of power has been found attractive because it implies an asymmetrical relationship. Some actors have more power than others. Causality also helps reduce 'the danger of tautology.' It recognizes that 'power must be stated in an empirical hypothesis' which can be tested and verified.[10] However, to say that power is a causation does not really define it. It does not say anything about how power causes outcomes. Harold Lasswell and Abraham Kaplan, Harold and Margaret Sprout, Dahl, Nagel, and Baldwin have all argued in effect that 'it is *essential* to specify or at least imply who is influencing whom with respect to what; in short, both scope and domain must be specified or implied.'[11]

Resources as Power

Political thinkers from Thucydides and Aristotle to Niccolò Machiavelli and Thomas Hobbes, and from the drafters of the U.S. constitution to Karl Marx and Friedrich Engels, have explained power in terms of resources. Their main hypothesis has been 'that the greater one's resources, the greater one's power' and, by extension, the more favourable one's negotiation outcomes.[12] Stressing military capabilities, Hans J. Morgenthau and the realist school refer to power as the overall resources of the state vis-à-vis the rest of the world.[13] 'Power is said to be a multidimensional phenomenon with both military and nonmilitary components.'[14]

Influenced by the bipolar domination of the U.S.–Soviet relationship in the post-war era, most studies of international negotiation have traditionally examined cases, which focus on symmetry of power between two actors – i.e., cases in which power resources are equal.[15] The work of Fred Iklé, published in the mid-1960s, is one such example.[16] Powerful states also have a predominant place in Arthur Lall's book of the same period on international negotiation.[17] Lall suggests that the position of the more powerful state will prevail. The realist view presupposes that 'powerful states make the rules.' Robert Keohane and Joseph Nye quote Thucydides, who wrote: 'The strong do what they can and the weak suffer what they must.'[18] Keohane and Nye also note that 'linkages [will be] drawn by powerful states through the use or threat of force.' In fact, this approach 'predicts a strong tendency toward congruence of outcomes among issue areas. When outcomes on one issue area are markedly different from those on others, we should expect shifts.' The stronger state will try to make outcomes 'in the deviant issue area more consistent with the world structure of military and economic power.'[19] Dale Dean and John Vasquez point out that the realist paradigm 'maintains that all issues in the system can be treated as if there were only one unidimensional issue in the system – the struggle for war and peace.'[20]

Some realist theorists have created frameworks for codifying the elements of national power. Ray Cline, for instance, has devised a formula for measuring aggregate structural power. It allows for economic capability, military capability, strategic purpose, and will to pursue national strategy.[21] However, the realist view of power has been challenged by many scholars. Baldwin notes that aggregate structural power so often fails to achieve expected results that it deserves a label, 'the paradox of unrealized power.'[22] Habeeb observes that the fact 'that the weak actor often gets much of what it wants ... cannot simply be ascribed to failure of will on the part of the strong.'[23] Raymond Aron, Annette Baker Fox, and Erling Bjøl have all argued that a small state may achieve its preferred outcome when negotiating with a larger and more powerful country. According to Aron, 'the small power sometimes takes the great where the latter would not have chosen to go.' Fox notes that small states can concentrate their energies on one issue while large states must focus on the whole system. Bjøl indicates that a small state can exercise its power simply by resisting a strong state.[24]

Zartman has found that 'the aggregate power position of a state cannot be directly translated into [successful negotiations]. Powerful states may turn out to be weak in a given [negotiation]' with smaller and weaker states.[25] Baldwin goes further: 'The notion of a single overall international power structure unrelated to any particular issue area is based on a concept of power that is virtually meaningless.'[26] By not taking into account the scope and domain of power, says Baldwin, realist theorists are suggesting 'either highly fungible resources or a single dominant issue-area,'[27] when in fact, as Charles Lockhart emphasizes, 'national resources must create options that are useful within the context of the specific encounters a nation faces.'[28]

Issue-Specific Power and Power Resources

Lasswell and Kaplan and Harold and Margaret Sprout were among the first to postulate that substantial power resources in one area may be totally useless in another.[29] Dahl concurred: 'The possibility cannot be ruled out that individuals or groups who are relatively powerful with respect to one kind of activity may be relatively weak with respect to other activities.' Contrary to the view held by realist theorists, 'power need not be general; it may be specialized.'[30] The concept of issue-specific power – the state's resources with regard to one individual matter – comes from the paradigm of interdependence put forward by Keohane and Nye. They argue that 'within each issue area one posits ... that stronger states ... will dominate weaker ones and determine the rules of the game.' Keohane and Nye stress that, 'unlike the overall structure explanation, issue structuralism does not predict congruence of power across issues.' Its basic premise 'is that power resources in one issue area lose some or all their effectiveness when applied to others.' Resources do not transfer easily.[31]

Issue structuralists find that force is rarely an option. Linkages reliant on force or coercion are thus ineffective. In fact, a basic assumption of issue-specific power is that 'although states may be tempted to draw linkages among issues, such linkages will be generally unsuccessful.'[32] Keohane and Nye, Kal Holsti and Thomas Allen Levy, as well as Allan Gotlieb, all point out that there are few linkages in Canadian–American relations.[33] In a book on transnational and transgovernmental relations between the two countries, edited by Annette Baker Fox, Alfred Hero, and Joseph Nye, an analysis of different issue areas shows that Canada was successful in some, even if it had fewer overall resources.[34] After having examined a half-century of bilateral relations (1920s–1970s), Keohane and Nye reached the same conclusion.[35] Gotlieb writes that Canadians have 'sensed that if linkage ever became the rule of conduct, the bigger power could always out-link the smaller.'[36] However, to the extent that issues become linked, the explanatory value of issue-specific power decreases, since, according to Keohane and Nye, 'outcomes in particular issue areas will no longer be accounted for simply by ... resources in those areas.'[37]

Both the realist school and the issue-specific approach have something in common. They argue that the negotiation outcome is explained by power resources. This hypothesis points to a serious problem. As Baldwin wonders, how are we to identify and distinguish power resources when we see them? 'It is difficult to imagine what is excluded, since almost anything could be used to influence someone to do something in some situation or another.'[38] Some authors have tried to define issue-specific power. Habeeb's description, for instance, builds on two paradigms – that of interdependence, as developed by Keohane and Nye, and that of social exchange, put forward by Richard Emerson, John Thibault, and Harold Kelley.[39] For Habeeb, issue-specific power derives from the power structure of a relationship. Actors are dependent on each other; 'each can unilaterally withhold agreement, prolong the process, or even end it.'[40] However, there are costs involved if the relationship is broken. Kenneth Waltz maintains that two parties 'are interdependent if the costs of breaking their relations or of reducing their exchanges are about equal for both of them.'[41] In fact, a state will develop an interdependent relationship with another when the costs of *not* doing so are too great, which is not to say that each actor will incur the same costs. Keohane and Nye stress that the actor who is more dependent will find it more costly to leave the relationship.[42]

Borrowing from Emerson and the social exchange theory, Habeeb constructs issue-specific power from three variables: alternatives, commitment, and control. These variables are to issue-specific power 'what material resources are to aggregate structural [power].'[43] Each can compensate for another. For instance, a strong commitment or greater control can compensate for lack of alternatives. First, alternatives increase the leverage of a state and its chances of achieving its preferred outcome. This factor is crucial for a negotiator at the 'security point' – i.e., the point at which he or she would favour deadlock over negotiation. Second, and in contrast, commitment can be either a positive or a negative resource. Greater commitment leads to greater dedication in realizing preferred outcomes, while greater need for a specific outcome becomes a liability, giving leverage to the other party. Finally, control, which Habeeb calls the single most important variable, is 'the degree to which an actor can achieve its objective unilaterally (i.e., outside the negotiation context).'[44] However, this definition of control does not really distinguish between 'having alternatives' and 'having control.' If an actor can achieve his or her objectives unilaterally without negotiating, it is obviously because he or she has alternatives.

The Fungibility of Power Resources

Several authors have shown that power resources are not sufficient to explain the outcomes of negotiations. Dahl writes that 'two individuals with access to ... the same resources may not exercise the same degree of power.'[45] Glen Snyder and Paul Diesing observe that the outcome may be different from what the power relations suggest.[46] How to solve this puzzle? Baldwin argues that the resources of the states involved in a negotiation may not have been estimated correctly. He also notes that it is wrong to assume that power resources are fungible.[47] Following the contextual analysis of power by Lasswell and Kaplan, Harold and Margaret Sprout, and Dahl, Baldwin indicates that political scientists have failed to place 'the capabilities (or potential power) of an actor ... in the context of a "policy-contingency framework" specifying who is trying (or might try) to get whom to do what.' Power-based predictions fail because political scientists assume that power resources are highly fungible, which they are not. Baldwin reminds us that 'political power resources ... tend to be much less liquid than economic resources.' Also, 'power resources ... in one policy-contingency framework may not only lose their effectiveness in another context; they may actually become liabilities rather than assets.' For Baldwin, 'power resources are situationally specific.' It is thus imperative to understand the context within which negotiators are operating.[48]

PROCESS: TACTICS

The Use of Tactics

Another explanation for the puzzle comes from the use of tactics in predicting outcomes. Keohane and Nye maintain that the concept of power resources or potential power 'provides a first approximation of initial bargaining advantages available to either side.' But resources are not enough to predict outcomes. When such predictions fail, the reason 'will often be found in the bargaining process that translates power resources into power over outcomes.'[49] Robert Bierstedt and Dennis Wrong also associate the notion of power with potential resources that can be used or not used.[50] Others have stressed that potential power is sometimes enough to influence outcomes.[51] Samuel Bacharach and Edward Lawler, for example, focus on the fact that 'a party with a substantial sanction potential or merely a reputation for power may have influence simply because others anticipate that party's wishes and act accordingly.'[52] For Dahl, 'A has power over B to the extent that he can get B to do something that he would not otherwise do.'[53] Power is thus not just a possession; it is also an *ability to use* in order to achieve preferred outcomes. Dahl, R. Harrison Wagner, and Henry Mintzberg have all pointed out that the English word 'power,' unlike its French equivalent, does not have a convenient verb form.[54] Mintzberg writes that the 'French word "pouvoir" stands for both the noun "power" and the verb "to be able." To have power is to be able to get desired things done, to effect outcomes.' It is, in the words of Bertrand Russell, 'the production of intended effects.'[55]

Some scholars view power in terms of tactics, patterns of interaction. Christer Jönsson observes that 'the exercise of power entails the conveyance of a message through some kind of signals, often a combination of verbal statements and non-verbal acts.'[56] Other scholars have also emphasized the role of tactics.[57] John Odell's analysis of bilateral trade negotiations between the United States and Latin American states confirms the value of strategies and tactics in predicting outcomes. He mentions, for example, that Latin American states would build alliances with domestic partners in the United States in order to influence outcomes.[58] Scholars such as François de Callières, Harold Nicolson, Snyder and Diesing, and Jeffrey Rubin and Bert Brown have focused on the personality of the negotiator.[59] As Habeeb points out, their approach to negotiation 'deal[s] more with the *characteristics* of the agent than with the *actions* of the agent.' Although the personality of an actor may explain his or her behaviour, including his or her choice of tactics, it does not say much about the negotiation process, while 'it is through process and action that power and power tactics are revealed.'[60]

Tactics *alone*, however, are not sufficient to explain negotiations' outcomes. Jönsson compares this situation to playing a poker game without knowing the rules: 'You may be a good bridge player or a good card player generally, but if you don't have the right cards and/or complete knowledge of the rules of poker – if that is the game you happen to be playing – it will not help you very much.'[61] Therefore the right combination of power resources and tactics is necessary to produce a 'win.' For Baldwin, bargaining skill – and, by extension, the use of tactics – constitute just another resource. Dahl also argues that 'skill could be treated as another resource.

Nonetheless, it is generally thought to be of critical importance.'[62] Both are right: bargaining skill and tactics could be treated as a resource, but one of a different kind. It is essential to be able to distinguish between structural and behavioural resources. The former are static, at least in the short run, while the latter are dynamic and movable throughout a process.

A Framework of Process

Negotiation is not static. It is a process in which power becomes a mode of interaction, a relation. To study negotiation is thus to develop a framework of process. As Habeeb explains, 'If each negotiation was characterized by a unique process, then the role of power could be analyzed only case by case; it would be difficult to reach any enduring theoretical conclusions.'[63] There are essentially two views of process in the negotiation literature. The first one, the offer–counteroffer approach, is based on concession/convergence theories: how each party reacts to the other's concessions. These theories of bargaining come from economics and focus on the concession rate of the parties: how parties make concessions and at what rate, how they respond to their opponent's concessions until the positions of the parties converge and an agreement is finally reached. Negotiators compare the costs and benefits of an agreement with their security point – i.e., the costs and benefits of no agreement. Among the main proponents of this view, Otomar Bartos argues that negotiators see the midpoint between each side's demands and offers as the solution.[64] The negotiation outcome is predictable if the bargainers' concession rates are known. John Cross writes that the strategies of each negotiator 'are contingent on each party's perception of the strategy of his opponent.'[65] Parties will modify their concession rate according to what they perceive or observe on the other side. As noted by Zartman, concession/convergence theories are in fact 'structural theories which indicate that the weaker party will concede until the tables are turned, at which point the other party will concede in its turn, and so on,' until the parties reach an agreement.[66] Some authors account for the notion of power simply by saying that the weaker party will concede at a faster rate. Others put the emphasis on the costs of holding out, and in so doing they imply that one party has power over its opponent if it can hold out longer.[67]

Although concession/convergence theories may provide a good indication of where parties 'will end up if they want to reach a mutually fair and maximizing outcome,' they are very deterministic and do not inform us about the negotiation process.[68] Zartman and Maureen Berman describe that process as having three phases – pre-negotiation, formula, and detail – while concession/convergence theories focus only on the third phase.[69] Daniel Druckman writes that a turning point will signal the passage from one phase to the next; impasse or crisis may, however, delay progress or lead to progress.[70] In the pre-negotiation, or diagnostic phase, parties are not negotiating; they are considering that option. Brian Tomlin identifies five stages in the pre-negotiation process. In the first, problem identification, 'an event or change in conditions ... prompts a reassessment of alternatives and adds negotiation to the range of options being considered.'[71] Second, there is a search for options to address this new issue. When negotiation is the preferred option, parties enter into a third stage, commitment to negotiation. Once one party communicates its decision to start negotiation, stage four begins – namely, agreement to negotiate. The final stage – setting the parameters – serves to set the agenda and define the issues that will be kept on and off the table. This stage may continue after formal talks have started and even throughout the entire course of the negotiations.

The second phase of the negotiation process involves developing a formula. Although negotiation has begun, there is no 'horse-trading' going on, no offer–counteroffer bargaining. The parties first exchange information and search for 'a shared perception or definition of the conflict that establishes terms of trade, the cognitive structure of referents for a solution, or an applicable criterion of justice.' In the third and final phase, parties bargain over details – offers and counteroffers – 'to implement the general framework set out in the previous phase.'[72] Negotiations end when at least one of the parties feels that the costs of continuing are higher than the costs of reaching an agreement.[73] Although the formula–detail approach suggested by Zartman and Berman is helpful and is used here to show how the parties move from pre-negotiation to a negotiated agreement, reality commands that this framework be very flexible, since the three phases may overlap.

COMBINING STRUCTURE AND PROCESS, RESOURCES AND TACTICS

This book combines structural and behavioural (process) conceptions of power. It is an attempt at exploring how the state's resources and tactics during the negotiation process helps explain the outcome and whether a party 'wins' in a given issue area. But how does one define 'winning' in a negotiation when, as Zartman observes, 'the nature of negotiation is to arrive at the largest mutually satisfactory agreement with any one (and therefore, each) getting at least enough to make it want to keep the agreement.' In fact, if parties reach and sign an agreement, it is 'a prima facie or nominal sign of success because it indicates a judgment by the parties that they expect to be better off with the agreement than without it, and that they can do no better by either continuing negotiations or choosing an alternative outcome.' One can, for instance, compare their positions before and after the deal.

This book evaluates negotiation outcomes by comparing the results of the NAFTA agreement in each issue area with the objectives of the party. It measures success against these objectives, not against the other parties. This type of evaluation obviously has limitations. Objectives may change, and policies may shift, during the negotiation process. Moreover, this measure does not indicate whether parties are in fact 'Pareto-optimally' better off – i.e., if the results have made at least one party better off without making another worse off.[74]

Although a few scholars have identified resources and tactics as determinants of negotiation outcome, some contend that tactics help determine outcomes by altering the issue–power balance: 'The process of negotiation involves moving from one issue-power balance (the prenegotiation balance) to another issue-power balance (the outcome balance) by the mutual practice of tactics.' Indeed, a negotiation's outcome becomes an asset, a future resource for the actor once the negotiation is over, but this conclusion does not imply that tactics have an indirect effect on a negotiation's outcome. Both resources and tactics are directed towards meeting the actor's objectives. But how to identify resources and tactics in a trade negotiation? As mentioned above, issue-specific power is defined as the state's resources in a given area. It centres on the power of a relationship between parties, which suggests that actors are dependent on each other.[75] An actor who has more resources will be less dependent than another who has fewer. We have already seen that it is also difficult to define resources. However, when analysing issue-specific power with respect to trade negotiations, one can identify a list of assets in an industry as resources for a state: its size and location; its share of the production and of the market; foreign control within it; its level of employment; and the importance of its trade with its counterpart(s) and access to its (their) and other markets. Other valuable assets in a negotiation are domestic laws, government intervention, and bilateral and international agreements.

All these resources may compensate one for another. For instance, greater protection from international agreements and from domestic laws help to reduce an actor's level of dependence. Moreover, the larger an industry and its share of production, the less dependent a state is vis-à-vis its counterpart in a negotiation. The larger the volume of trade between two actors, however, the more dependent they are on each other if there is no alternative market. Further, if the industry is also highly concentrated in one region and/or has a significant labour force, the state is even more dependent on it. Likewise, a high level of foreign control increases a state's dependence if these multinationals have headquarters in the country with which it is negotiating.

Although resources may compensate for one another, they do not necessarily have the same weight. In some situations, one resource may be more valuable than another. It is not just how many resources a state has that matters, but their significance. For example, an existing international agreement may have more weight in a negotiation than the overall share of production captured by a state's industry if it provides the negotiator with a strong fall-back position or the option to walk away from the table without jeopardizing his or her objectives.

Tactics – the other variable that explains negotiation outcomes – are defined as 'plans and means adopted in carrying out a scheme or achieving some ends.'[76] They are an actor's manoeuvres, tech-niques, and actions during negotiations. They serve to convey preferences and convince other parties. Tactics are aimed at ob-taining an actor's desired outcome. They have to be credible, be believable, and give leverage to the negotiator. The literature of-fers a long list of tactics available to the parties. In trade negotia-tions, however, some are more important than others. First, states have to take advantage of the fact that international negotiations are a two-level game by mobilizing public support and domestic groups for their objectives.[77] Trade negotiations are fashioned by the political and economic environment in which they take place. Today they are by definition two-dimensional. They encompass an international component and a domestic element. In addition to negotiating with its external partners, a state has to take into account the interests of the 'stakeholders' and use this to its ad-vantage. Involving them allows it to be firm at the negotiating table (i.e., to show commitment, by not moving if necessary) and to be taken seriously by its counterparts.

For example, industry consensus is a tactic that has proved to be vital. When an industry is divided, other parties are able to play one sector against another, which leaves a state without much leverage and a major political problem. Which side of the indus-try is a negotiator going to favour? But if an industry is protec-tionist and the government wants to liberalize this sector, the state may accept conditions that will lead to more openness. Building coalitions and alliances with another party or transnational ac-tors on a given issue also enhances the state's chance of achieving its preferred outcome in that sector.

Other tactics such as making concessions, manipulating dead-lines, and withholding signatures are more time-sensitive; if used at the appropriate moment, they can bring success. For instance, if negotiators have hammered out most differences, a party can increase its leverage by withholding its signature until the other parties address some of its demands. Pursuing alternatives is also a tactic that can affect outcomes. If no agreement is possible on a given issue, seeking other routes may allow all states to meet their objectives. A negotiator must also be ready to take advantage of contextual factors (such as domestic events) and use them to his or her benefit. Finally, tactics such as drafting the agreement (or being involved in the drafting process) help a state to exercise control over the process of negotiation.

Once a tactic has been selected, a negotiator must communicate it to the other parties. Good managerial and organizational skills, as well as solid technical expertise, can strengthen an actor's choice of tactics and thus increase his or her bargaining leverage. These skills also allow a negotiator to respond quickly to another party's tactics. As Winham mentions, countries 'should create a team that can handle large amounts of information, and can generate the additional information that is needed.' He adds: 'Once proposals are on the table, negotiators must be prepared to evaluate quickly and communicate effectively to their government the effects of position changes on the overall package.'[78] Negotiators must also be able to imagine themselves in their opponents' position, 'to see the situation as the other side sees it.'[79]

This book thus argues that negotiation outcome has two dimensions: structure and process. 'Structure' refers to the resources of the parties; 'process,' to the patterns of their interaction, or their tactics. An actor's resources and tactics during the three phases of the negotiation process help explain its outcomes. Neither factor alone can determine the outcome. A state that possesses more resources and uses stronger tactics over a given issue area is more likely to 'win' than one that has fewer resources and weaker tactics. An actor with the right mix of resources and tactics 'wins.' In multi-issue negotiations such as NAFTA, outstanding issues not resolved at the negotiating group level are also explained by the same approach. It is the actor's resources and tactics – for example, the commitment to achieving a particular objective – that determine the outcome at the level of chief negotiator or minister.

CASE SELECTION

Before examining the four cases in NAFTA, we should remind ourselves that we are measuring the concepts of 'winning' and 'losing' against the objectives of the state actors. Therefore these measures do not represent an assessment of the economic or welfare impact of the outcome in a particular sector.

Chapter 3 examines culture. In culture, the argument presented above suggests that, *a priori*, the Canadians' resources (especially the exemption included in the Canada–U.S. Free Trade Agreement, or FTA, which entered into force on 1 January 1989), if accompanied by strong tactics, should give them a 'win' in NAFTA.

In textiles and apparel (chapter 4), three factors – namely, Canada's lack of resources, i.e., the strict rules of origin negotiated in the FTA; the expiration (on 31 December 1992) of the FTA's tariff rate quota for non-wool fabrics and made-ups, allowing non-originating goods to enter the U.S. market duty free; and the industry's consensus in the United States and Mexico in favour of more restrictive rules of origin in NAFTA – should produce a 'loss' for Canada.

Chapter 5 considers the automotive sector. Canada 'won,' even though it appeared at the outset to lack issue-specific power – i.e., the resources necessary to 'win.' The U.S. Customs Service was challenging the interpretation of the FTA's rules of origin put forward by Honda and CAMI, which is a joint venture between General Motors and Suzuki, in their Canadian operations. Such a move raised questions as to the benefit for Japanese and other Asian carmakers of producing or assembling motor vehicles in Canada.

The *New York Times* reported on 17 June 1991, just a few days after the launching of the NAFTA negotiations, but well before the completion of the audit of Honda's North American operations, that U.S. Customs had found that the Honda Civics assembled in Alliston, Ontario, between 1 January 1989, and 31 March 1990, with engines manufactured in Ohio, did not satisfy the

FTA content requirement and thus did not qualify for duty-free treatment when entering the United States. Later, and after a series of rulings, Honda was asked to pay U.S.$17 million in duties.

Two of these rulings had a major impact on the overall decision of U.S. Customs. The 'intermediate material' ruling made a distinction between manufacturers that are vertically integrated and those that are not, whereas the FTA never intended to do so. The 'assembling/processing' ruling, in contrast, claimed that 'direct cost of processing' and 'direct cost of assembling' had distinctive meanings, even though Article 304 of the FTA states that they share the same definition. In the case of CAMI, the United States had made a unilateral decision in May 1991 to exclude non-mortgage interest from the 'direct cost of processing' formula of the FTA's rule-of-origin requirement.[80]

As mentioned above, although Canada appeared not to be protected by the FTA, it won in the auto sector in NAFTA. The *New York Times* wrote: 'The Canadians successfully insisted that the agreement [i.e., NAFTA] apply retroactively.'[81] In fact, the U.S. implementing legislation allows Honda to use the NAFTA rule of origin in order to determine if vehicles exported on or after 1 January 1989 are eligible for duty-free treatment. The Americans also acquiesced in Canada's demand to clarify both the rules of origin and the method used by U.S. Customs to calculate North American content.

Chapter 6 examines the case of the pharmaceutical industry, in which Canada appeared to possess both of the factors necessary to 'win' in NAFTA at the beginning of the negotiations. Canada's initial objective was to keep its compulsory licensing system, which allowed generic firms to apply for a licence to import (after 10 years of market exclusivity) or to manufacture (after 7 years of protection) pharmaceutical products in exchange for a royalty payment to the patent owner. In 1987, with Bill C-22, Canada had added an extra three years of protection for brand-name drugs without eliminating compulsory licensing. In the FTA negotiations, the U.S. administration did not succeed in convincing Brian Mulroney's Conservative government to reopen Bill C-22. Canada refused to abolish its special regime for pharmaceuticals.[82] But in NAFTA, Canada agreed to do so.[83]

Chapters 5 and 6 attempt to show whether these two cases – autos and pharmaceuticals – call into question the argument put forward in this book. In fact, by comparing the four cases, this book seeks to demonstrate that a small country with fewer over-all resources can win in negotiations on given issues if it has the right mix of resources and tactics – i.e., if it has *both* issue-specific power and strong tactics – but can lose if it lacks one or both of these factors. However, should it shift its policy during the nego-tiations, measuring a 'win' or a 'loss' against its initial objectives becomes much less meaningful.

Finally, the analysis of these four cases relies heavily on over 100 interviews with the NAFTA negotiators and members of the private sector who followed the negotiations very closely. They gave interviews in return for a promise of anonymity and confi-dentiality. Secondary sources also assisted in the reconstruction of the actual course of events. As Fen Osler Hampson and Michael Hart observe, this method may produce 'incomplete or inaccu-rate information.' They write that 'the historical case-study method ... has obvious limitations, which derive from the inherent limita-tions of circumstantial inference.'[84] Obviously, negotiators from all sides may not all share the same recollection of the same events. However, we have tried to minimize this risk by interviewing a number of people from all three countries involved in the NAFTA negotiations.

CHAPTER TWO

Towards a North American Free Trade Agreement

AN UNEASY PAST

When the *Wall Street Journal* reported on 27 March 1990 that representatives of Mexico and the United States had met secretly in February of the same year and agreed to negotiate a bilateral free trade agreement, this came as a surprise to most Mexico watchers.[1] Market-focused and outward-oriented reforms initiated by the Mexicans in mid-1985 had not gone unnoticed, and recent bilateral agreements aimed at improving trade between the two partners had fortified the relationship. But the decision to sign a free trade agreement with the United States meant that Mexico's economic relationship with its northern neighbour had entered a new phase.[2]

Since the Second World War, Mexican animosity towards the United States had focused on the domination of Mexico's trade and production by American interests.[3] The war marked the affirmation of a more protectionist Mexican economic policy. Like other Latin American countries, which sought to reduce their dependence on exports of primary products and imports of manufacturing goods, Mexico embraced the import-substitution model and turned inward. Tariffs and non-tariff barriers sheltered Mexican products from foreign competition. Import permits grew steadily, to cover 28 per cent of imports in 1956, 68 per cent in 1970, and virtually 100 per cent during the 1982 balance-of-payments crisis.[4]

This protectionist wall, along with investment incentives to the private sector, attracted U.S. foreign direct investment (FDI) across the border. The United States was Mexico's largest trading partner, accounting for at least 60 per cent of its exports and two-thirds of its imports. U.S. firms were also controlling major sectors of Mexico's production. For example, in 1972, approximately half of the 300 largest industrial firms were controlled by foreigners, and two-thirds of these were based in the United States.[5] Such a situation led to enactment in 1973 of the Law for the Promotion of Foreign Investment, which put a ceiling of 49 per cent on foreign participation in any Mexican company.

North American Economic Integration:
A Common Market for Energy?

Major oil discoveries in the 1970s allowed the Mexican government to increase its expenditures while becoming much more dependent on oil exports. It financed its fiscal deficit by external borrowing. In the United States, news of the oil discoveries and the effects of two oil crises convinced prominent Americans such as presidential candidates John Connally, a Republican, and Jerry Brown, a Democrat, to propose the establishment of a North American Common Market for energy. The Republican Ronald Reagan declared his candidacy in New York on 13 November 1979 by calling for a North American accord with Canada and Mexico on a much broader scale: 'I would be willing to invite each of our neighbors to send a special representative to our government to sit in on high level planning sessions with us, as partners, mutually concerned about the future of our Continent.' He then added: 'It is time we stop thinking of our nearest neighbors as foreigners.'[6] On 26 February 1980, the U.S. state governors adopted a resolution calling 'for a U.S.–Mexico–Canada council to serve as forum for developing policies for economic cooperation.'[7]

Both Canada and Mexico strongly opposed the proposed common market. During his visit to Ottawa in May 1980, Mexican President José López Portillo (1976–82) emphasized that his nation's 'energy resources would not be used to sustain the "very high standard of living" of others.'[8] Canadian Prime Minister Pierre Elliott Trudeau quickly added that a common market with the United States was not for Canada either. However, members of Canada's Progressive Conservative party, the official Opposition, expressed some interest in the idea of a regional common market. A Canadian journalist wrote in July 1980: 'The national president of the party is already talking about the desirability of a North American Common Market, and a former policy adviser to the party is promoting the concept of a "Treaty of North America" to formalize the extraordinary network of relations which already link the US and Canada, and to a lesser extent, Mexico.'[9] Although the idea of a North American accord seemed far-fetched, the Canadians were about to embark on bilateral free-trade negotiations with the United States.

THE FIRST STEP: THE CANADA–U.S. FREE TRADE AGREEMENT

The new Reagan administration opposed the energy policy of the Trudeau government, Canada's National Energy Program, and the extensive role of the Foreign Investment Review Agency. To try to reduce these irritants, in 1981 senior officials at the Canadian embassy in Washington held informal discussions with their counterparts in the Office of the U.S. Trade Representative about the possibility of broad sectoral free trade agreements. The talks did not succeed because of opposition from Canada's Department of Industry, Trade and Commerce (ITC). A year later, a major reorganization of the department resulted in the shift of the trade portfolio to the Department of External Affairs (DEA). The trade policy review initiated by ITC was completed by DEA in 1983. The report reaffirmed the multilateral trading system as Canada's main priority. It also mentioned the idea of pursuing sectoral free trade arrangements with the United States. In so doing, it confirmed the demise of the 'Third Option,' an unsuccessful attempt by the Trudeau government in the 1970s to diversify Canada's trade with other countries in order to become less dependent on the United States.[10] Canada had signed three sectoral agreements with the ments with the United States covering agricultural machinery, defence products, and automotive products. Although the Americans were more enthusiastic about a comprehensive free trade agreement, they initially went along with the Canadian proposal. But as the U.S. private sector showed little interest in this idea, the discussions went nowhere.[11]

The new government of Brian Mulroney, elected in September 1984, waited for the release of the report of the Royal Commission on the Economic Union and Development Prospects for Canada in September 1985 before announcing that it had decided to seek freer trade with the United States. Appointed by Prime Minister Trudeau in 1982 and chaired by a former Liberal minister, Donald Macdonald, the commission endorsed free trade between Canada and the United States. Earlier, in March 1985, at the Shamrock Summit held in Quebec City, Mulroney and President Reagan had instructed Trade Minister James Kelleher and U.S. Trade Representative William Brock to study ways to eliminate trade barriers between the two countries and to report in six months.[12] By August, Ottawa had decided to go ahead with the negotiations, and all the premiers, with the notable exception of Ontario's David Peterson, had expressed their support.

On 26 September 1985, Mulroney informed the House of Commons that he had asked Reagan 'to explore with Congress Canada's interest in pursuing [bilateral] negotiations to reduce tariffs and nontariff barriers.'[13] Two months later, on 10 December, Reagan formally notified Congress of his intention to negotiate a free trade agreement with Canada. Under the 'fast-track' procedure, Congress had sixty working days to reject the idea, which it didn't. Talks opened in Ottawa on 21 May 1986. Canada suspended them on 23 September 1987, when they broke off over subsidies and trade remedies. The negotiations resumed in early October and were completed on 3 October 1987. On 2 January 1988 Mulroney and Reagan signed the Canada–U.S. Free Trade Agreement (FTA), which entered into force on 1 January 1989.

The agreement marked a new beginning in the Canadian–U.S. economic relationship. It was an event of historic proportions for Canada. The country had toyed on several occasions since Confederation in 1867 with the idea of free trade with the United States.[14] Time had finally come for an agreement that would remove trade barriers in goods and reduce several impediments to trade in other areas such as services and investment. Canadian goods received free access to the U.S. market, and Canadian firms were able to benefit from much-needed economies of scale. But the agreement also meant that Canada had to become more competitive.[15]

Mexico Recovers from the Debt Crisis with Trade Liberalization

While Canada was busy negotiating a free trade agreement with the United States, Mexico was trying to recover from the 1982 debt crisis. Under Presidents Miguel de la Madrid (1982–8) and Carlos Salinas (1988–94), it undertook a series of reforms to liberalize trade, ease restrictions on foreign investment, rationalize public enterprises, liberalize and privatize the financial system, and deregulate some economic activities. Fiscal discipline and tight monetary policy, combined with a wage–price pact and a debt-restructuring deal – Mexico was the first beneficiary of the U.S. Brady Plan – helped lower inflation, restore confidence, and foster economic growth.[16]

On the trade front, Mexico was moving closer to the General Agreement on Tariffs and Trade (GATT) and finally joined in 1986. Maximum tariffs were lowered to 20 per cent, and import licences were eliminated on all but 20 per cent of imports. However, GATT membership could not eliminate peak import tariffs in the U.S. market or protectionist measures against Mexican exports. Prior to joining GATT, Mexico had signed a Subsidies and Countervailing Duties Understanding with the United States in 1985. This agreement provided Mexico with the injury test in U.S. countervailing duty cases in return for its eliminating export subsidies. In 1987, the two countries signed the Understanding Concerning a Framework of Principles and Procedures for Consultations Regarding Trade and Investment Relations. This agreement established a consultation mechanism to resolve trade disputes and identified subjects to be addressed in the bilateral relationship: agriculture, textiles, steel, electronics, intellectual property, investment, and technology transfer. As a result, in 1988 Mexico's access to the U.S. steel and textile markets increased, while import restrictions on U.S. beer and wine were relaxed.

Sectoral Agreements or Comprehensive Free Trade?

Mexico, in order to pay its external debt, which represented almost 22 per cent of total exports of goods and services in 1990, and to finance its economic development to absorb the one million young people entering the job market every year, needed economic growth through export markets and foreign investment.[17] Given its growing trade relationship with the United States, it had a clear incentive to try to liberalize trade further with its neighbour. However, because of deeply rooted mistrust towards the Americans, talk about free trade in Mexico was risky. Former U.S. Secretary of State Henry Kissinger told the Forum for the Americas conference, held in Washington, DC, in 1992: 'A few years ago, in the beginning of the Salinas term in Mexico, I spoke to one very highly placed official, and he was outlining some of the ideas that would dominate the new administration. And I said, "What about a free trade area?" "Don't ever mention that in Mexico," he said. "That will be perceived as exploitation by North America. We can go step by step. We can make sectoral agreements. But don't ever mention a free trade area if you don't want to damage all of us who believe in free trade."'[18]

Nevertheless, since the election of President Salinas, members of the Mexican private sector had been flirting with the idea of a closer relationship with both the Americans and the Canadians. The integration of Mexico into a North American common market was often mentioned. Salinas and Commerce Secretary Jaime Serra Puche, however, denied that Mexico had any such aspirations. The Salinas administration preferred bilateral sectoral agreements.[19]

In October 1989, during his testimony before the Senate Committee on Banking, Housing, and Urban Affairs, U.S. Secretary of

Commerce Robert A. Mosbacher was asked by Senator Bob Graham (Dem., Florida): 'Do you see, for instance, in the [case of] Mexico ... the development of a treaty analogous to the Canadian treaty?' Mosbacher responded: 'I do, and we've had some talks with our Mexican counterparts about this and they are cautious and I think we should not try to push them too fast, too hard. But they are interested, extremely interested, as we are, in moving toward this. But they want to take it a step at a time.'[20]

The first step was to sign, in October 1989, the Understanding Regarding Trade and Investment Facilitation Talks. This framework agreement mandated a series of bilateral negotiations between Mexico and the United States and complemented the 1987 agreement. The initial stage was to identify areas of mutual advantage and then decide whether to start negotiating.

The other element of the Mexican strategy was to attract foreign investment. This theme, along with trade, dominated Salinas's eight-day tour of Europe in late January and early February 1990. In Portugal, Britain, Germany, Belgium, and Switzerland, the message was the same: Mexico had changed and was open for business. But Salinas was worried that new opportunities in eastern Europe might divert European investment from the 'new Mexican' environment. Although European business leaders congratulated him on his country's achievements, they expressed little interest in investing in Mexico. At the World Economic Forum in Davos, a senior executive of a European automaker reportedly told Salinas that although he was amazed at how Mexico had put its house in order the Mexican market was too small for his firm to invest there. 'How many luxury cars could we sell in Mexico?' he asked the president. The senior executive then added that the prospect for an investment in Mexico would look much brighter should his firm be able thereby to serve the U.S. market.

A NEW BEGINNING: MEXICO'S DECISION
TO APPROACH THE UNITED STATES

The World Economic Forum in Davos marked a turning point in Mexican–U.S. relations. Salinas came to the conclusion that Mexico had to think in bigger terms and join a trade bloc. As reported later by Hermann von Bertrab, Mexico's co-ordinator for the NAFTA negotiations in Washington, DC, Salinas then asked Serra Puche: 'Jaime, what do you think about asking the United States to enter into a free trade agreement?' The next day in Davos, the minister approached U.S. Trade Representative Carla Hills, who suggested that they discuss the issue with President George Bush.[21] After an assessment by its economic cabinet, Mexico decided to approach the United States formally.

In an article published in the *Houston Chronicle* in January 1993, Mosbacher recalled how Serra Puche asked him to arrange a meeting in Washington with Carla Hills, Secretary of State James Baker, and National Security Advisor Brent Scowcroft. Mosbacher observed: 'When meeting time arrived, Serra was accompanied by President Salinas' chief of staff, José [María] Córdoba, a man of considerable strength. This was important. These talks could nominally have been carried on between the two nations' trade officials [but] by sending his own top aide, Salinas was laying his prestige on the line and expressing his personal commitment to an agreement.'[22]

The Bush administration was overwhelmingly supportive. In the 1988 presidential campaign, George Bush had suggested the possibility of a hemispheric trade area. None the less, his administration was divided over the issue. Bush, Mosbacher, and Baker, all from Texas, were enthusiastic, but Hills worried at first that these negotiations could jeopardize progress in the Uruguay Round of multilateral trade negotiations at GATT.

TAKING A STAND: CANADA ASKS TO JOIN IN

The Canadians, who already had a free trade agreement with the United States, were not included in these talks but were aware that Mexico was *very* interested in learning about their experience with free trade and the FTA. In December 1989, Salinas invited Brian Mulroney to Mexico City for an official visit as soon as possible. 'We have important things to discuss,' he told the Canadian prime minister. In January 1990, Mulroney sent one of his aides to

Mexico City to prepare his official visit. The Mexicans informed the aide that they wanted to talk about the FTA. On 22 and 23 January, the most senior Mexican cabinet secretaries attended the seventh meeting of the Canada–Mexico Joint Ministerial Committee in Ottawa.[23] This larger-than-usual participation took the Canadians by surprise. Shortly after, Córdoba told his Canadian counterparts that he wanted to make a 'discreet' two-day visit to Canada to meet those who had helped negotiate the FTA.

When Mulroney visited Mexico City in March 1990, he knew full well that the Mexicans had asked the United States to negotiate a bilateral free trade agreement. Derek Burney, Canada's ambassador to the United States and Mulroney's former chief of staff, had conveyed to the prime minister the information provided by Secretary Baker. Once in Mexico City, Mulroney met privately with Salinas at Los Pinos, the official residence of the Mexican president. They did not speak publicly about a free trade agreement between the two countries, but Mulroney alluded to the possibility of a trilateral agreement. On 17 March the news agency UPI reported: 'Canadian Prime Minister Brian Mulroney said ... he would not be surprised if a North American common market is established over the next decade ... "The policies of President Salinas lead me to conclude he is more and more interested in greater access to the North American market," Mulroney said. "Whether this emerges into a formal association with North America over the next decade I don't know, but I wouldn't be scandalized at the prospect," Mulroney said.'[24] Mulroney also made it clear that Canada would not allow itself to be hurt by a U.S.–Mexican bilateral agreement. 'We have no intention of being left out.'

During this visit, both countries signed 10 joint cooperation agreements including a Memorandum of Understanding Regarding the Framework for Trade and Investment Consultations, which provided for a dispute resolution mechanism, laid out an agenda for future discussion, and established working groups dealing with specific products.

Back in Canada, Trade Minister John Crosbie told the House of Commons on 19 March that Canada had no immediate plans to conclude a bilateral free trade agreement with Mexico or a trilateral agreement with the United States and Mexico. But when the *Wall Street Journal* broke the news on 27 March that Mexico and the United States had agreed to negotiate such an agreement, Canada had to take a stance and entered the first stage of the pre-negotiation process, as defined in chapter 1. External Affairs and International Trade Canada (EAITC) established a task force, headed by Robert Clark, later Canada's deputy chief negotiator in the NAFTA negotiations. The task force, composed of Clark and three staff members, reported directly to Deputy Trade Minister Donald Campbell. Its mandate was to review the implications of a Mexican–U.S. free trade agreement, thus opening the second stage of pre-negotiations for Canada.

After consulting with other departments, the task force presented its memorandum to Crosbie, who took it to the cabinet on 22 May 1990, with two options. The first called for a passive reaction – i.e., to follow developments. The second, recommended by the task force, required more active positioning. In fact, the task force urged the government 'to participate in exploratory discussions, without prejudice to any subsequent Canadian decision on whether to participate in the negotiations.'[25] The cabinet selected the second option and mandated the task force to prepare a more comprehensive report on the impact of a Mexican–U.S. free trade agreement on Canada.

Meanwhile, after the leak by U.S. officials to the *Wall Street Journal* reported on 27 March, the Mexicans were trying to play down the event and denied that any decision had been taken. They had hoped to build support for an agreement before it became public. Serra Puche declared that a working group was studying the impact of a free trade accord with the United States. On 17 April, Salinas called on the Mexican Senate to hold a national forum on trade relations with the world. A month later, on 21 May, the Senate recommended negotiation of a free trade agreement with the United States. It urged the president to focus on the United States but also to seek closer trade ties with Canada, Europe (especially Britain), Latin America, and the nations of the Pacific Basin.

In June 1990, Salinas travelled to Washington, DC, to meet with

President Bush. On 11 June, they announced that they had asked Hills and Serra Puche 'to undertake the consultations and pre-paratory work needed to initiate ... negotiations' on free trade and to report as soon as possible, but before December.[26] The Canadi-ans were kept informed. Bush had called Mulroney, and follow-ing the Washington meeting Serra Puche met with Crosbie in Montreal. On 8 August, Hills and Serra Puche recommended to Bush and Salinas that they begin formal negotiations on a com-prehensive free trade agreement.

The Canadians could no longer wait. They had to make a deci-sion. The task force had consulted the provinces, the business sec-tor, academe and labour. On 29 August 1990, the cabinet reviewed the four new options put forward by the task force: 'continue to monitor developments; seek observer status at bilateral Mexican–U.S. negotiations; negotiate a bilateral Canada–Mexico free trade agreement; or join Mexico and the United States in trilateral ne-gotiations.'[27] The task force favoured the fourth option. Academ-ics, Richard Lipsey among others, had warned that a bilateral agreement on free trade between the United States and Mexico 'would put the United States in a highly privileged position as the *only* country with free access to large, and growing North American markets.'[28] It was thus necessary to avoid the hub-and-spoke model, in which the United States would sign bilateral agreements with each country of the Americas and benefit from cumulative liberalization, including elimination of tariffs and non-tariff barriers. The United States would thereby have gained an additional advantage in attracting investors interested in the re-gion.

Because Canadian–Mexican trade was fairly modest, represent-ing less than half of one per cent of total Canadian imports in 1989, the Canadians were not really worried about their access to the Mexican market. They were concerned, however, about the impact of bilateral U.S.–Mexican free trade on their access to the U.S. market. According to economist Ronald Wonnacott: 'Whereas a bilateral US–Mexican agreement would not leave Canada fac-ing *tariff* discrimination in the US market, it might leave Canada facing *non-tariff* discrimination. This would occur if the Mexicans were able bilaterally to negotiate less restrictive quotas or some other more secure form of access to the United States than Canada now gets. Thus one of the specific reasons for Canada to wish to trilateralise the negotiations would be to ensure Canada receives at least as favourable treatment in the US market as does Mexico.'[29]

Therefore, in order to protect the gains made in the FTA, to remain an attractive location for foreign investment, and to take advantage of a growing Mexican market, the Canadian government announced on 24 September 1990 that it would seek to negotiate a trilateral free trade agreement with the United States and Mexico (the third stage of the pre-negotiation process for Canada).

Canada Has Some Convincing to Do

Following this announcement and until the formal decision on 5 February 1991 to initiate negotiations, the Canadians had some convincing to do. John Crosbie explained to his counterparts that while Canada had taken a long time before making its decision, that slowness should not convey lack of commitment. Rather, the federal government had to build a consensus with industry and the provinces. However, the Mexicans were worried. At first, they had been receptive to the idea of Canada's joining the talks, but the longer it took for Canada to make up its mind, the more reluctant they became. They wanted to secure ratification of the agreement before the 1992 U.S. election and saw Canada as a complicating factor.

The Canadians already had a free trade agreement with the United States and could therefore withdraw from the NAFTA negotiation with less penalty. So as to address the Mexican concerns about Canada's withdrawing, the three parties worked out the modalities of engagement and disengagement in a one-and-a-half-page agreement. It was understood that discussions would be structured in such a way as to make it possible for the other parties to continue the bilateral negotiation without losing the benefits negotiated under a trilateral arrangement. A country would withdraw in a manner that would not prejudice the prospects for success of the other two. A Canadian trade official observed: 'What the Mexicans wanted was assurances that they would not be left holding "a political bag," that they would have to turn back to their people and say: "The seventh largest economy in the world just walked away from the table but don't worry it is good for us." They did not want to be put in that kind of situation. Naturally, they asked for a sensible pre-understanding. Should Canada withdraw, it would do so in a low key manner.'

In fact, the Mexicans would have preferred that the Canadian experience in the FTA be available only to them in NAFTA. The Americans were also not thrilled at having to negotiate with Canada. Several U.S. agencies were advocating a bilateral approach. They were less preoccupied about the consequences of such a strategy for the trading system than about promoting free trade per se. However, U.S. Deputy Trade Representative Julius Katz, a seasoned negotiator, championed the inclusion of Canada. A few years later, he explained: 'Were the U.S. to embark on a policy of bilateral agreements, we would encourage others to do the same. What would result would be a greatly complicated trading system, with different schedules for phase-out of customs duties, different rules of origin, and different standards for investment and intellectual property. The benefits of free trade would be undermined by the increased complexity of the new structure of trade relationship.'[30]

Although Katz's arguments were very convincing and did prevail, the determining factor was undoubtedly the close relationship between Canada and the United States and their leaders. Once the concerns of both Mexico and the United States had been addressed with respect to potential Canadian withdrawal during the negotiations, it was almost impossible for the United States and the Bush administration to tell their closest ally that it was not welcomed at the NAFTA table.

There were nine groups set up to examine the issues to be dealt with in the trilateral negotiation. After several months of quiet meetings, the Mexicans organized a wrap-up session in Cancun. Reports from the nine groups and additional discussions finally led the three countries to announce on 5 February 1991 that they would begin talks on creating a North American free trade agreement (the fourth stage of the pre-negotiation process).

THE FAST-TRACK PROCEDURE

President Bush had notified Congress on 25 September 1990 of his intention to negotiate a free trade agreement with Mexico. Since Congress has authority over foreign commerce under the U.S. constitution, the Trade Act of 1974 engineered a mechanism to allow the executive branch to fashion trade deals without having Congress pick them apart piece by piece, thus necessitating renegotiation with foreign partners. The 'fast-track' authority gives the executive branch the leeway to negotiate a trade agreement, which Congress then accepts or rejects as a whole and without changes. Under the Trade Act of 1988, the president must inform the House Ways and Means Committee and the Senate Finance Committee of his or her intention to enter into a bilateral negotiation. Congress has then sixty working days to rebuff the executive branch. The chairman of the Senate Finance Committee, Lloyd Bentsen, another Texan, insisted that the administration notify the two committees separately for Mexico and for Canada, so that if a trilateral accord could not be achieved, bilateral talks could be pursued. Bentsen also wanted to set a precedent for future negotiations under the Enterprise for the Americas initiative. Congress was notified on 5 February in the case of Canada. On 23–24 May 1991, the House and Senate approved the request made on 1 March to renew for two years the fast-track negotiating authority. But in order to 'get the votes,' the administration had to put forward an Action Plan addressing Mexican–American environmental issues and to promise environmental organizations that their voice would be heard in the Office of the U.S. Trade Representative during the negotiations. This Action Plan, made public on 1 May 1991, helped gain the support of several law-makers for the renewal of the fast-track authority. A memorandum of understanding on workers' health and safety signed by Mexico and the United States also helped mobilize votes in the House and the Senate.

PRE-NEGOTIATION: THE FINAL STAGE

During the final stage of the pre-negotiation process, each party tried to shape the agenda of the negotiations. While Salinas had hinted in October 1990 that he would press for the free entry of Mexican workers across the U.S. border as part of the negotiations, his chief negotiator, Herminio Blanco Mendoza, told a conference sponsored by the Overseas Development Council in late October 1991 that workers' rights, immigration, and the environment were not topics for a free trade agreement. He also restated what his president had earlier said – that the basic tenets of the Mexican constitution were not negotiable. The constitution bars foreign ownership of border or coastal lands and prohibits foreign control of certain natural resources, including oil exploration and development. The Americans were pushing for a comprehensive agreement, including tariffs, non-tariff barriers, government procurement, investment, services, intellectual property, dispute settlement, safeguards, and rules of origin. The United States made it clear that *nothing* was off the table, except its immigration laws and ownership of the Mexican oil.

Once they had been formally invited to the table, the Canadians kept repeating that the FTA would not be reopened and that their cultural industries and the Auto Pact were off the table. One main result of the pre-negotiations was the need to have a 'rolling draft' during the negotiations. The experience of the FTA where there was no draft until the very end, had shown how complicated things could become in the absence of a draft.

NEGOTIATIONS

The Players

The three countries were finally ready to start negotiating. The talks were launched in Toronto on 12 June 1991 and ended at the Watergate Hotel in Washington, DC, on 12 August 1992, exactly fourteen months later. After the talks began in June, nineteen working groups, established under six major negotiating groups (market access, trade rules, services, investment, intellectual property, and dispute settlement), were set up. Each group had its own dynamic and was led by one negotiator for each country. The leading departments were the U.S. Trade Representative (USTR), the Mexican Ministry of Commerce and Industrial Development (SECOFI), and External Affairs and International Trade Canada (EAITC). Both the Americans and the Canadians relied on other departments and gave them responsibility for several groups (twelve in the case of the United States and ten for Canada). Both countries wanted to benefit from the expertise of these departments and to ensure that they would support the final agreement. The Mexicans assigned most of their leads to SECOFI. Chief negotiators – Julius Katz for the United States, Herminio Blanco Mendoza for Mexico, and John Weekes for Canada – met regularly to try to iron out difficult issues. Finally, seven ministerial meetings between Carla Hills, Jaime Serra Puche, and Michael Wilson[31] (who had replaced John Crosbie in April 1991) served to review the progress of the negotiations, so as to give some impetus to the talks and ultimately to resolve the toughest issues.

The private sector also played a major role in these negotiations. In Canada, business leaders were consulted through the International Trade Advisory Committee (ITAC) and the Sectoral Advisory Groups on International Trade (SAGIT), which had been conceived in the mid-1980s to advise the government on trade issues. ITAC had thirty-eight members representing mainly the private sector, but also labour and academe. It included the chairs of the fifteen SAGITs. In the United States, seven policy advisory committees, thirty technical, sectoral, and functional advisory committees, and the President's Advisory Committee for Trade Policy and Negotiations made sure that the interests of the business community were well-served. In Mexico, the private sector's input was channelled through the Co-ordinator of Foreign Trade Business Organizations (COECE), recently set up under Juan Gallardo.

Searching for a Formula

The negotiators spent the first few months sharing information and getting to know each other. On 19 September 1991, the parties exchanged their first tariff offers. After the third ministerial meeting, held in Zacatecas, Mexico, at the end of October, the talks entered a second phase, in which negotiators started drafting texts and searching for formulas. Earlier that month, at a meeting of chief negotiators at Meech Lake, near Ottawa, Weekes had suggested that each country table a paper explaining its position and exchange it with its counterparts by the end of November. These texts, in which several issues were not covered, were presented by the Americans on 21 November, the Mexicans on 2 December, and the Canadians on 4 December.[32] A small group of lawyers then organized the material and prepared a 'run-on' text. On the political front, Presidents Bush and Salinas held a meeting at Camp David, Maryland, on 13 and 14 December to help push the negotiations forward. The Mexican president declared that the two leaders ratified their political commitment to a free trade agreement, and soon. Mulroney was kept informed.

Working groups met at the Leavey Center at Georgetown University in Washington, DC, on 6–10 January 1992, to prepare a 'composite' text. A month later, on 9–10 February, at the fourth ministerial meeting, in Chantilly, Virginia, the three ministers examined the bracketed text. The Americans were complaining that the Mexicans were 'sitting on their hands' and were unwilling 'to discuss substantive matters.'[33] However, a Mexican negotiator commented that 'his country [had] comprehended that NAFTA would be based not on horse-trading over the removal of barriers but on a set of principles – a concept that Washington and Ottawa had endorsed from the beginning.'[34]

Approximately 400 negotiators gathered in Dallas, Texas, for a 'jamboree' plenary session on 17–21 February. In Chantilly, the ministers had asked their negotiators to concentrate in Dallas on areas that were close to resolution. During the Dallas session, however, frustration ran high in the American camp. The Mexicans were not moving significantly on any major issue. Finally, Katz told them that their 'tit-for-tat concessions' were unacceptable and that they would have to reduce their barriers by more than the United States and Canada would in order to get a deal. Being the most closed economy meant that Mexico had to open more; after the Mexicans acknowledged this reality, the negotiators got a boost.[35] The Dallas meeting was a turning point for several working groups searching for an appropriate formula. However, major roadblocks were still present in agriculture, autos, energy, and textiles, to name a few sectors. The Dallas Composite Text was leaked to the media in March 1992. The 400-page document showed that there was no chapter on autos and energy and that the text still contained 1,200 brackets.

In late March, Salinas talked to Bush and Mulroney. The Mexicans were worried that the talks were losing momentum. Salinas indicated that Mexico was willing to compromise to bring the negotiations to speedy resolution. Even though the talks were advancing, there were still some major disagreements. At the fifth ministerial meeting, in Montreal in April 1992, Wilson observed that progress had been achieved in many areas, including customs procedures, rules of origin, and safeguards and temporary entry for foreign workers. But a final agreement was still far away.

More advances took place at a meeting in Mexico City in late April and early May. Mexico signalled that it was willing to narrow 'the list of basic petrochemicals from which it [was banning] all foreign investor participation.'[36] In May, the three parties agreed to negotiate separate bilateral agreements on agriculture, with the Canadian–American provisions being those included in the FTA. Canada refused to accept in the NAFTA negotiations what it was later forced to approve in the Uruguay Round – i.e., changing into tariffs the quotas protecting its supply-management approach. The Canadians were also playing with the possibility of excluding apparel from a trilateral agreement but learned from their counterparts that they would also have to exclude the textile industry – a decision that would have been too costly (see chapter 4).

The End Game and the Packages

By June 1992, negotiations in several working groups were either completed or near completion, but major differences persisted in groups such as autos, energy, government procurement, investment, and textiles. The negotiators kept repeating that the negotiations were a single undertaking: 'Nothing is agreed until everything is agreed.' The meeting of Bush and Salinas at the All-Star baseball game in San Diego, California, in mid-July marked the beginning of the end of the negotiations. Bush declared to the press: 'We're in the ninth inning.' The Mexicans had just agreed to allow U.S. banks to set up branches in Mexico; to open all but fourteen petrochemical products to foreign investment; to accept performance contracts; and to open up the procurement of PEMEX and of the Federal Electricity Commission to U.S. and Canadian companies. The Americans had hoped to have an agreement by 1 July, but the Canadians were putting up a surprising degree of resistance in several areas. Just before the sixth ministerial meeting in Mexico City on 25–26 July, Wilson reaffirmed that the key issues in the FTA would not be reopened in NAFTA. Canada would walk away before weakening the FTA.

Beginning in late July and until the very end, the negotiators held the final round of talks at the Watergate Hotel in Washington, DC. For the Canadians, the main outstanding issues were their tariff-rate quota for wool apparel, rules of origin in textiles and apparel, regional content value for autos, cultural industries, government procurement, policies for screening foreign investment, and the dispute-settlement mechanism in anti-dumping and countervailing-duty cases. The Canadians clashed with the Americans over this last issue. The United States wanted 'to strengthen the existing extraordinary challenge procedures of [the FTA] by increasing the time available for review of panel decisions.'[37] The Canadians had argued in the case of fresh pork in 1991 that the provisions of the FTA's chapter 19 were meant to be used in specific circumstances – i.e., in cases of 'gross misconduct or conflict of interest, departure from a fundamental rule of procedure, or when the panel exceeds its authority or jurisdiction.'[38] To change that would mean to call 'into question the binding nature of the dispute settlement process.'[39] Moreover, the Canadians, who were later successful, strongly disagreed with the Americans about suspending any decision of a NAFTA panel and transferring the matter to a national court in cases involving subsidies and countervailing duties. Canadian sources mentioned that Canada interrupted negotiations for two days over this issue. The Americans, in contrast, say that Carla Hills was prepared 'to excuse the Canadians from the negotiations.'[40] Another issue of friction was energy. Since Mexico was refusing to agree not to treat U.S. buyers of Mexican oil and gas differently from its Mexican customers in the event of a shortage, Canada was trying to go back on its FTA commitment to the Americans. Moreover, the Canadians, who were playing a very defensive game in the beginning, became over time much more proactive. Hermann von Bertrab recalls that the main Canadian tactic during the end game was to wait for a deal to be about to be made in one area before 'seizing' the issue until Canada's concerns were addressed. This negotiating tactic, though quite effective, infuriated the Mexicans and the Americans, who were both eager to cut a deal – a bilateral one, if necessary.[41]

Formulas had been engineered for most working groups in the spring. But the 'detail phase,' which had begun at about the same time, was far from over. At the Watergate, negotiators tried to resolve the outstanding issues. The chief negotiators were trying to get rid of the battles and to look at the draft agreement in a broader context. As one trade official put it: 'The pressure forced people to begin to think in terms of packages. We would say: What do we have left here? Mexico wants this, Canada wants that and the U.S. want this. We would bring this out on a grid and then say: Why don't we all retire and think about this? People wanted to make sure that there was no extreme.'

Negotiators emphasized that there were no linkages in NAFTA but that there were packages. The chief negotiators and the three ministers, who provided guidance, reviewed the outstanding issues and eventually made the final decisions. They wanted a balanced agreement to accommodate the three parties. At the end, the ministers got together and made deals on specific issues within the context of the so-called packages. Commitment to a particular issue became a key factor. Countries had to 'prioritize' their objectives. The chief negotiators had tried all along to narrow down the number of issues referred to the ministers, because these issues, once moved to the political level, had nowhere else to go. Asked if they were satisfied with the agreement, several negotiators commented: 'We got the best agreement possible under the circumstances.' The U.S. chief negotiator kept reminding his colleagues that 'the perfect was the enemy of the good.' Some negotiators would have preferred to have had more time to debate some issues, but a deal had to be struck, and it was done in the early morning of 12 August 1992.

POST-NEGOTIATION PHASE

The senior legal counsel for each of the three countries remained in Washington for a few more weeks to review the text – the 'legal scrubbing' phase, which translates agreements struck in principle into legally binding language. In some cases, such as autos, there was virtually no text on 12 August. A comprehensive draft legal text was released on 8 September. A month later, on 7 October, another version was made public when Bush, Mulroney, and Salinas witnessed the initialling of the agreement by their trade ministers in San Antonio, Texas. A few changes were made to the text released on 17 December 1992, when each head of government signed the agreement, in his own capital. NAFTA was now ready for domestic approval.

Side Accords

In mid-March 1993, the three countries started negotiating side agreements on labour and the environment. The U.S. Democratic candidate Bill Clinton had promised during the 1992 U.S. presidential campaign that should he be elected president he would negotiate these accords. The pressure from labour, environmental groups, and key members of his party had convinced him that these accords were necessary. An agreement was reached between the three NAFTA partners on 13 August 1993. NAFTA was now ready for ratification.

Ratification: The Battle in Congress

On 25 February 1993, Michael Wilson tabled Bill C-115, the NAFTA-implementing legislation. On 23 June, Canada became the first country to ratify NAFTA, but royal assent was withheld until after the U.S. vote. In the United States, the battle proved difficult. Approval was less certain in the U.S. Congress than in Canada (parliamentary system) or Mexico (one-party domination at that time). U.S. opponents to NAFTA included Pat Buchanan, Ralph Nader, Ross Perot, labour, and some environmentalist groups, and a large number of Democrats, including House Majority Leader Richard Gephardt and House Whip David Bonior. More deals were needed to convince enough senators and representatives to vote for NAFTA. With the exception of culture, durum wheat, and NAFTA's Chapter 19 (review and dispute settlements in anti-dumping and countervailing duty matters), Canada was not the target of these opponents. It was Mexico, with its low wages and low-skilled labour, that was the focal point of NAFTA's opponents. While the Americans were debating NAFTA, Canadian business leaders tried to put more pressure on their neighbours by urging their government to negotiate a separate deal with Mexico should the United States reject the agreement.[42]

The new Liberal Canadian prime minister, Jean Chrétien, elected in late October, had campaigned on a pledge to renegotiate parts of NAFTA. He wanted a subsidies and anti-dumping code in NAFTA and to amend the energy provisions of the FTA. The three parties to NAFTA issued a statement in early December 'pledging to set up trilateral working groups to develop common rules on antidumping and subsidies within two years after NAFTA enters into effect.'[43] They stressed that 'the two working groups on antidumping and subsidies rules will "build as appropriate" on the results of the Uruguay Round in those areas.'[44] But no progress had been made on this issue at the time of writing and the groups are essentially dormant. As for the energy provisions, Chrétien's other priority, the Clinton administration refused to give up. As mentioned earlier, 'The NAFTA and FTA language on energy requires Canada and the U.S. to ensure that supplies of oil and other basic energy products to the other party are not disrupted in the event of an emergency in which the government decides to restrict energy exports. The language requires that energy be maintained at the same proportion relative to overall supply even if restrictions are imposed. It also requires that energy exports be priced no higher than the domestic price.'[45] Mexico opposed such a provision in NAFTA and was granted an exemption. The Canadians sought unsuccessfully to get similar treatment.

The U.S. House of Representatives finally approved NAFTA on 17 November 1993, followed by the U.S. Senate on 20 November and by the Mexican Senate on 23 November 1993. President Clinton signed it into law on 8 December, and it entered into force on 1 January 1994.

PART TWO

Four Cases

CHAPTER THREE

Culture: Preserving the Status Quo

The Canadian and Mexican cultural industries are generally more extensively subsidized, regulated, and protected than their U.S. counterparts. In Canada, protecting cultural industries has always been a matter of the utmost importance for the government. Lacking a unifying culture and sharing a long border and, for the majority of the population, a common language with the United States, Canadians have consistently felt that state intervention was not only justifiable but necessary to increase Canada's cultural resources and build a national identity.

As early as 1867, the politician and poet Thomas D'Arcy McGee argued that supporting what we now call cultural industries was a 'state and social necessity.'[1] In fact, from the very beginning, Canadians have been concerned with the large U.S. influence on Canadian culture and the small size of their own market – in short, their lack of resources in what is now known as the cultural sector. In 1889, for instance, James Bell wrote that 'American papers, magazines, books, periodicals, secular and religious, for children and for adults, fill Canadian homes'; other commentators worried that 'because of Canada's great size and small population ..., cultural products could have no impact – could not, indeed, even get produced and distributed – without state intervention.'[2] A century later, in 1987, Canada's federal Department of Communications put forward these same arguments in its survey of Canadian cultural industries. Quoting John Gray, a Canadian playwright, the document noted: 'Increasingly, American mass culture is being seen by Canadians as "normal" culture, and Canadian mass culture as "abnormal" culture.' The survey also emphasized the small size of Canada's two main linguistic markets. 'The Anglophone market ... is widely dispersed across a vast geographical area ... The positive characteristics of Canada's Francophone market – geographical compactness, a separate language and physical remoteness from the major importing nation, France – are offset by its size ..., which renders economies of scale even more difficult than in English-speaking Canada.'[3]

The nationalist approach to Canadian culture is therefore based on protectionist measures aimed at ensuring that domestic cultural products will be available at home. Instruments such as content rules, ownership restrictions, subsidies, and tax incentives have been among the major devices used by the federal and provincial governments to foster their development. In fact, very few experts in Canada have challenged this conventional wisdom and asked whether these instruments were the most effective way to promote domestic content in the domestic market.[4] The FTA exempted culture, securing continuance of these measures. The Macdonald Commission had urged the Canadian government in its 1985 report to negotiate 'explicit treaty provisions that would authorize public funding of ... cultural industries and permit affirmative discrimination for Canadian producers.'[5] At the outset of the NAFTA negotiations, the pressure was enormous on the Canadian government to preserve the cultural exemption. As they had before and during the FTA negotiations, nationalists argued that existing protectionist measures were necessary to ensure the survival of domestic cultural products.

This chapter opens with the main objectives of the three parties in NAFTA, and then it describes the outcome of the negotiations. It next reviews the key resources of each state actor – first, market share and industry control, and second, government intervention – the different policy instruments implemented by the players over the years in order to increase their resources in the cultural sector. Then it identifies the key components of issue-specific power for each country. Finally, it looks at the main tactics used during the negotiation process. The chapter concludes with a reflection on how Canada used both its issue-specific power and its tactics to meet its objectives in NAFTA.

NEGOTIATORS' OBJECTIVES

The main Canadian objective was very clear in NAFTA: the cultural exemption obtained in the FTA was *not* negotiable; culture was *not* on the table, which meant that the FTA's exemption would be carried over in NAFTA without any discussions.

The Americans saw the situation differently. They were eager to negotiate a comprehensive treatment of all intellectual property rights and to resolve two major irritants – Canadian compulsory licensing in pharmaceuticals (to be covered in chapter 6) and the cultural exemption. Their idea was to put as much pressure as possible on the Canadians in order to make at least some inroads in the cultural exemption. The Americans also had other priorities, such as excluding moral rights of authors from the NAFTA agreement so as not to impede the economic benefits of the right holder, who can be a legal person in a common law system. Civil law countries generally protect both the moral rights of authors and their economic rights. Moral rights are inalienable rights that preserve the integrity of an author's work, his or her right to be known as the author, and his or her right to determine in what form the work will be made public. As moral rights are usually not transferable, they may impede the economic rights associated with a given work, since the owner of these rights may not be the author. Another major goal for the United States was to convince Mexico, a country with a civil law tradition, to agree that transfers of rights by an author to a legal person imply that the transferee must receive remuneration for these rights. The Americans also wanted Mexico to accept the work-for-hire doctrine, under which the work created in a contractual relationship belongs to the party that paid for the work. Moreover, the Americans were determined to prohibit parallel importation – i.e., the import of protected works whose distribution and sale is not authorized by the right holder in a given country. They also wanted to prevent the importing of unauthorized works and to establish a commercial rental right for producers of sound recordings.

For the Mexicans, in contrast, culture was not a major problem. Unlike the English-speaking Canadians, they did not feel threatened by the presence of American culture but nevertheless had issues that needed to be addressed. Mexico called for the restoration of copyright protection for motion pictures that had fallen into the U.S. public domain under the old U.S. copyright regime. Also, being a member of the Convention for the Protection of Performers, Producers of Phonograms and Broadcasting Organizations (the Rome Convention, signed in 1961), the Mexicans did not want to apply national treatment to all intellectual property rights. They were specifically concerned with performers' rights, which are covered in the Rome Convention by the principle of reciprocity.

NEGOTIATION OUTCOME

Canada Keeps Its Cultural Exemption

Canada was able to preserve the status quo and maintain the cultural exemption negotiated in the FTA. Although there are many provisions in NAFTA that address culture-related issues, for Canada, the most important ones are article 2107 and annex 2106. Article 2107 defines cultural industries as being the publishing industry (books, magazines, periodicals, and newspapers), the film and video industry, the music recording industry, the music publishing industry, and the broadcasting industry (radio, television, cable, and satellite). Annex 2106 stipulates that the FTA governs rights and obligations between Canada and any party with respect to cultural industries, except for Article 302 of NAFTA on tariff elimination.[6] FTA 2005(1) exempts Canadian cultural industries from its provisions and allows, under 2005(2), measures of equivalent commercial effect in retaliation for measures inconsistent with the agreement.

Exceptions to the Cultural Exemption

The cultural exemption in the FTA comprises four exceptions. First, it does not apply to tariff elimination on cultural products (article 401). Second, forced divestiture as provided for in FTA 1607(4) requires Canada to purchase a business from an American investor at fair open market value should Canada demand the divestiture of that business enterprise pursuant to its review of an indirect acquisition of such a business. Third, the exemption does not apply either to the only FTA provision dealing with copyright issues. Article 2006(1) requires that a copyright holder of the other party receive 'equitable and non-discriminatory remuneration for any retransmission to the public ... of the copyright holder's program ... carried in distant signals.' At the time of the FTA negotiations, Canadian copyright law did not provide for such remuneration to copyright holders. Under paragraph 2 of article 2006, each party's copyright law has to provide for the copyright holder's authorization, whether transmission of the program is intended for free reception by the public or not. Paragraph 3 allows each party to maintain several measures in effect on 4 October 1987. Fourth, the FTA's cultural exemption eliminates the obligations under section 19 of Canada's Income Tax Act to print and typeset a newspaper or periodical in Canada in order to be able to deduct advertising expenses. FTA 2007 is in accordance with article 2012 of the same agreement, which does not include printing and typesetting as part of the cultural sector. Therefore, with the exceptions of FTA 401, 1607(4), 2006 and 2007, NAFTA, exempts Canadian cultural industries from having to apply the FTA provisions. However, as mentioned above, article 2005(2) of that agreement stipulates very clearly that 'a Party may take measures of equivalent commercial effect in response to actions that would have been inconsistent' with the FTA.

Exemption Allows Departure from the NAFTA Obligations

Since NAFTA specifically refers to the FTA, Canada could adopt measures that would depart from the NAFTA obligations, if these obligations are not included in the FTA, without being subject to retaliation by the United States or Mexico. The U.S. General Accounting Office (GAO) confirms this analysis with respect to intellectual property, an issue not covered in the FTA: 'Canada, without violating the agreement, could take broad exemptions from all NAFTA intellectual property obligations relating to cultural industries except those deriving from its adherence to other international agreements.[7] The right of retaliation would also not apply to any actions taken by Canada in a cultural service industry – broadcasting, for example – because FTA's chapter 14 lists one cultural activity – wholesale dealing in books, periodicals, and newspapers – in Canada's schedule of covered services.[8]

Therefore, except for the FTA exemption carried over in NAFTA, Canadian cultural industries would be bound by the intellectual property provisions of NAFTA's chapter 17, particularly those on national treatment (article 1703), copyright (article 1705), sound recordings (article 1706), and enforcement (articles 1714–18), and by those in the NAFTA chapters on investment (chapter 11) and cross-border services (chapter 12). The investment and services provisions oblige parties to apply national treatment (articles 1102 and 1202) and the most-favoured-nation (MFN) treatment (articles 1103 and 1203), thereby prohibiting discrimination in favour of a party's own nationals (national treatment) and nationals of other countries (MFN treatment). For instance, as mentioned by Jon Johnson, under the MFN obligations of chapters 11 and 12, Canada would have 'to extend the same benefits to the United States as it presently extends to other countries under its co-production agreements.'[9] Chapter 11 also prohibits performance requirements (article 1106) with regard to the investment made by a national of another party, while several Canadian-funded programs, such as Telefilm Canada and capital cost allowances (CCAs) for investors in Canadian films, impose requirements on domestic content as a condition to get subsidies. Other NAFTA provisions that relate to cultural industries are article 1107, prohibiting requirements that individuals in senior management positions be of any particular nationality, and article 1205, precluding the imposition of 'local presence.' In fact, NAFTA not only protects the status quo, but it goes beyond the FTA by extending protection for Canadian cultural industries to any other party and by broadening the definition of cultural industries to include both enterprises and individuals (NAFTA 2107 and 201), while the FTA covers only enterprises.

U.S. Victories

Moral Rights

The United States was unable to convince Canada to do away with its 'carve-out' of cultural industries but met most of its other objectives. NAFTA requires member countries to apply the substantive provisions of the Convention for the Protection of Literary and Artistic Works (Berne Convention, signed 1971) but does not impose any obligations on the United States to give effect to article 6*bis* on moral rights, pursuant to NAFTA Annex 1701.3(2). The exclusion of moral rights represents a major victory for the United States, because it allows authors to transfer their rights to companies and employers without later disrupting the exploitation of their works to the disadvantage of the holder of the economic rights.

Contractual Rights

Another article, NAFTA 1705(3), covers both copyright and related rights and provides for the free transfer of economic rights by contract for purposes of their exploitation and enjoyment by the transferee. This means that the transferee receives remuneration for these economic rights. The United States was particularly concerned with the tradition in civil law countries, such as Mexico, where the transferee may not be allowed to collect royalties. Article 1705(3) also recognizes the work-for-hire concept for works and sound recordings, another principle new to Mexico. Employment contracts, in which the employer becomes the author and right holder of a work or sound recordings created by an employee, are common in the U.S. entertainment industries (sound recordings, motion pictures, and television productions). NAFTA guarantees to these right holders the economic benefits derived from their rights. The incorporation of such contractual rights into NAFTA is a major achievement for the United States. It reverses the trend in other countries – namely in Europe – where regulations often restrict the transferability of copyright and related rights.[10] NAFTA 1705(3) is also strengthened by article 1703(2), which requires that no formalities or conditions be imposed, as a condition of according national treatment, for the acquisition of rights in respect of copyright and related rights.

Importation of Unauthorized Works

The Americans also succeeded in prohibiting the importation of unauthorized works. Article 1705(2) allows authors and their successors the rights enumerated in the Berne Convention, including the right to authorize or prohibit importation of unauthorized copies, first distribution of the original and each copy of the work, communication of a work to the public, as well as commercial rental of the original or copies of a computer program. However, the United States failed to persuade Mexico to agree on prohibiting parallel importation. The Mexicans see banning this practice as being anti-competitive,[11] while, as explained by Washington-based lawyers Charles Levy and Stuart Weiser, the Americans believe that 'to gain full benefit from their rights, right holders should be able to make, use, or sell the subject matter of their rights on a country-by-country basis.'[12] Parallel importation takes this control away from right holders.

Rental of Sound Recordings

Another victory for the United States was the establishment in NAFTA of a commercial rental right for producers of sound recordings. Article 1706(1)(d) provides that a producer of a sound recording has the right to authorize or prohibit the commercial rental of the original or a copy of a sound recording, except where expressly otherwise provided in a contract between the producer of the sound recording and the authors of the works fixed. This means that the author or owner of a sound recording cannot rent it to someone else without the authorization of the producer. The exception was included after the Mexicans insisted that authors should have the right to ask the producer to waive his or her rental right.[13]

Results for Mexico

Restoration of Copyright to Mexican Films: Mixed Results

Mexico's efforts to restore copyright to motion pictures that had fallen into the public domain in the United States under the old U.S. Copyright Law met with some success. The 1909 act granted a 28-year initial term of protection, beginning on publication. A renewal term of 28 years was conferred only after the author or his or her heirs had filed an application during the twenty-eighth year. The Copyright Act of 1976 sets up a term of life of the author plus 50 years for copyright in works created after 1 January 1978. For works copyrighted before 1978, the 1976 act lengthens the renewal term to 47 years. Failure to comply with the renewal and other formalities (such as the addition of the copyright notice from copies or phonorecords publicly distributed by authority of the copyright owner) led to forfeiture of copyright to the public domain. In June 1992, Congress eliminated the requirement to file an application to renew the term of copyright. This 'automatic renewal amendment' applies for works first published between 1964 and 1977 inclusively.

What NAFTA Annex 1705.7 does is to oblige the United States to provide protection to motion pictures produced in another party's territory between 1 January 1978 and 1 March 1989 (the Berne Convention, to which the United States acceded in 1989, does not allow formalities), to the extent consistent with the U.S. constitution and subject to budgetary considerations. This allows the restoration of copyright in some Mexican or Canadian motion pictures that had fallen into the public domain in the United States through right holders' failure to comply with the notice formality. Film producers had until 31 December 1994, to request the resurrection of a work under section 104A(b) of the Copyright Act. What NAFTA does *not* do is to restore copyright protection for thousands of Mexican motion pictures that entered the public domain because they were published without notice before 1 January 1978. NAFTA also does not resurrect copyright for motion pictures published before 1 January 1964 and whose registration was not renewed for a second term during the last year of the first copyright term.

Secondary Uses of Sound Recordings: U.S. Concession to Mexico

The United States made a major concession to Mexico when it accepted an exception to national treatment. In respect of sound recordings, article 1703(1) requires national treatment for producers and performers of another party. However, it allows a party to apply the principle of reciprocity in the case of secondary uses of sound recordings – a tenet of the Rome Convention. Under this convention, Mexico gives its performers neighbouring rights on sound recordings – i.e., grants them the right to receive a royalty for public performance of their sound recordings (for example, on radio and television). But the principle of reciprocity allows Mexico the right not to give such remuneration to Americans whose sound recordings are performed in Mexico, since the United States is not a party to the Rome Convention.

Other Provisions

Term of Protection, Limitations to Copyright Protection, and Compulsory Licensing

Other provisions in chapter 17 are relevant to the cultural industries. They include the requirement for parties to comply with the substantive provisions of the Convention for the Protection of Producers of Phonograms against Unauthorized Duplication of their Phonograms (the Geneva Convention 1971) and, as mentioned above, the Berne Convention. NAFTA also determines the standard term of life of the author plus 50 years for copyright protection and 50 years from first fixation for the duration of sound recording protection. Under NAFTA 1705(5), limitations and exceptions to the rights provided for in article 1705 are allowed only in certain special cases that do not conflict with normal exploitation of the work and do not unreasonably prejudice the legitimate interests of the right holder. This provision is based on article 9(2) of the Berne Convention. NAFTA 1705(6) restricts the right permitted to developing countries under the appendix to the Berne Convention to grant translation and reproduction licences. Although Mexico has never used compulsory licensing under this appendix, NAFTA requires that translation and reproduction licences should not be allowed by a party where legitimate needs for copies or translations in that party's territory could be met by the right holder if it were not for obstacles created by that party.[14]

U.S. and Mexican Reservations

Finally, with respect to cultural industries, Mexico has taken reservations under NAFTA's annex I to protect existing measures that do not conform with obligations taken in chapters 11 and 12. For instance, Mexico has determined, for the protection of copyrights, that the holder of a concession for a commercial broadcast station or for a cable television system must obtain an authorization from the Secretaría de Gobernación to import in any form radio or television programming for broadcast or cable distribution within the territory of Mexico.[15] Mexico also wanted to make sure that the use of the Spanish language for broadcast, including advertising broadcast, cable, or multipoint distribution system, was required; that 'a majority of the time of each day's live broadcast programs must feature Mexican nationals'; and that a radio or television announcer or presenter who is not a Mexican national must obtain an authorization from the Secretaría de Gobernación to perform in Mexico.[16] Annex I stipulates that 'advertising included in programs directly from outside the territory of Mexico may not be distributed in those programs when they are retransmitted in the territory of Mexico.'[17] Other reservations deal with ownership and concessions in the cable industry and with screen time for films produced by Mexicans either within or outside their country.[18]

Both Mexico and the United States have taken reservations under annex II to protect existing measures or to adopt new or more restrictive measures that do not conform with obligations imposed in chapters 11 and 12. With respect to national treatment, MFN treatment, local presence, and senior management, Mexico reserves 'the right to adopt or maintain any measure relating to investment in, or provision of, broadcasting, multipoint distribution systems, uninterrupted music and high-definition television services.'[19] U.S. reservations address issues related to ownership in the cable industry, the newspaper publishing industry, and investment in radiocommunications.[20] Pursuant to NAFTA 1207, the United States decided to list non-discriminatory quantitative restrictions in annex V that it wanted to maintain at the time of the negotiations, while in accordance with NAFTA 1208 both Mexico and the United States set out their commitments to liberalize non-discriminatory measures in annex VI.

RESOURCES

Canadian nationalists have long argued that Canada lacks resources in the cultural sector and therefore needs to protect and subsidize its cultural industries. They point out that 60 per cent of books sold in Canada are foreign, as are 80 per cent of English-language magazines available on newsstands, 95 per cent of feature films, 84 per cent of sales of sound recordings, 70 per cent of radio, and over 60 per cent of English-language television programming. They also emphasize that Canada's trade balance of cultural goods and services is highly negative, with heavy dependence on the United States as an export market (85 per cent of cultural goods). However, at the time of the NAFTA negotiations in 1991–2, the data also show that foreign-controlled firms accounted for less than 50 per cent of domestic sales both in book publishing (47 per cent) and periodicals (45 per cent) and for 44 per cent of revenue in the distribution of films and videos. U.S. television stations got no more than 25 per cent of audience share in Canada, but there was a wide gap between anglophones and francophones in television viewing in 1991. Domestic programming represented 27 per cent of total viewing among anglophones in 1991, and 63 per cent among francophones.

Market Share and Industry Control

Canadian Cultural Industries

The arts and culture generated more than $20 billion in revenue in Canada in 1991–2, and over 600,000 jobs. In book publishing, 8,722 titles were released, 5 per cent more than the previous year. Canadian products captured approximately 40 per cent of market share. Canadian-controlled firms accounted for 80 per cent of title production, 60 per cent of overall sales (domestic market and exports) of 'Canadian-authored' 'own titles' (i.e., including titles originated by publishers and for which they cover costs and risks and titles whose rights they buy for publication in Canada), and 53 per cent of domestic sales. They also monopolized 97 per cent of export sales, receiving 33 per cent of their total revenue from these sales in international markets.[21]

In the periodical industry, there were 1,055 publishers in Canada in 1991–2, compared with 810 in 1984. Of these 1,055, only 140 were publishing more than one periodical. The largest four accounted for 37 per cent of the revenue of the industry (46 per cent for the eight largest) and 33 per cent of the circulation (45 per cent for the eight largest). The highly concentrated industry is mostly Canadian-owned, and the content is overwhelmingly domestic (93 per cent). The number of periodicals has been relatively stable over the years, reaching 1,440 in 1991–2 and capturing 55 per cent of the total domestic market share – a slight decline from 59 per cent in 1988–9. U.S. magazines, however, have been dominating Canadian newsstands since the beginning of the century. In fact, seven out of 10 Canadian magazines are not available on newsstands. The best space is usually given to bestselling periodicals, most of which are American. The situation is different in Quebec, where Canadian French-language periodicals generally occupy more space.

Single-copy sales represented only 12 per cent of paid circulation and 7 per cent of total revenue in 1991–2. Moreover, the industry relies heavily on advertising sales, which accounted for 64 per cent of total revenue that same year.[22] The problem facing the industry is the smallness of the Canadian market, which limits the possibility of reaping the benefits of economies of scale. Unit cost of production is generally higher than in the United States, and 'because of their strong position in the Canadian market, U.S. periodicals have become the price-setters, restricting the prices that can be charged by comparable Canadian publications.'[23]

In film and video production, there were 742 (mostly small and predominantly Canadian-owned) establishments in 1991–2. Revenues totalled $688.2 million, the bulk of which came from the non-theatrical market (advertising, government, educational, and industry), with 45 per cent, and home entertainment (video, conventional, and pay television), at 42 per cent. The theatrical market captured slightly over 1 per cent of the total.[24] The market share of American feature films is traditionally very high, reaching over 95 per cent in English Canada and 83 per cent in Quebec. Films made in Canada generally capture an insignificant market share (2 per cent), while non-U.S. foreign films have a substantial market share (14 per cent) only in Quebec.[25]

A small number of American companies were dominating the distribution market. Foreign-controlled companies generated 83 per cent of the theatrical distribution revenues from motion picture theatres and drive-ins and received 48 per cent of the revenues from home entertainment. The Canadian theatrical market is vertically integrated with the U.S. film industry. There were two major theatre chains in 1991–2. Famous Players was established by a group of Canadian investors in 1920 and bought by Paramount Pictures in 1930. Since 1994, it has been owned by the entertainment giant Viacom. Odeon was formed by Canadian investors during the Second World War, purchased by British interests a few years later, and bought by Canadian-based Cineplex in 1984. In May 1998, Sony's Loews merged with Cineplex Odeon.

In sound recording, 1,101 new recordings[26] with Canadian content represented 15 per cent of the total in 1991–2. Recordings with English lyrics and Canadian content[27] captured 13 per cent of the anglophone market, while new recordings with French lyrics and Canadian content took 66 per cent of the francophone market.

Canadian-controlled firms released 79 per cent of these new recordings and earned 62 per cent of sales revenue from Canadian-
content recordings. Foreign-controlled companies released
72 per cent of *all* recordings and earned 84 per cent of total sales
revenue and 77 per cent of total revenue.[28] Facing tariffs on importing recordings, several multinationals set up subsidiaries in
Canada starting in the 1960s. Such tariffs (14 per cent) were abolished in the FTA. These multinationals are vertically integrated
and also control the distribution market.

U.S. Cultural Industries

The Americans have never complained that they were lacking resources in culture. The statistics prove them right. The core copyright industries contributed 3.67 per cent of U.S. gross domestic
product (GDP) in 1991–2, and their share of national employment
was 2.46 per cent. Employment reached almost 3 million in 1992.[29]
Approximately 50,000 new books or editions appear every year
in the United States. Shipments – value of products and services –
increased in 1992 to reach U.S.$17.4 billion. The (U.S.) Interna-
tional Trade Administration notes that exports account for approximately 10 per cent of the sales. At the time of the NAFTA
negotiations in 1992, the largest markets for U.S. exports were
Canada (42.9 per cent), the United Kingdom (14 per cent), Aus-
tralia (7.5 per cent), Japan (5.5 percent), and Germany and Mexico
(3.1 per cent each). The United States is also an importer of books.
The leading exporters were the United Kingdom (20.8 per cent),
Hong Kong (18.9 percent), Japan (9.2 per cent), Singapore (9 percent), and Canada (8.7 per cent). Mexico's share was 2.5 per cent.[30]
In the periodical industry, U.S. exports grew at an average rate of
18 per cent annually between 1989 and 1992. The single most sizeable market for U.S. magazines in 1992 was Canada, with 73.6 per
cent of total exports, followed by the United Kingdom (7.1 per
cent), Mexico (4.7 per cent), and the Netherlands (4.1 per cent).
Canada was also the largest source of foreign magazines in
the United States in 1992, with 57.6 per cent of the total; the
United Kingdom supplied 14.8 per cent, Japan 6.2 per cent, and

Mexico 3.5 per cent. In 1992, U.S. exports totalled approximately U.S.$731 million, and U.S. imports an estimated U.S.$136 million. To increase their revenues, several of the 11,143 U.S. magazines have launched national editions of their publications.

The entertainment industries (films, prerecorded music, video, and cable television) have been extremely successful, with a trade surplus of U.S.$4 billion in 1992, making them the second-largest U.S. export industry, just after commercial aircraft. Box office receipts rose in 1992 but did not reach the 1989 record of U.S.$5 billion. The Motion Picture Association of America (MPAA), the voice of the major studios, has estimated that foreign revenues from box office, television, video cassettes, and pay TV increased by 0.6 per cent in 1992, to U.S.$6.6 billion. The majors account for approximately 80 per cent of foreign revenues from U.S. films. The independent sector captures the remainder. The MPAA also reported that, for the eighth consecutive year, Japan was the leading export market in 1992, with approximately U.S.$165 million in film rentals; Canada moved from second place in 1989 to fourth in 1991, with U.S.$134 million. The Hollywood studios also produce film and television shows in Canada.

The U.S. Department of Commerce's Bureau of Economic Analysis (BEA) found that exports of film and television tape rentals amounted to U.S.$2.5 billion in 1992, while imports reached U.S.$90 million. This does not, however, take into account receipts of foreign affiliates, which in 1991 totalled U.S.$4.8 billion.[31] Finally, U.S. sales of prerecorded music – i.e., all formats, including music videos – reached U.S.$10.4 billion in 1993, up 15 per cent over 1992. Although the United States is the world's single largest exporter of prerecorded music, the real value of foreign sales is extremely difficult to calculate. As emphasized by the International Trade Administration, 'a large percentage of music sold abroad is manufactured by subsidiaries of U.S. companies or under license agreements.'[32]

Mexican Cultural Industries

Book publishing goes back almost five centuries in Mexico. In fact, it is widely believed that the first book to be printed in the Americas was published in Mexico City in 1535. Fray Juan de Zumárraga, who arrived in Mexico City in 1528 to serve as the first bishop of the city, saw the printing and publishing of religious books as a powerful tool to convert the native population. He arranged negotiations between Juan Cromberger, a printer in Seville, and Juan Pablos, an Italian from Brescia, to bring book printing and publishing to Mexico. Pablos came to Mexico City, opened a branch office for Cromberger, and printed his first book in 1539.[33]

The close relationship between Spanish and Mexican publishing is thus nothing new. According to the Cámara Nacional de la Industria Editorial (National Chamber of the Publishing Industry), Mexicans owned 30 per cent of publishing enterprises at the end of the 1980s, foreigners held 10 per cent, and Mexicans and foreigners (publishers from Madrid and Barcelona) together owned 60 per cent. Books and periodicals accounted for 0.45 per cent of GDP in 1989.[34] During the same year, approximately 10,000 books were published, down 50 per cent compared to annual figures from the 1960s. There were 1,106 firms in these two industries in 1989, of which 863 were owned by the private sector, 104 by government, 50 by academe, and 89 by other groups (such as professional associations). Only 200 have been able to publish more than ten books a year, and only nine more than fifty.[35]

Although the Mexican film industry is still the strongest in Latin America, it has been producing fewer films in the past few years. Long gone are the days of the golden age (1940–54). While the total number of films produced in Mexico reached 138 in 1958, it fell in the early 1960s, increased again in the early 1970s (82 movies in 1971) at the beginning of the Echeverría administration, then fell to 35 in 1976. It rose again in the early 1980s, only to plummet a few years later. The early 1990s witnessed a dramatic reduction – 98 in 1990, but only 32 in 1991 and 44 in 1992. Most of these movies were produced by the private sector – 89 in 1990, 17 in 1991, and 33 in 1992. The Hollywood majors dominate distribution, with 65 per cent of movies presented. Mexican films captured 23 per cent of the market between 1989 and 1994.[36] The music market is also controlled by a few companies. In 1991, Mexico's big five (BMG, EMI, PolyGram, Sony, and Warner) captured 77 per cent of the market. The whole music market was worth U.S.$267 million in 1991, which represented two and one-half times the U.S. Hispanic domestic market.[37]

Government Intervention

Canada: A Plethora of Policy Instruments

From the Aird Commission appointed in 1929 to help define Canada's radio broadcasting policy to the Task Force on the Magazine Industry, which submitted its report in 1994, and the Mandate Review Committee, which examined film and broadcasting and made its report public in 1996, the federal government has made great use of royal commissions, task forces, and committees to find ways to protect and promote its cultural industries.[38] The most important agency subsidizing arts and culture is the Canada Council for the Arts (first known as the Canada Council), founded in 1957. Grants from Parliament and income from an endowment fund constitute the main sources of its funding.

Book Publishing: Copyright Protection, Subsidies, and the Baie Comeau Policy

Early attempts in Canada at protecting the book publishing industry took place when the Statute of Anne, the first copyright act enacted for both England and Scotland in 1709, began to apply to British colonies in 1814.[39] A few years later, in 1832, Lower Canada (now the province of Quebec) adopted its first copyright statute. This legislation was essentially a copy of the 1831 U.S. law, an interesting development given Lower Canada's French civil law tradition. The 1832 legislation protected, among other things, books, maps, charts, and musical compositions for a period of 28 years from registration, with a renewal term of 14 years when the author's immediate heirs (spouse and children) were still alive at the end of the first period. Parliament enacted the first Canadian statute in 1868, following the U.S. model, which was confirmed in the statute adopted in 1875. However, as mentioned by William Hayhurst, 'whereas the U.S. was in 1875 still denying copyright to foreigners, the Canadian statute accorded copyright to persons domiciled in Canada or in a British possession as well as to citizens of countries having an international copyright treaty with the U.K.'[40] Copyright registration, printing, and publishing had to take place in Canada for copyright to be protected. Notwithstanding the U.S. model, the United Kingdom greatly influenced Canadian copyright statutes. Both in 1872 and in 1889, Canadian copyright legislation was denied royal assent under Britain's Colonial Laws Validity Act of 1865 because it was deemed inconsistent with U.K. legislation.[41] The United Kingdom had become a member of the 1886 Berne Convention in 1887. Canada and the rest of the empire were also covered by the convention, under which an author could register his or her work and publish in any member country as long as he or she complied with the formalities of such country.

Canada thus modelled its main Copyright Act, enacted in 1921, on Britain's Copyright Act of 1911. It entered into force on 1 January 1924. Over the years, Canadian nationalists complained about the practice of 'buying around,' whereby books could be bought directly in the United States and imported to Canada without the consent of Canadian right holders. The old Copyright Act allowed authors to prevent parallel importation of their works, but book distributors did not benefit from such rights. Current copyright legislation, which received royal assent on 25 April 1997, grants these rights to book distributors.[42] It permits parallel importation for specific uses of books by non-profit libraries, archives, museums, educational institutions, and governments, as well as for personal use (two copies) – an important dimension, given the growth of Internet-based ordering. Copyright protection also covers other literary and artistic works such as motion pictures, sound recordings, information products, and computer programs.

Provincial and federal subsidies have affected book publishing. Ottawa became more active in the 1970s, increasing assistance to publishers through the Canada Council in 1972. It launched an industrial development assistance policy in 1979 with the Book

Publishing Development Program and set up the Book Publishing Industry Development Plan in 1986 and the more comprehensive Cultural Industries Development Fund in 1990. It also provided indirect support to the industry in the form of a postal subsidy, which in March 1993 was replaced with a program of direct assistance for books of Canadian authors distributed by domestic publishers.

Another key element of federal strategy has been to restrain the acquisition of Canadian-controlled publishers by foreign companies. In July 1985, Communications Minister Marcel Masse persuaded his cabinet colleagues at a meeting held in Baie Comeau, Quebec, the childhood home of Prime Minister Mulroney, to adopt a foreign investment policy in book publishing and distribution, to be implemented under the Investment Canada Act. The 'Baie Comeau policy' allowed foreign investors to acquire publishing companies if they did so through a joint venture with a Canadian-controlled firm. For indirect acquisitions – i.e., when a Canadian subsidiary was sold as part of the assets of a foreign corporation – the foreign investor had to sell control to Canadians within two years at fair market value. In January 1992, Communications Minister Perrin Beatty revised the policy: 'Foreign investments in new businesses would be limited to Canadian-controlled joint ventures; [and] foreign acquisition of Canadian-controlled publishing and distribution businesses would not generally be permitted.'[43] Indirect acquisitions would be permitted as long as they benefited Canada. A foreign investor selling a business operating in Canada would have to give Canadians the opportunity to bid.

Periodicals: Section 19 of the Income Tax Act,
Tariff Code 9958, and Postal Subsidies

In addition to the allocation of grants, government intervention in periodical publishing has been historically based on three measures: section 19 of the Income Tax Act, Customs Tariff Code 9958, and postal subsidies. As Paul Audley mentions, the Royal Commission on Publications (O'Leary Commission) pointed out in 1961 that Canadian editions of foreign magazines were receiving more than '40 per cent of the total amount spent on consumer magazine advertising in Canada.'[44] The report's major concern was that Canadian editions were essentially composed of foreign – mostly American – editorial content, with Canadian advertising appended. In 1965, section 19 of the Income Tax Act was amended to give a tax deduction for advertisement placed in Canadian magazines, except for *Time* and *Reader's Digest*, which were 'grandfathered.' The Davey Report in 1970 reached similar conclusions. Section 19 had not helped the Canadian periodical industry grow. That led the federal government to adopt Bill C-58 (effective 1 January 1976) and revise the Income Tax Act once again to allow tax deductions only for advertisements placed in Canadian-owned periodicals. As was noted above, FTA 2007 eliminated the obligation to print and typeset periodicals in Canada.

In 1965, Ottawa enacted Customs Tariff Code 9958 to prohibit entry of 'split-run advertising' editions of foreign periodicals into Canada, so as to discourage use of foreign editorial content in conjunction with Canadian advertising. At the time of the NAFTA negotiations, the code was still playing a significant role. However, new technology allowed *Time Canada* in 1993 to beam copy of *Sports Illustrated* electronically to its printing plant in Richmond Hill, near Toronto, and add a few pages of Canadian content. In fact, *Time Canada* printed several issues of *Sports Illustrated* in 1993. The 30-year-old customs regulation required Revenue Canada to seize split-run editions of foreign periodicals when they actually *crossed* the border. *Sports Illustrated* had succeeded in electronically evading the measure. To study the implications of this problem for the periodical industry, the Mulroney government set up the Task Force on the Magazine Industry, which in March 1994 recommended a tax of 80 per cent on foreign magazines that printed Canadian-advertising editions. The task force also suggested grandfathering *Reader's Digest*, *Sports Illustrated*, and *Time*. In December 1994, Canadian Heritage Minister Michel Dupuy proposed an 80 per cent excise tax on the advertising revenue of every periodical in which more than 20 per cent of the editorial content came from a foreign edition. The measure, imposed in

December 1995 through adoption of Bill C-103, grandfathered magazines that were publishing Canadian editions prior to 26 March 1993, which meant excluding *Sports Illustrated*.

In March 1996, the United States took the issue before the World Trade Organization (WTO). A year later, on 14 March 1997, the final report of the WTO panel ruled against Canada. An Appellate Body confirmed the panel's ruling on 30 June 1997. Canada was found to violate GATT article XI with its import ban and article III:2 on national treatment with its excise tax. The Americans also challenged the Canadian postal subsidy, first established in the Postal Act in 1875 and aimed at helping the domestic periodical industry. In 1990, the federal government decided to gradually phase out this program and to replace it with direct funding. The program was set to expire on 30 April 1996 but was extended for three years. The WTO Appellate Body reversed the WTO panel's report and ruled in favour of the United States, arguing that the postal subsidy was in contravention of GATT article III:4.

In October 1998, Canada abolished its prohibition on split-run imports and its excise tax, changed its postal policy, and introduced the Foreign Publishers Advertising Services Act (Bill C-55) in order to comply with the Appellate Body's decision. The objective of Bill C-55 was to forbid foreign-owned magazine publishers from accepting advertisements aimed at Canadian consumers. Instead of taxing the magazines with foreign content, Ottawa preferred the option of focusing on the 'advertising services' – an issue not covered under Canada's General Agreement on Trade in Services (GATS) schedule in the WTO. The bill was going to make it illegal for Canadian companies to advertise in foreign split-run magazines which would result in large fines. When the U.S. government threatened to retaliate, Canada negotiated a bilateral agreement with its southern neighbour in June 1999. Canada agreed to amend Bill C-55, and the United States in return would take no action under the WTO Agreements, NAFTA, or section 301 of the (U.S.) Trade Act of 1974 (as amended). Canada agreed to exempt from its legislation foreign-owned magazines with 12 per cent or less Canadian advertising space; this proportion was to increase to 15 per cent after eighteen months of the entry into force of Bill C-55 and to 18 per cent after thirty-six months. Except for Canadian-owned businesses, Ottawa also agreed to permit up to 51 per cent foreign ownership in the establishment and acquisition of businesses intending to publish, distribute, and sell periodicals, effective from ninety days after the June agreement entered into force. The proportion was to rise to 100 per cent after one year (the previous ceiling was 25 per cent). Foreign investments still have to meet the 'net benefits clause' under section 38 of the Investment Canada Act. Such provision takes into consideration the effect of the investment on competition, its contribution to the Canadian economy, and its compatibility with cultural policies.

The bilateral agreement requires that, within one year of its entry into force, Parliament amend section 19 of the Income Tax Act to allow advertisers deductions for ads in periodicals irrespective of the nationality of the publisher or place of production, as long as the periodical contains the requisite levels of original editorial content. The agreement also calls for the Income Tax Act to be amended to change the amount of the allowable deduction and of original editorial content required to permit deduction of half of the advertising costs for advertisers in publications with zero to 79 per cent of original editorial content. A full deduction is required for publications with 80 per cent or more original editorial content. Foreign periodicals published under a licensing agreement with a Canadian are also eligible to take advantage of the deductions.

The Film Industry: Tax Shelter, Subsidies,
and Distribution Problems

In order to foster a national film industry, the Canadian government undertook a series of steps. It set up the National Film Board (NFB) in 1939 to produce, distribute, and promote films focusing on Canada. The NFB, which is known for its award-winning documentaries and animation movies, has never been a threat to the Hollywood majors. In the mid-1960s, Ottawa set up the Canadian Film Development Corporation (CFDC), which began its operations in 1968, helping to finance Canadian feature films. The CFDC, whose first budget of $10 million was extended for another $10 million in 1971, never became self-sufficient, partly because of its investments and the decisions made by both distributors and exhibitors. Quotas negotiated by the federal government with the theatre chains in the 1970s also failed to give more screen time to Canadian films. In 1978, the CFDC started financing projects that were benefiting from capital cost allowances (CCAs), a tax deduction for investors in Canadian feature films. The CCA, introduced in 1974, allowed a tax credit for capital costs of 100 per cent a year. Such credit was reduced to 50 per cent in 1983 and to 30 per cent in 1988.[45]

The CFDC in 1983 gave way to Telefilm Canada when Communications Minister Francis Fox created the Canadian Broadcast Development Fund to stimulate television programming. In 1986, the government established a Feature Film Fund under Telefilm Canada, following the recommendations of the Special Task Force on the Film Industry in 1985. Telefilm distributes grants to help produce and finance theatrical and television movies, provided that certain content requirements are met. Several provinces have also set up funding agencies for the film and video industry. The Canadian Film or Video Production Tax and provincial tax credit programs aim at helping production companies. Other measures include co-production treaties with foreign countries.

Government measures have generally ignored the most important problem facing Canadian cinema, which is the lack of access of domestic feature films to a good distribution system. The government of Quebec, however, chose to address the issue in its Cinema Act of 1983. Bill 109, aimed at licensing and regulating distributors of films and videocassettes, required that distributors be at least 80 per cent Canadian-owned and that a portion of the gross distribution income be reinvested in films made in Quebec. Though ratified unanimously on 23 June 1983 by Quebec's legislature, the National Assembly, Bill 109 was strongly opposed by the Hollywood majors, who threatened to boycott Quebec. On 22 October 1986, the majors and the government of Quebec agreed to leave non-English-language movies to Quebec-based distributors and allow the majors to distribute the English-language movies that they are distributing in the United States. At the federal level, the Special Task Force on the Film Industry issued its report in 1985. It recommended giving more control to Canadian-owned distributors. That led Communications Minister Flora MacDonald to announce in February 1987 that Ottawa would establish a licensing system for the importation of foreign films to be distributed in Canada. However, the bill was never tabled. The pressure from the majors and letters from U.S. congressmen and President Ronald Reagan convinced Canada not to go ahead with the bill.

Sound Recording: Content Regulations and Copyright Protection

Besides federal and provincial grants and loans, one of the most important government measures in sound recording has been the Canadian-content regulations ('CanCon'), adopted by the Canadian Radio Television Commission (CRTC), known since 1976 as the Canadian Radio-television and Telecommunications Commission (also CRTC). These regulations require that 30 per cent of all music played on AM radio stations between 6 a.m. and midnight be classified as Canadian. For FM stations, the regulations vary from 7 per cent for ethnic stations to 30 per cent for most popular-music FM stations. In the francophone market, the French-language requirement is 65 per cent. Moreover, in 1986, the Canadian government created the Sound Recording Development Program (SRDP), a $25-million program over five years aimed at supporting the production, promotion, marketing, and distribution of domestic music products. It renewed this program in 1990.

Copyright protection has also affected the music industry. Examples have included the Sound Recording Licence Amendment of 1971; the 1988 amendments to the Copyright Act abolishing compulsory licences for the recording of musical works; and the new definition of musical works in the Copyright Amendment Act of 1993 that eliminates the need for graphic requirements and ensures that broadcasters, cable companies, and pay and specialty services, among others, have to pay royalties. The current Copyright Act entitles performers and producers of sound recordings to receive royalty payments from broadcasting and public performance. These new 'neighbouring rights' are recognized in the Rome Convention of 1961. The Copyright Act also imposes a levy on blank audio cassettes and tapes, domestic or imported, that are sold in Canada. Proceeds go through their associations, to eligible composers, lyricists, performers, and producers.

Broadcasting: Government Regulations and
Investment Policy

The Canadian government has been involved in the broadcasting industry since the beginning of the century.[46] In its 1929 report, the Aird Commission recommended creation of a publicly owned radio network similar to the British system. As noted in its 1996 report by the Mandate Review Committee on Canadian Broadcasting and Film for the 21st Century, the Aird Commission was lamenting 'the rapid expansion of American network radio, the flow of American programming across the border, and the fear that "Canada was fast becoming a mere satellite of American broadcasting."'[47] The Broadcasting Act of 1932 established the Canadian Radio Broadcasting Commission, which was replaced by the Canadian Broadcasting Corporation (CBC) in 1936. The CBC's mandate was to offer public radio programming and to oversee the entire radio system. The 1950s saw the first television broadcasting in Canada – on September 6, 1952 – from station CBFT in Montreal; the publication of the Fowler Report on broadcasting in 1957; and the Broadcasting Act of 1958, which established the Board of Broadcast Governors to regulate the entire system. Privately owned channels became available in 1961 with CTV and Télé-Métropole.

A few years later, in 1964, Canada's Secretary of State appointed the Fowler Committee to analyse the influence of American content in programming. The committee's recommendations led to the Broadcasting Act of 1968 creating the independent CRTC to regulate the broadcasting industries and to grant and to renew licences. As explained by the CRTC itself, 'the Commission was given special responsibilities to ensure that ownership and control of broadcasting remained in Canadian hands, that programming would be of high quality with substantial Canadian content, and that Canadian broadcasting would serve to safeguard, enrich and strengthen the nation of Canada from sea to sea.'[48] In Canada, as in many other countries, foreign control of broadcasting industries is not allowed. Foreigners may now own up to 33.3 per cent of the holding company of a Canadian broadcasting firm, 20 per cent at the licensing level, and 100 per cent of the non-voting shares, as long as Canadians exercise control. The old rules, which were in force until 1997, required that Canadians own 80 per cent of voting stock.

Content regulations are also a major feature of the broadcasting industry. To promote domestic programming, the CRTC mandates a 60 per cent share for Canadian programming on a yearly basis and 50 per cent (60 per cent for the CBC) during prime-time hours (6 p.m. to midnight). The CRTC also regulates cable television, pay and specialty television, direct-to-home satellite (DTH) systems, multipoint distribution systems, subscription television, and pay audio. The Canadian Television Fund, which receives funds from Telefilm Canada and contributions from the cable industry and the Department of Canadian Heritage, supports the production and distribution of Canadian programming. Since 1997, DTH services have been required to give 5 per cent of their gross annual revenues to the Fund, which is available only to Canadian-owned and -controlled firms fulfilling the regulations about Canadian content.

Finally, other federal measures include Bill C-58, which denies tax deductions to Canadians advertising on U.S. border stations, and the Canadian priority carriage regulations, which require cable companies to substitute the Canadian signal for the U.S. signal when both are broadcasting the same television program. Following a 1980 determination under section 301 of the (U.S.) Trade Act of 1974 against Bill C-58, the United States enacted similar legislation against Canada in its Trade Act of 1984. Another protectionist measure is the licensing of specialty channels by the CRTC, which led to the delisting of a U.S. country-music cable service, Country Music Television (CMT). In 1984, CMT received authorization to be carried by Canadian cable companies. That same year, the CRTC adopted a policy that would terminate the eligibility of an American specialty channel when a competitive Canadian service becomes available. In 1987, this policy became optional. However, in June 1994, the CRTC delisted CMT in favour of a new Canadian channel, New Country Network (NCN). CMT filed a petition under section 301, and Canada was found to have acted in an unreasonable and discriminatory manner. While the Office of the U.S. Trade Representative (USTR) threatened retaliation, CMT and NCN reached a settlement on 6 March 1996. The licence is now owned by a holding company, with CMT as a minority holder and NCN as a majority holder.[49]

Government Intervention in the United States

Reluctance to Subsidize the Muse

Government support for the cultural industries in the United States has always been rather timid. Attempts at creating an arts council failed on numerous occasions because of a lack of congressional appropriations.[50] The case against federal funding for the arts was based essentially on the premise that culture was not important enough to justify congressional votes and tax dollars. Many also thought that government intervention could lead to interference and a loss of artistic freedom. Nevertheless, Congress in 1891 created the National Conservatory of Music in New York City. In 1910 President William Howard Taft established a Commission on Fine Arts. Lacking a precise mandate, the commission dealt almost exclusively with the architecture of Washington, DC. In 1950, President Harry Truman asked the commission to consider how the federal government could help the arts sector. In its report, the commission recommended establishment of a cultural centre in Washington. In 1958, President Dwight Eisenhower signed Public Law 85-874 creating the National Cultural Center, which opened in 1971 as the John F. Kennedy Center for the Performing Arts. After a few other, ill-fated attempts in the late 1950s and early 1960s, Congress agreed in September 1965 to create the

National Foundation for the Arts and Humanities, with two administrative branches: the National Endowment for the Arts (NEA) and the National Endowment for the Humanities (NEH). Once President Lyndon B. Johnson signed Public Law 89-209, the NEA became an independent agency, which reports to the president and is directly funded by Congress. Its large-scale direct subsidy program represented a major shift in U.S. policy. The NEA has been at times at the centre of controversies but remains the main instrument of government subsidy for the arts in the United States. Additional public funding is also available from agencies such as the United States Information Agency, which supports international cultural programs, as well as state and local arts councils. In fact, the legislation creating the NEA requires that at least 20 per cent of its budget be directly available to state arts councils.[51]

Two other major U.S. federal initiatives undertaken to support employment had an unprecedented impact on the arts. The programs of the Works Progress Administration (WPA) were launched in the 1930s to create temporary employment during the Depression. Inspiration for the arts program, from which more than 40,000 artists benefited, came from the Mexican government's subsidizing of the mural movement in that country. In the 1970s, the (U.S.) Comprehensive Employment and Training Act (CETA) focused on helping the unemployed. Its arts program (1975–81) became one of the largest funding sources for the cultural industries, exceeding at times the NEA's expenditures.[52] As in the case of Canada, other measures to support the arts came in the form of indirect aid, such as deductions given to individual taxpayers and corporations, both at the federal and state levels, for their contributions to charitable organizations, including arts institutions.

Special 301

Special 301 protects intellectual property rights of U.S. right holders. The (U.S.) Omnibus Trade and Competitiveness Act of 1988 amended the Trade Act of 1974 to include the 'Special 301' provision requiring the USTR to identify each year those foreign countries that deny adequate and effective protection for intellectual property rights or that deny fair and equitable market access to persons who rely on protection of intellectual property. 'Priority' countries are those with the 'most onerous or egregious acts, policies, or practices,' whose policies or practices have 'the greatest adverse impact (actual or potential) on the relevant U.S. products,' and who are not negotiating in good faith or making significant progress bilaterally or multilaterally to provide adequate and effective protection. The USTR must initiate a section 301 investigation within thirty days of identifying such a country. Countries listed on the 'priority' watch list and on the watch list are subject to close monitoring from the USTR. For instance, Canada was put on the watch list from 1989 to 1992, removed in 1993, then got 'special attention' in 1994, and was back on the watch list again starting in 1995 because the United States had serious concerns in the copyright sector.[53] Mexico was on the priority list in 1989, removed in 1990, and put 'under observation' in 1998 for problems related to piracy.

Copyright Protection and the Manufacturing Clause

Copyright protection has over the years fostered the development of U.S. cultural industries. Among the illustrative categories of works of authorship covered under the Copyright Act of 1976 are literary works; musical works, including any accompanying words; dramatic works, including any accompanying music; motion pictures and other audiovisual works; and sound recordings. In 1998, the Digital Millennium Copyright Act added copyright works in cyberspace. The Sonny Bono Copyright Term Extension Act, also in 1998, extended by twenty years copyright protection in the United States. The duration of copyright protection is now life of the author plus seventy years.

The book publishing industry was the first to benefit from copyright protection. The act of 1790, modelled after the English Statute of Anne and enacted by Congress on 31 May 1790, protected books, maps, and charts by U.S. citizens or residents. Foreign authors such as Charles Dickens later suffered from lack of protection and often complained that American publishers pirated their books. In 1837, a bill was introduced in Congress to extend copy-right protection to anyone, regardless of nationality, provided that the edition was published and printed in the United States. The bill failed to gather much support but marked the first attempt at restricting copyright protection to works manufactured in the United States. The Chace Act of 1891 was more successful and became a landmark event; a manufacturing clause secured pro-tection for U.S. publishers and book manufacturers who feared British domination. Foreign authors received copyright protec-tion as long as their books, photographs, chromos, or lithographs were 'printed from type set within the United States or from plates made therefrom.'[54] Almost twenty years later, the Copyright Act of 1909 increased the manufacturing requirements by mandating that printing, binding, and typesetting of an English-language book or periodical be performed in the United States. Under cer-tain restrictions, exceptions allowed importation of one copy for individual use. Congress amended the Copyright Act in 1949 to permit the importation of up to 1,500 copies of books or periodi-cals of foreign origin in the English language if an ad interim, five-year copyright was requested. This right was extended to U.S. citizens and residents in 1954.[55]

The U.S. State Department called, albeit unsuccessfully, for the repeal of the manufacturing clause in 1949. Along with other for-malities, this clause had been preventing the United States from joining the Berne Convention, under which copyrights could not be subject to such requirements. In 1952, the Universal Copyright Convention (UCC), negotiated under the auspices of the United Nations Educational, Scientific, and Cultural Organization (UNESCO), was signed by forty countries, including the United States. To allow ratification of the UCC, Congress amended the Copyright Act on 31 August 1954 to exempt citizens of UCC coun-tries, except Americans, from the manufacturing clause. There-fore U.S. authors were still discriminated against. Several attempts at revising the Copyright Act of 1909 took place in the 1960s. The U.S. Copyright Office commissioned studies aimed at a complete overhaul of U.S. copyright law. The Register of Copyrights re-ported in 1961 that there was 'no justification for denying copyright protection, or cutting it off after 5 years, for failure to manufacture an edition in the United States.' He also noted that 'the effects on authors is severe. They lose not only the right to reproduce their works in printed form, but also the other rights, often more remunerative, to use their works in motion pictures, broadcast, plays, etc.' In the course of congressional hearings on the 1965 Revision Bill, the Department of Commerce recommended elimination of the manufacturing clause and called into question the protection afforded to the printing industry. Another issue discussed during those hearings was an exemption for Canada. Representatives of the U.S. book manufacturing industry championed this idea. They explained that since Canada acquires approximately 50 per cent of U.S. book exports, removal of the manufacturing clause and Canada's eventual elimination of customs duties and other charges on imported printed books would allow book manufacturers to manufacture for the entire North American market. Canadian and U.S. representatives of the printing and publishing industries reached an agreement in Toronto on 16 February 1968 to eliminate the manufacturing clause, provided that Canada became a member of the United Nations' Agreement on the Importation of Educational, Scientific and Cultural Material, signed in Florence in 1950, which eliminated tariffs and other charges on importation of printed books, newspapers, periodicals, and other documents. The United States had signed the Florence Agreement in 1966. Despite strong opposition from the U.S. State Department, which worried about its potential violation of GATT's article XIII, the Copyright Act of 1976 incorporated the exemption for Canada. Other new exemptions included works by Americans residing abroad for more than a year, U.S. authors unable to publish in the United States, and works made-for-hire under certain conditions. The 1976 act required that preponderantly non-dramatic English-language literary material be manufactured in the United States or Canada. Although the manufacturing clause was set to expire on 1 July 1982, printers and labour unions convinced Congress in June 1982 to extend the expiry date to 1 July 1986. President Reagan vetoed the measure, but Congress overrode his veto (324–86 in the House and 84–9 in the Senate).

The European Community (EC) lodged a formal complaint against the manufacturing clause before the GATT on 8 March 1983, arguing that it constituted a breach of GATT articles XI:1 and XIII. A panel was established in July 1983, and the GATT Council approved its decision in May 1984. The United States was found to have violated its GATT obligations, and the EC announced in 1986 that it planned to retaliate should the United States extend the manufacturing clause, due to expire on 1 July 1986. Intense lobbying came from intellectual property associations; from industries such as tobacco, chemicals, and machinery, which stood to lose from European retaliation; and from U.S. Trade Representative Clayton Yeutter and Commerce Secretary Malcom Baldridge. They convinced Congress in the spring of 1986 not to extend the manufacturing clause indefinitely. After almost a century of trade protection aimed at protecting domestic book printing, the clause's demise signalled the beginning of a new era in U.S. copyright protection, allowing for more active promotion of the protection of intellectual property rights in bilateral and multilateral trade negotiations.

Periodical Industry: Indirect Assistance

In the U.S. periodical industry, indirect assistance has come from the United States Postal Service. First, the Post Office Act of 1794 allowed magazines to be transported in the mail as long as their size permitted it. New postal regulations in 1852 required each magazine (not the subscriber) to pay for postage. The establishment of a second-class postal rate a few years later led to rapid growth in the periodical industry.[56]

Foreign Ownership of Motion Picture Studios and Protection of Sound Recordings

The motion picture industry has always been rather insulated from government intervention, with the notable exception of the blacklisting period during the McCarthy era just after the Second World War. Government measures in sound recordings have been mostly the result of state laws. In fact, before 1972, sound recordings were protected only by state laws. The first federal law protecting sound recordings, the Sound Recording Act of 1971, and the Copyright Act of 1976 apply to recordings fixed after 1972. In 1984, the Record Rental Amendment was adopted, it prohibits rental of phonorecords of a sound recording embodying a musical work.

In the mid-1980s the increase in the foreign ownership of U.S. entertainment industries raised some serious concerns. The acquisition by foreigners – mostly Japanese – of major Hollywood studios (for example, Columbia Pictures, by Sony, in 1989, and MCA, by Matsushita, in 1990), record companies (for example, RCA, by BMG/Bertelsmann, in 1986, and CBS Records, by Sony, in 1987), and television stations (for example, Metromedia, by Rupert Murdoch, in 1985) in the late 1980s sent shockwaves to Congress. These foreign acquisitions convinced the House Telecommunications Subcommittee to hold hearings on the global media market. The chair of the House Budget Committee, Democrat Leon Panetta of California, went a step further and introduced legislation in October 1991 that would have put a ceiling (50 per cent) on foreign ownership in the U.S. cultural industries.[57]

FCC and Public Broadcasting

The first U.S. statute dealing with broadcasting, which had begun at the turn of the century, was the Radio Act of 1912, which authorized the secretary of commerce to license 'and, to a limited extent, regulate the dot-and-dash wireless communications to which radio was then limited.'[58] The Radio Act of 1927 created the Federal Radio Commission (FRC). With the arrival of Franklin D. Roosevelt's administration in 1933, Congress adopted the Communications Act of 1934 establishing the Federal Communications Commission (FCC), an independent federal agency responsible directly to Congress. Leaders of the industry had been calling for a single regulatory commission encompassing the authority of the FRC (broadcasting) and the Interstate Commerce Commission (telephone and telegraph). As in other countries such as Canada and Mexico, security concerns convinced legislators in the United

States to prohibit foreigners from controlling broadcasting companies. The Radio Act of 1912 required licences to be given only to citizens of the United States and Puerto Rico, while section 310(b) of the Communications Act of 1934 limits foreign involvement to a maximum of 20 per cent of direct ownership of companies with a broadcasting licence and 25 per cent of a holding company that controls a licensee. The 1934 act also provides for a waiver should the FCC conclude that such a decision is in the public interest. However, the only such waiver ever granted was given in 1995, when the FCC agreed to give a licence to the Australian-based News Corporation, owned by Rupert Murdoch, for Fox Broadcasting. The Telecommunications Act of 1996 did not remove the restrictions on foreign ownership but allowed foreigners to serve as officers or directors of a corporate licensee.[59]

In addition to regulating broadcasting, Congress created the Corporation for Public Broadcasting (CPB), established under the Public Broadcasting Act of 1967. CPB is a private and non-profit organization that oversees public telecommunication (radio, television, and online). It is a public–private partnership, in which financial support for public broadcasting comes overwhelmingly from non-federal sources (86 per cent). The 1967 act also led to creation of the Public Broadcasting Service (PBS) in 1969 and National Public Radio (NPR) in 1970.

Government Intervention in Mexico

A National Council for Culture and the Arts

It is through direct involvement that the Mexican government has tried to increase cultural resources. National unity and the promotion of a Spanish-language, homogeneous culture have always been the main objectives of its cultural policy. Since 1988, cultural affairs have been handled by the Consejo Nacional para la Cultura y las Artes (National Council for Culture and the Arts, or CNCA), created on 7 December 1988. Functioning under criteria of rationalization and efficiency, the CNCA has the mandate to co-ordinate, modernize, and give institutional coherence to the cultural institutions that aim at preserving, promoting, and diffusing the Mexican culture, including the Instituto Nacional de Bellas Artes (National Institute of Fine Arts, or INBA), the Instituto Nacional de Antropología e Historia (National Institute of Anthropology and History, or INAH), the Fondo de Cultura Económica (Economic Cultural Fund, or FCE), the Biblioteca de México (Library of Mexico), and Radio Educación.[60] The Fondo Nacional para la Cultura y las Artes (National Fund for Culture and the Arts, or FONCA) has been helping Mexican artists since 1989. Funding comes from the government and the private sector.

Book Publishing and Periodical Industries:
Subsidies and Copyright Protection

The Mexican government has long been involved in the book publishing and periodical industries, by, for example, supporting publication of textbooks distributed free of charge to children. Books are published by the CNCA, FCE, and the INBA. Several periodicals covering different aspects of Mexican culture are also published by the CNCA, the INAH, the INBA, and other public organizations.[61]

Property rights for the publication of literary works have been available in Mexico in one form or another since 1846. The civil codes of 1870, 1884, and 1928 also addressed the issue. The first federal copyright law was enacted in 1947. A new law was introduced in 1956 after Mexico joined the UCC; amendments to this law were adopted in 1963.[62] The current law published in the *Diario Oficial* on 24 December 1996, covers several categories, including literary, musical, and dramatic works, motion pictures and other audiovisual works, radio and television programs, and computer programs.

The Film Industry: The Powerful Role of the State

Intervention by governments in the Mexican film industry has been instrumental in the development of the domestic cinema. During the Second World War, the U.S. government, through the Office of the Coordinator for Inter-American Affairs, gave a major boost to the industry by providing funding, equipment, and Hollywood advisers. The supply of raw film stock by the United States helped Mexico supplant Argentina as the leading exporter of Spanish-language films for Latin America.[63] The Mexican state's involvement in the film industry has also been significant. Between the mid-1930s and the mid-1970s it created or purchased (total or mixed participation) several institutions aimed variously at financing (Banco Cinematográfico, set up in 1947), producing (Conacine, Conacite 1 and 2), distributing (Pel-Nal, Pel-Mex, and Cimex), publicizing (Procinemex), and exhibiting (Operadora de Teatros) Mexican movies. In addition, movie studios such as Churubusco – the largest in Latin America – and Estudios América were also part of the government's strategy to support domestic film making.

The arrival of the Echeverría administration (1970–6) marked a turning point. Under the guidance of the actor Rodolfo Echeverría, the president's brother, a plan for restructuring the industry was introduced in January 1971. Echeverría regretted that domestic production was low and of poor quality, with films largely financed (over 80 per cent) by the Banco Cinematográfico. Echeverría, the Banco's new director, proposed to nationalize the industry and encourage the production of films espousing social and political themes. This led to establishment of three state production companies (Conacine, Conacite 1, and Conacite 2) in 1974–5, government purchase of Estudios América in 1975 (it had bought Churubusco in 1959), and building of the Centro de Capacitación Cinematográfica, a filmmaking school, in 1975 and the Cineteca Nacional, an archive for Mexican movies. But the results were mixed at best. Production fell, and private participation all but disappeared.

When José López Portillo (1976–82) succeeded Luis Echeverría, he appointed his sister, Margarita López Portillo, to head the Dirección General de Radio, Televisión y Cinematografía, a new government-sponsored agency controlling state activities in film, radio, and television. Nationalization and a state-sponsored film industry were no longer fashionable. The Banco Cinematográfico and Conacite 1 and 2 were dismantled in favour of stimulating private-sector productions and co-productions. In fact, the overwhelming majority of films produced during that period were financed by the private sector. Miguel de la Madrid's term as president (1982–8) brought a return to a more 'hands-on' government policy with establishment in 1983 of IMCINE,[64] whose financial support, however, does not cover all production costs. Filmmakers have to assume part of the risk or find private investors. IMCINE and all the other government-owned film enterprises have been part of the CNCA since 1989. The CNCA also helps fund videos with the Unidad de Producción Audiovisuales (UPA), created in 1989.

The Salinas administration (1988–94) sought to discourage funding from the state and protection in the film industry. A new law, Ley Federal de Cinematografía, published on 29 December 1992, superseded the Ley de la Industria Cinematográfica of 1949. The government privatized several government-owned companies, such as the largest exhibitor chain, COTSA (Compañia Operadora de Teatros), and the production studio, Estudios América. It deregulated ticket prices, previously frozen. A new cinema law of December 1998 requires movie theatres to reserve 10 per cent of screen time for domestic productions and created a new fund to encourage local productions.

Sound Recordings: Protection and Piracy

The Mexican government's involvement in the sound recording industry is minimal. The Plan Nacional de Apoyo a la Música (National Plan to Support Music), implemented in 1989, has been addressing various aspects of the music industry (composition, records, music publishing, fabrication of musical instruments, and so on), while since 1991 the Copyright Law has protected sound recordings. However, piracy was still a major problem at the time of the NAFTA negotiations. The International Intellectual Property Alliance (IIPA), a consortium of trade associations representing U.S. copyright companies, reported in 1991 that losses in Mexico because of piracy had reached U.S.$75 million a year in sound recordings and U.S.$15 million in cable and video. Mexico had been placed on the USTR's Special 301 priority watch list in 1989 but had been removed in 1990 after Mexico pledged in its

National Industry and Foreign Trade Modernization Program to strengthen its legislation on intellectual property. At the beginning of 1997, the Recording Industry Association of America (RIAA) expressed concerns about the new Mexican federal Copyright Law, which entered into force on 24 March 1997, because of its vague language about the inclusion in the penal code of sound recordings as protected works. The new law provides for a maximum penalty of 15,000 times the daily minimum wage, while the previous law had had a much lower fine, at 500 times that figure.[65]

Broadcasting, Regulations, and Foreign Ownership

Wireless telegraph was introduced in Mexico in 1902. The first radio broadcasting was transmitted in 1921, and the first television program on 1 September 1950. The broadcasting industry (radio and television) is now regulated by the Ley Federal de Radio y Televisión (Radio and Television Federal Law) of 19 January 1960, and cable television, by the Reglamento del Servicio de Televisión por Cable (Cable Television Regulation). The Foreign Investment Law, last modified on 24 December 1996, prohibits foreigners from participating in radio and television companies except through 'neutral investment' – 'investment made in nonvoting or limited voting shares issued with the prior authorization of SECOFI' (the Ministry of Commerce and Industrial Development).[66] However, for cable companies, foreign investment is allowed for up to 49 per cent of the total investment. The government also regulates the multipoint multichannel distribution system (MDDS), or subscription-based wireless cable, and direct-to-home satellite television.[67]

ISSUE-SPECIFIC POWER

Canada: The Cultural Exemption

The previous sections on government intervention have shown that all three countries – but most specifically Canada – have adopted a great number of measures aimed at protecting and increasing their cultural resources. But despite the overwhelming presence of American cultural products in Canada, Ottawa had issue-specific power at the outset of the NAFTA negotiations. Over the years, it had implemented a series of policy instruments to encourage creation of domestic cultural products. Ownership restrictions, content regulations, tax shelters, and subsidies have served as a way to promote development of and access to Canadian content. But above all, the federal government had convinced the Americans to exempt the Canadian cultural industries from the FTA, thereby shielding these protectionist measures, at least in the short run, against any type of liberalization. In the worst-case scenario, Canada could have walked away from the NAFTA table and achieved its main objective unilaterally, because the FTA would still have protected its cultural industries. In fact, the cultural exemption more than compensated for the low level of Canada's other resources, such as the size of its market and the small share of that market captured by Canadian books, films, and recordings.

The United States and Mexico

The United States and Mexico also had resources of their own at the beginning of the negotiations. The U.S. cultural industries account for a large share of North American cultural production and have captured a significant share of the market. Their level of employment and contribution to the GDP is high. Their trade has been flourishing, especially with Canada, their single largest export market. Government intervention has taken the form mainly of regulation of broadcasting ownership and copyright protection. Key resources for the United States in the copyright sector included a 'carve-out' provision with respect to Berne article 6*bis* and moral rights. As mentioned by Richard Neff and Fran Smallson, the (U.S.) Berne Convention Implementation Act indicates 'that the domestic law of the United States (including moral rights protection – or the absence thereof) is adequate to satisfy the obligations of the United States in adhering to Berne.'[68] At the time of the NAFTA negotiations, U.S. copyright legislation did not formally provide for recognition of moral rights, except for visual artists (under the Visual Artists Rights Act of 1990). U.S. copyright legislation also had long recognized the work-for-hire concept. For instance, section 26 of the 1909 act includes work for hire – i.e., work created for another – in its definition of author. For the Mexicans, in addition to providing subsidies for their cultural industries like the Canadians and Americans, their main resources rested with government regulation and infrastructure. One essential resource that would prove to be determinant was Mexico's ratification of the Rome Convention.[69]

TACTICS

Cultural Industries: On or Off the Table?

During the pre-negotiation phase, the United States and Canada raised the issue of culture, but for very different reasons. The Americans made it clear to the Canadians that they did not like the cultural exemption. In February 1991, the *Globe and Mail* reported that U.S. Trade Representative Carla Hills had told a House of Representatives committee that the United States did not favour cultural exemptions because they were protectionist. She also mentioned that 'Canada and the U.S. agreed to disagree on the question of Canadian protection for cultural industries, and said the two countries ... [were] still debating the issue.'[70] On 8 April, five congressmen sent a letter to Ambassador Hills calling on her not to exempt cultural industries in NAFTA.[71] They believed that to do so would send the wrong signal to the Europeans, who had 'already cited Canada's cultural exemption as a precedent for the European Community's Broadcast Quota' – an issue that would later be at the heart of the deadlock over audiovisual trade between Europe and the United States in the Uruguay Round. The representatives ended by asking Hills 'to use the new negotiations as an opportunity to reverse the damaging precedent ensconced in the Canadian F.T.A.'[72]

The Canadians and their new minister of international trade, Michael Wilson, promised that Canada was 'not going to let the

United States get through the back door what it could not get through the front door.' Wilson said: 'The FTA is signed, sealed and delivered. We will not negotiate it twice.' This stance was a signal to the Americans that the Canadians were going to be very firm, knowing that they had the backing of the Canadian population. At the Financial Post Conference held in Montreal on 25 April 1991, Wilson added: 'That applies in particular to pressure from U.S. lobby groups to challenge Canada's special measures of support for its cultural industry. That pressure will not work. This Government insisted on maintaining special measures of support for its cultural industries when it negotiated the FTA. It is not prepared to negotiate now what was settled then.'

Another successful Canadian tactic was to take advantage of the ongoing constitutional crisis by playing the 'unity card.' Wilson was trying to convince the Americans that the cultural exemption was essential 'particularly when the capacity of Canadians to reflect their nationhood to each other has never been more important.'[73] In an address to the Central Canada Broadcasters' Association in June 1991, he pleaded passionately for a cultural exemption: 'This is not just a question of protecting an industry. It is a matter of preserving the soul of a nation at a crucial time in our history. We are defending a culture.'[74] Maclean Hunter's chairman, Donald G. Campbell, echoed Wilson's statement at his company's annual meeting: 'Our national media are needed today to protect this country in precisely the same way an east–west railroad was needed at the time of confederation.'[75]

The Americans kept putting pressure on Canada until the end. After the beginning of the negotiations in June 1991, Ambassador Hills told reporters that 'the only thing I know that's off the table is the ownership of the oil mineral rights in Mexico and our immigration laws.'[76] The Mexicans were of no help to the Canadians. Knowing that the Americans were so adamantly opposed to cultural exemptions, Commerce Secretary Serra Puche declared that culture was an issue 'not so relevant for Mexico.'[77] The Mexican tactic was to go along with the Americans and later to negotiate specific exemptions. The U.S. tactic was to isolate the Canadians by pressing Mexico not to side with Canada. A Mexican official told the *Toronto Star*: 'The Americans are surprisingly forceful in this area and lobbying us surprisingly hard.'[78]

Industry Consensus in Canada and the United States

At the first ministerial meeting held in Seattle in August 1991, even though culture was not part of any working group, the United States raised issues pertaining to the Canadian exemption. The *Globe and Mail* quoted a Canadian official: 'Culture is an issue that was raised and continues to be discussed.'[79] In the following months, the private sector in both Canada and the United States reiterated the industry's consensus in each country. In Canada, the industry was opposed to any liberalization. There was a sectoral advisory group on international trade (SAGIT) dealing with cultural issues, one of the fifteen sectoral advisory groups on international trade. Also, the Canadian Culture/Communications Industries Committee, which had lobbied Ottawa for a cultural exemption during the FTA negotiations, was very active. On the U.S. side, representatives of the Motion Picture Association of America (MPAA) and the Recording Industry Association of America (RIAA) were very persistent in advocating elimination of the Canadian exemption.

In November 1991, a conference entitled 'North American Private Sector Meeting on Services in the North American Free Trade Agreement,' took place in Washington, DC, attended by representatives of cultural industries from all three countries. The Americans told their counterparts that culture was a trade commodity, a business, and that an exemption made no sense. They confirmed that the U.S. government was being lobbied very hard by the private sector not to extend the FTA exemption to other trade agreements. The Mexicans complained that U.S. films dubbed in Spanish were flooding their market, while the Canadians repeated their stance that the overwhelming U.S. cultural presence in Canada made the exemption necessary. Also, in November 1991, the U.S. Council for International Business told the Bush administration that it had to 'seek a comprehensive intellectual property agreement' in NAFTA.[80] On cultural issues, specifically copyright, the council said that 'Canada should be willing to consider substantial roll-back.'[81]

Canadians Say 'No' to Negotiations on Cultural Industries

Canadian negotiators had the mandate not to negotiate anything relating to the Canadian cultural industries.The status quo was the *formula* that Canada sought to 'sell' to its counterparts. This does not mean that there was no discussion related to culture. On the contrary, besides tariffs in the market access group, at least three working groups (on intellectual property, investment, and services) dealt with cultural issues. In March 1992, a Canadian official told the *Toronto Star* that the Americans had 'backed off': 'We have been under no pressure on that for several months, it just hasn't been part of the negotiations.'[82] But the issue had not been forgotten altogether. In a letter of 26 February, the Intellectual Property Committee, a coalition of thirteen American companies, urged Carla Hills to include national treatment in the chapter on intellectual property and to eliminate the cultural exemption.[83]

The real debate pertaining to culture 'happened at the end of the negotiations,' a Canadian trade official acknowledged. 'The discussion at all levels was whether the status quo was sufficient or not sufficient,' he noted. By July 1992, the end game had begun, and the Americans thought that it was time to press the Canadians to liberalize their cultural industries. Quoting unidentified sources, the *Toronto Star* confirmed that Hills 'renewed demands that Canada eliminate barriers on cultural trade during a private meeting with [Minister] Wilson in New York on July 18.'[84]

Mexico Demands Exemptions à la carte and Restoration of Copyright Protection for Old Movies

Mexico decided during the negotiations to negotiate exemptions à la carte from free trade, which made Canada more vulnerable. The American tactic of isolating Canada was once again at play. Moreover, Mexico and, to a lesser extent, Canada were trying to convince the United States to protect films that had been declared in the public domain under the old U.S. copyright regime. The Mexicans, in particular, were eager to 'resurrect' copyright protection for these films. The United States agreed but narrowed down the period (1 January 1978 – 1 March 1989) for which restoration was to be allowed.

National Treatment and Broad Cultural Exemption

For both the Mexicans and the Canadians, the main outstanding issue, according to one Canadian official, had to do with 'how extensive national treatment should apply to intellectual property where national treatment was not a rule, particularly neighbouring rights, and to future intellectual property rights.' Having ratified the Rome Convention, which protects performers, producers of sound recordings, and broadcasters, Mexico did not favour national treatment, because that meant granting U.S. performers the right to collect royalties for public performance (radio and television) of their sound recordings, even though the United States is not a signatory to the Rome Convention. Canada was also questioning an across-the-board provision on national treatment. The Canadians were in the second phase of the revision[85] of their copyright law and were analysing the possibility of applying the Rome Convention and its reciprocity principle. Canada was also worried about future intellectual property rights and the development of new technologies. Its main concern was that because these new rights would fall under the national treatment provision, no discrimination would be possible.

Since all parties were unwilling to make any concession, while the Americans kept pushing very hard, 'the matter did not get resolved until the very end, until the whole package was put in place. It was *the* final issue on intellectual property,' a Canadian negotiator acknowledged. A compromise was struck at the ministerial level. There would be an across-the-board provision for national treatment. But to satisfy Mexico, this provision would also allow a party to 'limit rights of performers of another party in respect of secondary uses of sound recordings to those rights its nationals are accorded in the territory of such another Party' (NAFTA 1703[1]). Canada would keep its cultural exemption.

The Canadians had realized that pressing for an overall cultural exemption was a better tactic than having to negotiate reservations chapter by chapter. The federal government had envisaged negotiating reservations for each chapter covering cultural issues. It asked the cultural SAGIT which option the industry would prefer: the Mexican or the status quo. The private sector was very reluctant to forgo the overall exemption and insisted on protecting the status quo. The Canadian government therefore stood its ground and accepted across-the-board national treatment in chapter 17, provided that it would keep the FTA cultural exemption. As mentioned above, the exemption, by specifically referring to the FTA, allows Canada to depart from the NAFTA provisions in intellectual property, except those deriving from its adherence to other international agreements, and to adopt or maintain any measure that could violate the NAFTA obligations on intellectual property without being subject to possible retaliation by another party. The retaliation right also does not apply to several provisions of the chapters on investment and cross-border services. For instance, the MFN treatment principle is not part of these two chapters in the FTA. The principle of national treatment covers only the establishment of new businesses in the FTA and the providers of a specific list of commercial services.

The Canadians could not afford politically to see the cultural exemption eroded, but the Americans kept pushing. A Mexican trade official remembers: 'It was the FTA revisited all over again.' Commenting on the fact that cultural industries were off the table, a senior Canadian trade official acknowledged: 'It was not obvious until the day of the agreement.' The Americans finally gave up, but not without a fight. 'We had to back away. The whole package was more important to us than Canada's cultural industries exemption,' an American participant said. In fact, Canada had enormous leverage on culture during the end game at the Watergate. The Americans, who had refused the concept of self-imposed deadline for ending the NAFTA negotiations, were now in a different situation. President Bush wanted a deal in time for the Republican convention in mid-August. The Canadians were in no hurry and used their leverage to get a concession from the Americans at the last hour. The cultural exemption was saved. It was 'a last minute concession to Canada before the negotiations were completed on Aug. 12.'[86] The detail phase did not last too long. The negotiators had agreed basically to use the FTA's wording.

CONCLUSION

It is undoubtedly clear that Canada performed well in culture. Trade Minister Wilson had repeatedly said that issues settled in the FTA would *not* be reopened: 'the U.S. will not get through NAFTA ... what it failed to achieve in the FTA.'[87] Canada desperately wanted to protect the status quo. As issues that would affect Canada's cultural industries were being discussed, Canada decided that a cultural exemption incorporating the whole agreement would be simpler. Moreover, by choosing to keep the reference to the FTA, Canada was ensuring that the status quo would be protected and that new obligations in intellectual property, for example, would not affect Canada's cultural industries.

The Americans had a different strategy. They view culture as a profitable business, with a $4-billion trade surplus a year. They also did not want to set another precedent that would force them to extend the cultural exemption to their European partners or any other countries.[88] The Industry Functional Advisory Committee on Intellectual Property Rights for Trade Policy Matters confirmed this position when it wrote in its report on NAFTA in September 1992 that Canada was a special case. 'The "cultural industries" issue is an outgrowth of the arguably unique geographic and linguistic proximity of the United States and Canada. It is for that reason that our other trading partners should not view the exclusion as a precedent in future bilateral or multilateral intellectual property negotiations.'[89]

Although the Canadians had issue-specific power in culture and could have walked away from the negotiations if necessary, they also knew that their overall objectives in NAFTA would be better served if they were part of the agreement. Given the strong backing of the Canadian population, an unshakeable industry consensus, and the invocation of an ongoing constitutional crisis threatening the future of the country, the Canadian tactics were clear from beginning to end: to be firm in maintaining that cultural industries were off the table and that issues pertaining to Canadian cultural industries would *not* be negotiated at any table. Canada was determined to persuade the Americans that it would not settle for less than what was agreed on in the FTA. The use of tactics was extremely important in that respect. The Canadians refused to negotiate anything related to culture. They also took advantage of a contextual event – the Canadian constitutional crisis – to try to convince the Americans that the exemption was necessary to preserve Canada as a country. But most important, Canada 'seized' the moment during the end game and withheld its signature until it got what it wanted in culture. This tactic, which was very time-sensitive, proved extremely successful.

The pressure from the U.S. lobby on the Bush administration not to extend the exemption to NAFTA because of the impact that such an action could have on the Uruguay Round had been constant and did not stop after 12 August 1992. In fact, shortly after the deal was struck, the MPAA pressed Congress to reopen NAFTA to eliminate the cultural exemption.[90] The RIAA also sounded the alarm to Congress about the consequences of that exemption on the GATT agreement. Moreover, in her testimony before both the Senate Finance Committee and the House Ways and Means Committee, Carla Hills warned Canada that the exemption provided for retaliation and that the United States was prepared to retaliate should Canada adopt any measure causing prejudice to the U.S. economy.[91] In fact, the Intellectual Property Committee sent a letter to her on 1 October 1992, calling for a three-step strategy should Canada invoke the exemption with respect to intellectual property rights: 'First ... the implementing legislation should ensure that strong measures will be taken so as to deter Canada from exercising the exclusion. Second, the exclusion should be renegotiated as soon as possible. Third, the United States should make it clear to our trading partners that such an exclusion would not be accepted again by the United States under any circumstances.'[92]

To make sure that the Canadians and the Europeans were aware that the United States was serious about retaliation, Representative Robert Matsui (Dem., California), a leading proponent of NAFTA, introduced a provision in the U.S. implementing legislation amending section 182 of the Trade Act of 1974 (19 USC 2242) and requiring the USTR to identify, no later than thirty days after it submits its annual report to Congress,

> any act, policy, or practice of Canada which – A) affects cultural industries, B) is adopted or expanded after December 17, 1992, and C) is actionable under article 2106 of the North American Free Trade Agreement.[93]

This section did not add anything new to NAFTA, but it sent a clear message to the Canadians that invoking the exemption would put them at risk. Canada had met its objectives and 'won' in NAFTA by protecting the status quo, but the United States reminded its northern neighbour of the real meaning of this status quo – that the United States has the right to retaliate should Canada invoke the cultural exemption to implement measures inconsistent with the Canada–U.S. Free Trade Agreement.

CHAPTER FOUR

Textiles and Apparel: Canada, the Odd Man Out

Textiles and apparel are among the oldest manufacturing industries in the world, 'with roots going back to the very beginning of civilization.'[1] They led the industrial revolution to become one of the primary employers in most developed countries. In the United States, one in ten manufacturing workers is still employed by these two sectors. As these industries grew, countries sought to protect themselves against foreign competition. The U.S. Congress enacted its first tariff on cotton and woollen goods in 1816. Mexico's early tariffs in 1821 and 1827 were aimed at shielding the Puebla-based artisan textile industry against imports. In 1829, cotton products were included on Mexico's prohibited import list.[2] Likewise, Canada's National Policy Tariff of 1879 focused on encouraging import substitution and thereby investment in the textile sector.

Textiles (fibres, yarns, fabric, and other products) are made from natural sources such as cotton, flax, hemp, ramie, silk, and wool; and from 'man-made' fibres such as acetate, acrylic, nylon, rayon, and polyester. Textile products include goods as diverse as automotive and apparel trimmings, canvas and related products, carpets and rugs, and curtains and draperies. Production is concentrated in three regions of the world: 'highly industrialized countries (North America, European Union, Japan) with generally high-value-added applications; newly industrialized countries (Korea, Taiwan) with medium and low-end applications; and emerging countries (Pacific Rim, China, India) with low-end applications.'[3] The textile industry has benefited from technological advances and is more capital-intensive and mechanized than the apparel sector, whose firms operate in all corners of the globe, from the most industrialized to the least developed. The apparel industry is essentially labour-intensive.

In view of the new competition coming from developing nations and the successive tariff reductions negotiated through GATT, industrialized economies tried to curb imports by devising a specific regime for textiles and apparel, because apparel and, to a lesser extent, textiles were providing much-needed jobs to low-skilled workers in developed countries. Since tariffs were no longer the favoured instrument to increase protection, quantitative restrictions became the most notable feature of this new regime. Voluntary export restraints (VERs), targeting only a few countries, quickly made room in the 1960s and early 1970s, albeit without great success, for two international arrangements in cotton textiles – the Short-Term Arrangement (STA) and the Long-Term Arrangement (LTA). But tighter protection was embraced as imports from non-member countries and of textile products and apparel manufactured from wool and man-made fibres kept growing in developed countries. This led to a more comprehensive solution in 1974, with the entry into force of the Multi-Fibre Arrangement (MFA) negotiated under the auspices of GATT. The MFA covered trade in textile and apparel products made from cotton, wool, and man-made fibres and established the rules for bilateral agreements on export restraint. Operating outside the aegis of GATT, the MFA allowed members to violate the most-favoured-nation (MFN) principle, the cornerstone of GATT, by discriminating among textile- and apparel-producing countries and by imposing quotas instead of tariffs. As observed by William Cline, the MFA set 'a precedent of imposing quantitative restrictions against developing countries (and in this case Japan as well) but not against industrial countries.'[4] The MFA was renewed several times until it was replaced in 1995 by the Agreement on Textiles and Clothing negotiated in the Uruguay Round. This agreement phases out the MFA quotas over ten years.

But intense lobbying from textile and apparel manufacturers was still at play in the industrialized world in the late 1980s and early 1990s. In North America, the Canada–U.S. Free Trade Agreement (FTA) had seen the emergence of a new protectionist instrument – a 'fabric forward' rule of origin. Although that represented a clear victory for the U.S. textile and clothing industries, Canada had negotiated tariff rate quotas (TRQs) to offset this rule somewhat, which was putting Canadian manufacturers at a disadvantage when using third-country inputs. At the beginning of the NAFTA negotiations, the stakes were high. U.S. manufacturers were calling for a tightening of the rule of origin in order to protect their domestic market.

This chapter first examines the objectives of the NAFTA negotiators, and then it considers the outcome of the negotiations. It next looks at the main resources of each state actor, reviewing, as in chapter 3, the market share and industry control in each country. It moves on to consider, at both the multilateral and the national levels, the role of government intervention in trying to increase resources in textiles and apparel. It then analyses issue-specific power. The chapter next discusses in detail the tactics employed by the negotiators to meet their objectives.

NEGOTIATORS' OBJECTIVES

The Canadian objectives in the textile and apparel negotiations were three-fold. First, Canada wanted to secure the access to the U.S. market it had obtained under the FTA. Second, it hoped to negotiate improvements to some areas of access arrangements in the FTA. For instance, it had concerns that the FTA's TRQs for non-originating goods were not going to be sufficient. Moreover, the Canadian industry had no guarantees for the TRQ for non-wool fabric and made-ups beyond the end of December 1992. Third, vis-à-vis low-cost Mexican competition, Canada wanted an appropriate adjustment period for both textiles and apparel – two very sensitive sectors, given their concentration in Quebec.

The United States had three objectives. The Americans wanted to strengthen the rules of origin in textiles and apparel in order to prevent Mexico from becoming an export platform for non-NAFTA countries. They also wanted appropriate safeguards and long adjustment periods for their most import-sensitive sectors. Finally, both the Americans and the Mexicans were eager to gain greater access to each other's market. The Mexicans also called for the immediate elimination of U.S. quotas and early removal of U.S. tariffs on Mexican textiles and apparel.

NEGOTIATION OUTCOME: STRICTER RULES OF ORIGIN

The United States was overwhelmingly successful in textiles and apparel. It negotiated more restrictive rules of origin than existed under the FTA. These rules determine which goods not wholly produced in North America are given preferential duty treatment. Non-originating components must undergo a tariff shift in the Harmonized System (HS) of tariff classification in order to receive preferential duty treatment or NAFTA tariff status. In a free trade area, rules of origin have two functions. First, they specify criteria determining which goods or services not entirely produced within the area are entitled to duty-free treatment. They also aim at preventing *trade deflection*, whereby imported commodities would enter the free trade area through the country with the lowest tariff.[5]

A Gain for the United States

The 'Yarn Forward' Rule

The NAFTA general rule of origin in textiles and apparel is known as 'yarn forward,' whereby apparel and made-up textile goods undergo a 'triple transformation.' There are three stages in the manufacturing process of most textile and apparel products. Fibre is first spun into yarn, yarn is then knitted or woven into fabric, and fabric is then cut and sewn into goods such as made-up textile products or apparel. To comply with the NAFTA rule, textile goods and apparel have to be manufactured within the free trade area from North American yarn knitted or woven into fabric cut and sewn in the NAFTA region. Thus, *only* imported fibre inputs are allowed. There are exceptions, however. A 'fibre forward' rule covers some textile and apparel products made of cotton and 'man-made' fibre (MMF).[6] Other products, including linings, fall under a 'fabric forward' rule.[7] Products not made in North America or deemed to be in short supply[8] have to meet a less stringent 'single substantial transformation' rule of origin.[9] Textile and apparel goods that do not comply with the NAFTA rules of origin but contain no more than 7 per cent by weight of non-originating material are eligible for NAFTA preferential duty. This provision is known as the *de minimis* rule.[10]

A general review of all the rules of origin in textiles and apparel must take place within five years of the date of NAFTA's entry into force. The objective of this review is to take into account the effect of increasing global competition on textile and apparel goods, the implications of the Uruguay Round agreement, the rules in other integration agreements, and developments relating to textile and apparel production and trade.[11] Moreover, parties may consult each other on request to determine whether particular goods should have different rules of origin, taking into account availability of supply within the area. They may also want to change the list of items subject to substantial transformation.[12]

Mixed Results for Canada

Offsetting NAFTA Rules with Tariff Preference Levels

The single most important objective of the Canadian negotiators was to preserve Canada's access to the U.S. market obtained under the FTA. However, whereas the FTA required a 'double transformation,' or what is known as a 'fabric forward' rule, NAFTA requires a 'triple transformation.' In the FTA, apparel and made-up textile goods had to be manufactured from Canadian or American fabric cut and sewn within the region. Imported yarn and fibres were allowed. In NAFTA, as we saw, only fibres can be imported. The Canadian government was not pleased with the new NAFTA rules because they were threatening Canada's access to the U.S. market. A Canadian official remarked during the negotiations that 'under the yarn forward proposal, 90 percent of U.S. and Mexican apparel production will qualify for trade preferences, while less than 50 percent of Canadian production, which relies heavily on imported yarn, will qualify.'[13]

Jack Kivenko, vice-president of Jack Spratt in Montreal and at that time president of the Canadian Apparel Manufacturers Institute, echoed this statement in his testimony before the Senate of Canada in June 1992: 'The problem with these rules is that Canada's apparel manufacturers, with few domestic textile facilities available, are unable to meet their needs and have been forced to source their inputs off-shore. Our knit fabric industry relies most exclusively on imported yarns, and over 60 per cent of the woven fabrics used in the Canadian garment industry must be imported. In addition, much of the fabric sold by Canadian textile firms is comprised of imported yarns or is merely converted and finished in Canada, meaning that garments made of those fabrics would not meet the NAFTA rules of origin. In other words, if NAFTA were adopted, the majority of Canadian garments would be ineligible for free trade.'[14]

To offset the impact of these more stringent rules, Canada convinced its negotiating partners to increase the special provisions negotiated under the FTA that allowed its manufacturers to export to the United States, at the preferential rate of duty, textile and apparel products that did not satisfy the FTA rules of origin. Three tariff rate quotas (TRQs) had been negotiated under the Canada–U.S. Free Trade Agreement. Above these annual levels, goods were subject to the MFN rate. Tariff preference levels (TPLs), or annual quotas, formerly known as TRQs, were negotiated in NAFTA for textiles and apparel that do not conform to the rules of origin. They allow access to the market of member countries for non-originating goods. As in the FTA, for quantities above these TPLs, goods are subject to the MFN rate. Tables 4.1–3 show the TPLs for Canada, the United States, and Mexico, respectively.[15] In addition, the United States agreed to a temporary TPL of 25 million square metres equivalent (SMEs) for apparel and made-up goods sewn and assembled in Mexico from imported fabric and re-exported to the United States under tariff item 9802.00.80.60.[16]

TABLE 4.1
Canada's tariff preference levels

	FTA (TRQs) Imports into the United States	Imports into the United States	Imports into Mexico
Cotton or man-made apparel	41,806,500 SMEs	80,000,000 SMEs + 2 per cent annual growth* (of which no more than 60,000,000 + 1 per cent annual growth can be made from offshore fabric)	6,000,000 SMEs
Wool apparel	5,016,780 SMEs	5,066,948 SMEs + 1 per cent annual growth (of which no more than 5,016,780 can be of men's or boy's wool suits of U.S. category 443)†	250,000 SMEs
Cotton or man-made fibre fabrics and made-ups	25,083,900 SMEs (until 31 Dec. 1992, and extended until 31 Dec. 1993)	65,000,000 SMEs + 2 per cent annual growth (of which no more than 35,000,000 for knitted fabrics and textile articles and no more than 35,000,000 for woven fabrics and textile articles)	7,000,000 SMEs
Cotton or man-made fibre spun yarn	Not applicable	10,700,000 kg + 2 per cent annual growth	1,000,000 kg

*The annual growth rates apply for five years commencing on 1 January 1995. In the general review of all the rules of origin, Canada and the United States must decide whether they wish to continue to apply annual growth factors to the Canadian TPLs. Should they decide not to continue with a growth factor, they may on request adjust any annual TPL based on the ability to obtain supplies of particular fibres, yarns and fabrics. Annex 300-B, appendix 6, section B, paragraphs 8(b) and 8(a). Subparagraph a already applies to imports into Canada from Mexico or the United States, imports into Mexico from Canada or the United States, and imports into the United States from Mexico.
†The annual growth rate does not cover wool suits.

TABLE 4.2
U.S. tariff preference levels

	FTA (TRQs) Imports into Canada	Imports into Canada	Imports into Mexico
Cotton or man-made apparel	8,779,365 SMEs	9,000,000 SMEs	12,000,000 SMEs
Wool apparel	919,740 SMEs	919,740 SMEs	1,000,000 SMEs
Cotton or man-made fibre fabrics and made-ups		2,000,000 SMEs (knitted fabrics only)	2,000,000 SMEs
Cotton or man-made fibre spun yarn	Not applicable	1,000,000 kg	1,000,000 kg

TABLE 4.3
Mexico's tariff preference levels

	Imports into Canada	Imports into the United States
Cotton or man-made apparel	6,000,000 SMEs	45,000,000 SMEs
Wool apparel	250,000 SMEs	1,500,000 SMEs
Cotton or man-made fibre fabrics and made-ups	7,000,000 SMEs	24,000,000 SMEs*
Cotton or man-made fibre spun yarn	1,000,000 kg	1,000,000 kg

*No more than 18 million SMEs for knitted fabrics and textile articles and no more than six million SMEs for woven fabrics and textile articles.

The results are mixed for Canada in TPLs. On the one hand, Canadian TPLs for the United States are the only ones that are allowed to grow. Five years after the entry into force of NAFTA, the two parties must decide whether to maintain these growth rates. Another piece of good news for Canada is that the new quota negotiated on cotton or man-made fibre-spun yarns was set at a level four times higher than Canada's 1991 exports to the United States. Moreover, in non-wool apparel and non-wool fabrics and made-up articles, the Canadian TPLs counterbalance the effects of the rules of origin, even though they include more articles. However, in the long run, the TPLs put a ceiling on Canada's ability to export to the United States. As well, there is clear erosion in Canada's access to the U.S. market in wool apparel. The small increase in the TPL for wool apparel does not offset the impact of the more restrictive rules of origin.

Wool Apparel

In an area of great Canadian export success – wool apparel – the quota has increased by 1 per cent from 5,016,780 SMEs to 5,066,948 SMEs (plus 1 per cent annual growth for five years). This small increase is a loss for Canada, as acknowledged by a senior Canadian trade official involved in the NAFTA negotiations: 'Personally, in wool apparel, I was quite disappointed.' In a letter to U.S. Trade Representative Carla Hills in the summer of 1992, before the end of the negotiations, Canadian Trade Minister Michael Wilson wrote: 'The existing 5 million square meters equivalent TRQ was negotiated as part of the FTA trade-off related to rules of origin in this sector. Clearly, the introduction of more restrictive rules of origin, without an offsetting increase in the TRQ, would represent an erosion in the access which Canada obtained under the FTA.'[17]

Moreover, the Canadian Apparel Manufacturers Institute argued that this new quota does not offset the impact of the NAFTA rules of origin because of the new definition of wool: 'Canada and Mexico have formally agreed to adopt the U.S. definition of wool. While this definition has been imposed administratively by the Americans under the Canada–U.S. Free Trade Agreement it has been consistently opposed by the Canadian apparel industry and was open to dispute from Canada. Using the American definition, woven apparel in chief weight of man-made fibres containing 36% or more of wool will be considered to be wool apparel. The minimum for knitted apparel is set at 23% wool. The impact of this agreement is to push more products into the items covered by the wool apparel TRQ, thus limiting flexibility and access to the U.S. market.'[18] The institute also mentioned that, for the first time, linings are counted to determine the origin of a garment. In addition, 'Under the NAFTA rules of origin a large portion of the knit garments made in Canada would no longer qualify for free access to the U.S. market. The majority of the yarns used by Canadian knitters are sourced off-shore. Under the proposed three-stage rule of origin, garments made of these yarns would, for the first time, be forced to use [TPLs] to access the American market. As a result, wool and wool-blend sweaters exported to the United States would be forced to use the [TPLs].'[19]

Canadian apparel manufacturers used 20 per cent of the wool quota in 1989 and 1990, 51 per cent in 1991, 70 per cent in 1992, and 88 per cent in 1993.[20] The growth rate in the wool apparel TPL does not mean much to Canadian apparel manufacturers. 'Translated solely into wool suits, the 1[per cent] annual growth would amount to roughly four days of production by one current suit exporter. That does not leave a lot of room for export growth.'[21]

A modest victory for Canada was the high sub-limit on men's wool suits, a sector in which Canada has been extremely successful, supplanting Italy in 1992 as the leading foreign supplier to the American market. The new sub-limit is equivalent to the FTA's TRQ for wool apparel – i.e., 5,016,780 SMEs. Alvin Segal, president of the Montreal-based Peerless Clothing, one of the industry's star performers, is very optimistic. His company manufactures only men's wool suits and exports 90 per cent of its production to the United States: 'Fortunately, in our product, wool suits, I don't see NAFTA as a threat because Mexico doesn't have the opportunity to use third world fabrics – not third world offshore fabrics, as we have here in Canada. The only opportunity we've had and the reason we've been a success in the U.S. market is because we're able to offer offshore fabrics to the U.S. market. The last thing American retailers need from a Canadian apparel manufacturer is what they already have ... They want us for Italian fabrics, French fabrics, English fabrics.'[22] One of the reasons his company has been so successful, Segal believes, is because the tariff on wool is lower in Canada than in the United States, a key policy decision on the part of the Canadian government that has contributed to the success of this industry.

Non-Wool Apparel

In non-wool apparel, Canada's TPL has expanded from 41,806,500 SMEs under the FTA to 80,000,000 SMEs under NAFTA, with a growth rate of 2 per cent per year. Of these 80 million SMEs, 60 million are for single transformation, and the balance is for double transformation. Clothing manufacturers had not made great use of the non-wool apparel TRQ, which seems to indicate that their ability to export to the United States will not be compromised.[23] However, the Canadian apparel industry was quick to point out that 'this growth will be offset by the far greater number of garments which will fall under the [TPL]. All garments knit to shape in Canada using off-shore yarns would need to use [the TPL] to export to the United States under NAFTA. All garments using woven fabrics made in North America from off-shore yarns will be forced to use [the TPL] to export to the United States.'[24] As in wool apparel, for the first time linings are also used in determining origin of non-wool apparel under NAFTA.

Non-Wool Fabric and Made-Up Articles and the Debit Clause

No quota was negotiated in NAFTA for wool fabrics and made-up goods. The TPL for non-wool fabric and made-up articles, in contrast, was nearly tripled, from 25 to 65 million SMEs. Here again the same arguments play. In the short run, the TPL offsets the effects of the rules of origin, but as more goods fall under this TPL, an increase of 160 per cent may not be as significant as it looks. However, the debit clause, which allows textile goods made with 50 per cent or less non-originating materials to debit this TPL by 50 per cent instead of the full 100 per cent, is certainly going to compensate for the effects of the rules of origin.[25] This provision applies only to 'dual sourcing' between Canada and the United States, and, unlike the FTA, NAFTA guarantees the TPL for non-wool fabric and made-ups.

A Major Victory for Mexico

Quota Elimination

Mexico was rewarded with the immediate lifting by the United States of its quotas on Mexican exports that met the NAFTA rules of origin or the requirements of the special regime on textiles established in 1988 (textile products and apparel imported from Mexico that are assembled from U.S.-cut and -formed fabric). For non-originating goods not satisfying the NAFTA rules of origin or the special regime but meeting the U.S. normal rule of origin, it was agreed that quotas would be phased out gradually over ten years.[26]

Other Issues

Tariff Elimination

Tariff elimination between Canada and the United States followed the schedule set forth under the FTA, which phased out all tariffs by 1 January 1998. During the NAFTA negotiations, Canada and Mexico agreed to reduce their tariffs according to the following timetable. First, clothing tariffs are being reduced to zero in ten equal instalments over ten years – the so-called C period, the longest adjustment period sought by Canada. Most textile tariffs are being eliminated over an eight-year period, a 'B+' phase-in – a reduction of 20 per cent the first year; no reduction the second year; annual reductions of 10 per cent during the five following years, and finally a 30 per cent reduction the last year. A few tariffs are being phased out in six equal stages (category B*l*). Others, particularly those already accelerated under the FTA, were eliminated immediately on NAFTA's entry into force.[27] Most tariffs between the United States and Mexico had been eliminated after the first five years of NAFTA. During the NAFTA negotiations, parties agreed to an immediate tariff elimination on 49 per cent of Mexican exports to the United States (an 'A' period), 45.3 per cent in five years (a 'B6' period), and five per cent over ten years (a 'C' period). The United States was successful in ensuring that tariffs on more sensitive products, such as rayon filaments and woven fabrics, certain man-made fibre-wool blend fabrics, and most women's wool apparel, are being phased out over ten years.[28] Mexican tariffs on U.S. exports are also being eliminated in three phases. Before NAFTA, approximately 3 per cent of U.S. exports were entering the Mexican market duty free. The United States and Mexico had agreed during the negotiations on three phases – immediate elimination of tariffs on 16.8 per cent of the goods ('A' period) representing key U.S. exports; an intermediate elimination over five years ('B6' period) for 60.7 per cent of the goods; and a long-term phase-out for the remaining products over ten years ('C' period).[29]

NAFTA contains an 'acceleration clause' that permits faster phase-in to reduce tariffs and quotas on goods mutually agreed on between two (or more) of the parties – NAFTA 302(3). On 29 April 1998, at their fourth ministerial meeting, held in Paris, NAFTA ministers agreed on a U.S.$1-billion package of tariff elimination. Among the textile items that were accelerated in one or more NAFTA countries are certain types of wool yarn, some wool textiles, certain types of cotton yarn, woven cotton fabrics, and certain man-made fibres, yarns, and woven fabrics.[30]

Safeguards

NAFTA contains two safeguard mechanisms. For originating goods – i.e., goods that satisfy the rules of origin – and goods covered by TPLs, tariffs can be temporarily increased to MFN rates during the transition period (ten years) if imports are determined to cause 'serious damage, or actual threat thereof,' to the domestic industry. This measure is weaker than the general NAFTA standard of 'substantial cause of serious injury, or threat thereof.' The 'tariff snapback' may be invoked only once during the transition period against any specific good, and for a maximum of three years. The party against whose good the action is taken must receive compensation in the form of concessions having substantially equivalent trade effects.[31] The United States and Canada were able to convince Mexico to accept a second safeguard mechanism, which applies to non-originating goods during the transition period, including TPL-eligible goods. This quantitative restriction safeguard allows a party to impose quotas for up to three and a half years against disruptive imports of another party. No compensation need be given, and the same standard of 'serious damage, or actual threat thereof,' applies. It does not cover Canadian–U.S. trade.[32]

Duty Drawback, Uniform Procedures, and Government-Private Sector Cooperation

NAFTA extended for two more years (from January 1994 to January 1996) the full duty drawback available under the FTA. With Mexico, the deadline for Canada and the United States is 1 January 2001.[33] As noted by the U.S. General Accounting Office (GAO), Mexican *maquiladoras*[34] and U.S. foreign trade zones[35] will have 'to pay duty on all non–North American components and raw material used to make products eligible for NAFTA duty-free treatment' after a seven-year transition period.[36] In order to prevent double taxation, NAFTA allows for limited drawback programs on goods as long as these goods are subject to duties. Duty drawback programs waive or rebate tariffs paid on imported components used in exported goods. For Canadian exports, the refund is equivalent to the lesser of the duty paid on non-originating inputs and the duty paid on textiles or apparel when exported to the United States or Mexico.[37] As under the FTA, duty drawback applies permanently to apparel exports between Canada and the United States traded at the MFN rates.[38]

NAFTA provides for customs co-operation and enforcement. Uniform procedures will be used to 'ensure that exporters who market their product in more than one NAFTA country do not have to adapt to multiple customs regimes.'[39] Exporters must maintain certificate-of-origin forms for a minimum of five years (see NAFTA 505). Each member's customs administration may audit books of exporting firms in other countries to verify if the products meet the rules of origin. The U.S. GAO notes that it may also 'conduct timely, on-site plant inspections to verify production and capacity in all NAFTA countries to prevent illegal transshipment of textile and apparel products.'[40] Advance rulings are also going to be issued on request.

Finally, NAFTA established two committees. The Subcommittee on Labelling of Textile and Apparel Goods comprises government and private-sector representatives from each country. Its mandate is to 'pursue a work program on the harmonization of labelling requirements to facilitate trade in textile and apparel goods ... through the adoption of uniform labelling provisions.'[41] The Committee on Trade in Worn Clothing has to 'assess the benefits and risks that may result from the elimination of existing restrictions on trade ... in worn clothing.'[42] Representatives of the three governments and the private sector work together on this committee.

RESOURCES

The textile and apparel industries have enjoyed an unprecedented level of protection compared to other manufactured goods over this past century. Dating back to the interwar period, the U.S. private sector, and to a lesser extent Canadian manufacturers, have helped to shape the trade regime that has governed these industries. When comparative advantage started shifting to developing countries because of their abundant labour resources, these economies began manufacturing and exporting textile products and apparel. But the sharp increase in their exports to industrialized nations soon became the target of schemes to restrict their access to North American and European markets. The main goal of developed countries – especially the United States and Canada – was to protect their resources in textiles and apparel from severe losses and cutbacks.

Developed countries were particularly concerned with these factors – their share of production and of the market; their level of employment in these industries, especially taking into account geographical concentration; and their growing trade with low-cost textile-producing countries. Japan's increasing textile exports in the mid-1930s led to its first voluntary export restraints (VERs) with the United States and the appointment of Canada's royal commission on the textile industry in 1936, following the temporary closing of Dominion Textile's rayon plant in Sherbrooke, Quebec. More recently, U.S. textile and apparel industries increased their resources during the FTA negotiations. The FTA resulted in very strict disciplines in rules of origin that favoured U.S. players, although Canadian producers received compensation through tariff rate quotas, as noted above.

Market Share and Industry Control

Canadian Textile and Apparel Industries

While the manufacture of woollen goods goes back to the early days of settlement in Canada, the first cotton mill on record was established in 1844 in Sherbrooke. Manufacturing of broad silk fabrics started in 1922 in Cowansville, Quebec. Two years later, the first rayon plant was erected in Cornwall, Ontario, by the British-based Courtauld Company. Canadian textile manufacturers[43] sell a wide range of products to more than 150 customer industries. They serve essentially three markets: household and institutional, which accounts for 45 per cent of total output; apparel, with 35 per cent; and industrial and commercial, with 20 per cent.[44] The industry is located in small urban communities in Ontario (57 per cent of shipments and 48 per cent of the workforce) and Quebec (37 per cent of shipments and 43 per cent of the workforce). The textile sector consisted of over 1,000 establishments at the time of the NAFTA negotiations, with concentration particularly high in primary textiles, even though the majority of firms have fewer than fifty employees. According to a 1991 publication of Industry, Science and Technology Canada, 'the value of shipments of the top 7 [per cent] of all textile firms (73 establishments, each with more than 200 workers) [accounted] for 50 [per cent] of total industry output' in the late 1980s and early 1990s. In textile products, low barriers to entry have led to more fragmentation, except for bedsheets, carpets and rugs, and pillowcases and towels. The presence of foreign-based multinationals is also significant in the primary textile area. Foreign-owned firms are responsible for 60 per cent of all shipments in that sub-sector, and several producers are vertically integrated. In textile products, the situation is reversed: the Canadian presence is predominant, and, except for carpets and rugs, most firms are not vertically integrated.[45] The textile industry devoted more than $2.8 dollars between 1987 and 1996 to buying new machinery, equipment, and buildings and to becoming more efficient and productive. Large firms have taken advantage of economies of scale and have been major users of new technology.

The industry employed about 60,000 persons in 1991 and 1992 and over 50,000 in 1997. It accounted for a little over 2 per cent of Canada's GDP and 3 per cent of its manufacturing employment at the outset of the NAFTA negotiations. The textile industry made total shipments of approximately $6.95 billion in 1991 and 1992 – a drop of $750 million from 1989, the industry's best year before implementation of NAFTA in 1994. Total shipments reached $8.2 billion in 1994 and over $9 billion in both 1996 and 1997. Until quite recently, the industry was not export-oriented. In fact, exports represented slightly more than 5 per cent of the value of shipments in the 1960s and about 11 per cent at the end of the 1980s. By 1997, however, they had reached close to 30 per cent. Imports as a proportion of total value shipments have also increased over the past few years. They accounted for 40 per cent of the domestic market in 1991, and more than 50 per cent in 1997. Exports to the United States grew substantially as a proportion of total exports after the signing of the FTA. They represented 54.9 per cent of total textile exports in 1989, 56.6 per cent in 1990, 64.3 per cent in 1991, and 69.1 per cent in 1992. By 1997, they had climbed to over 77 per cent. Textile imports from the United States also increased as a proportion of total Canadian imports – 49 per cent of the total in 1989, 52 per cent in 1990, 56 per cent in 1991, and 66 per cent in 1997. Canada has had a trade deficit in textiles with the United States and Mexico for several years.[46] Canada's trade with Mexico is fairly small. Canadian exports to Mexico accounted for 1.03 per cent of total Canadian textile exports in 1989,

0.73 per cent in 1990, and 0.41 per cent in 1991. Imports from Mexico were greater, though still very small – 1.3 per cent of total Canadian textile imports in 1990 and 1.06 per cent in 1991.

The apparel industry manufactures a wide range of goods and has recently crafted new niches for itself. It produces high-quality garments for the retail market and also serves industrial and institutional users by producing functional apparel.[47] Although the apparel sector is now present in every province and territory of Canada, it has always been concentrated in Quebec, which has about 67 per cent of establishments, 63 per cent of shipments, and 56 per cent of employment. Apparel accounted for 10 per cent of Quebec's manufacturing employment in 1994. Ontario, Manitoba, and British Columbia are the other main producers. Canadian-owned, mostly family-run firms dominate, accounting for 98 per cent of the 2,000-plus total. Three-quarters of the firms have fewer than fifty employees and produce approximately one-third of industry shipments. At the beginning of the 1990s, only 12 per cent of the firms had more than 100 employees. Foreign-owned establishments are generally larger and controlled by U.S.-based multinationals.

The apparel industry employed about 100,000 people in the early 1990s. Employment had fallen to slightly more than 84,000 by 1995. Most workers are women (75 per cent) and immigrants (over 50 per cent). The industry accounted for 1.6 per cent of Canada's manufacturing GDP in the mid-1990s and almost 6 per cent of manufacturing employment. It suffered huge losses during the recessions of the late 1980s and early 1990s. More than 800 firms, or about 30 per cent of the total, closed between 1988 and 1993, and employment dropped at the average annual rate of 5.2 per cent over this period, with the most severe decline occurring during the NAFTA negotiations in 1991 and 1992. Shipments also fell dramatically, from $6.4 billion in 1989 to $5.1 billion in 1992 (in constant 1986 dollars). Shipments started increasing again in 1993, to reach $8.5 billion in 1995.

Like textiles, the apparel industry has not traditionally been export-oriented, but this trend was reversed starting with the FTA. Apparel exports accounted for 21 per cent of total shipments in

1995, up substantially from 1989, at only 5 per cent. Canadian manufacturers have been especially successful these past few years with exports of men's and boy's apparel (38 per cent of total exports in 1995). Imports have also increased substantially, from 18 per cent of the domestic market in 1981 to 42 per cent in 1995. Exports to the United States have risen consistently, representing 85 per cent of total apparel exports in 1989, 86 per cent in 1990 and 1991, and 92 per cent in 1997. Imports from the United States also grew, from 7 per cent of total apparel imports in 1989 to 20 per cent in 1997. Canada has had a trade surplus with the United States since 1984. Trade with Mexico is smaller in apparel than it is in textiles. Exports there represented 0.09 per cent of exports in 1991, while imports from Mexico accounted for 0.52 per cent of imports.

U.S. Textile and Apparel Industries

U.S. textile manufacturing started in New England in the early seventeenth century, with flax and wool being the two major fibres commonly used. The first cotton mill was established by Samuel Slater in Blackstone River, Rhode Island. Slater was a young Englishman who in 1782 emigrated to the United States as an agricultural labourer while he was in reality a skilled mechanic. At the time, England banned exportation of machinery designs and prohibited emigration of skilled mechanics. Slater had memorized how to build the water power–based machine patented in 1769 while working with the inventor's partner in England.

The U.S. 'Textile Complex' has since grown to include more than 26,000 firms in the fibre, textile, and apparel industries. Most of the 5,000 textile companies are located in non-metropolitan areas of the southeast – i.e., in descending order, North Carolina, with 30 per cent of U.S. textile GDP, Georgia, South Carolina, Alabama, and Virginia.[48] Concentration was increasing in the textile industry at the outset of the NAFTA negotiations. At the end of the 1980s, 16 per cent of the plants employed 84 per cent of the workforce.[49] These are large plants of 100 employees or more. In order to become more competitive, the industry invested over

U.S.$4,000 annually per worker between 1989 and 1993 to buy new equipment and modernize plants.

The textile industry employed 600,000 persons in 1992, down from a peak of 1.3 million in 1948. Automation in the 1960s and 1970s, and the rising dollar and recessions of the 1980s, led to significant reduction in employment. The sector enjoyed an increase in job growth after 1990–1, to approximately 636,000 workers in 1996. As in Canada, a higher proportion of women and minorities are present in the textile and apparel industries than in other sectors of manufacturing. Close to 60 per cent of textile jobs are located in the Carolinas and Georgia. The industry is also the largest manufacturing employer in Alabama, accounting for one-third of all such work. In fact, the Textile Complex is a key element of the U.S. economy, providing 10 per cent of manufacturing employment.

The value of textile shipments dropped during the 1990–1 recession but grew in 1992 by 4 per cent, to U.S.$70 billion. The value of shipments had reached U.S.$80 billion by 1997. As a whole, the industry is less export-oriented than its Canadian counterpart. In 1989, exports represented only 4.2 per cent of shipments, and in 1997 about 8 per cent. Canada took approximately 25 per cent of total U.S. exports in 1992 and 27 per cent in 1996, making it the leading market for U.S. textile exports. Mexico came second in 1992, with 13 per cent, and in 1996, with 16.6 per cent. Imports as a proportion of domestic production remained very low during the 1970s, at 4.5 per cent, and rose slightly during the 1980s, to 7 per cent. The figure climbed slowly, to 8 per cent in 1992 and 9 per cent in 1997. Imports from Canada represented 7 per cent of total U.S. textile imports in 1992 and almost 13 per cent in 1996, while Mexico accounted for 1.9 per cent in 1992 and 6.7 per cent in 1996.

Because of low barriers to entry, the U.S. apparel industry is not very concentrated. Most of its 21,000 firms are small and have an average of forty employees. Apparel establishments are located mainly in California, which has one-fifth of the workers, and in New York, with 10 per cent. Texas, North Carolina, Tennessee, Georgia, and Pennsylvania are the other largest employers. The industry reached its highest level of employment in 1973, with 1.4 million jobs. By 1992, it had fallen to 960,000, and by 1997 to fewer than 850,000, partly because of new technology and import penetration. However, although firms have been investing in new equipment and technology, it is often more difficult for small apparel firms than for large textile companies to buy the latest technology. This explains why the apparel industry is spending only 40 per cent of the textile industry's budget on capital investments.[50]

The value of shipments of apparel grew modestly in the 1990s, to reach over U.S.$70 billion in 1992 and U.S.$80 billion in 1997.[51] Exports as a percentage of product shipments more than doubled between 1989 (4 per cent) and 1993 (9 per cent). This export growth is partly explained by shipments of garment parts for assembly in low-cost countries under item 9802 and the Special Access Program (both explained below in the section on government intervention), with duty being paid only on value added at re-entry to the United States. A special regime with Mexico had also been in effect from 1989 to 1993. U.S. apparel exports to Canada and Mexico accounted for 6.6 per cent and 17.8 per cent of total exports in 1992, respectively, and 8.1 per cent and 23.9 per cent in 1996. Import penetration has consistently increased in the United States, from 13 per cent in 1980 to 26 per cent in 1988. At the time of the NAFTA negotiations, approximately 40 per cent of apparel consumed came from abroad.[52] U.S. apparel imports from Mexico, the Caribbean, and Central America grew rapidly in the 1990s because of tariff item 9802 and the Special Access Program. In 1992, imports from Canada and Mexico combined represented a small 5.1 per cent, while in 1996, Mexico became the top supplier of apparel imports in the United States and Canada's share increased slightly, reaching approximately 2.6 per cent.

Mexican Textile and Apparel Industries

The artisan industry started well before the arrival of the Europeans, with the production of yarn and fabric, but the modern textile sector began when Estevan de Antuñano opened a water power–based factory on a river bank near Puebla in the 1830s.[53] The industry flourished and developed, mainly with the help of now-dismantled protectionist measures implemented by the government after 1945. The country is home to more than 14,000 textile and apparel firms. Textile establishments are located all over the country, and major producing centres include Estado de México, Puebla, the Federal District, Tlaxcala, Aguascalientes, Querétaro, Oaxaca, and Baja California. At the time of the NAFTA negotiations, the Ministry of Commerce and Industrial Development (SECOFI) reported that the textile industry counted 2,249 businesses, of which 86 per cent were small or micro firms. Most firms were Mexican-owned, and foreign investment did not exceed 10 per cent.[54] The industry comprised more than 2,800 firms in 1994 and more than 2,600 in 1997.

The textile industry generated approximately 210,000 jobs in 1990, representing 5.6 per cent of Mexican manufacturing output and 9 per cent of manufacturing employment.[55] In the mid-1990s, the number of employees fluctuated between 142,000 in 1994 and approximately 160,000 in 1997. The industry accounted for 3.6 per cent of manufacturing GDP in 1994 and roughly 4.1 per cent in 1997.[56] Value added dropped between 1980 and 1993 at an average rate of 1.8 per cent a year, while total textile output fell in nominal terms in 1995 after the peso crisis (which began in December 1994) but grew again in 1996 and 1997. Total output stood at 8.3 billion pesos in 1994, 7.98 billion pesos in 1995, 9.56 billion pesos in 1996, and over 11 billion pesos in 1997.

Apparel firms are present throughout the country but concentrated in the Federal District and along the U.S. border. The 'fashion belt' includes the states of Jalisco, Aguascalientes, and Guanajuato. There were 9,125 firms in the clothing industry generating 600,000 jobs at the time of the NAFTA negotiations. By 1997, the number of companies had increased to 11,700, while fluctuating between 10,000 and 12,000 during the mid-1990s. The overwhelming majority – 96 per cent – of these firms are small or micro. The sector employed approximately 460,000 workers in 1997.[57] The industry's share of GDP was about 1.48 per cent in 1994 and rose to over 1.7 per cent by 1997.

Both the textile and apparel industries have traditionally been targeting the once highly protected domestic market. Textile and apparel exports (excluding the *maquiladora* sector) were worth U.S.$330 million in 1991, while total output exceeded U.S.$10 billion. Imports amounted to U.S.$796 million. By 1994, exports had increased to U.S.$990 million and imports to U.S.$2.1 billion. The 1995 recession and peso crisis led to significant export growth (86 per cent) and a drop in imports (40 per cent). Except in 1995, Mexico has usually registered a trade deficit in textile and apparel (combined). Moreover, the United States is by far Mexico's largest supplier and buyer of textiles and apparel, accounting for 69.2 per cent of Mexico's imports in 1993 and 86.4 per cent in 1994. Mexican exports to United States have also grown, from U.S.$1.4 billion in 1993 to U.S.$4.2 billion in 1996.

As was mentioned in the report on the impact of NAFTA's first three years published in July 1997, 'on a value basis, almost two-thirds of Mexico's textile and apparel exports to the United States are currently manufactured using U.S. components parts.' In 1990, 42 per cent of total U.S. imports from Mexico were assembled in Mexico from U.S. components, by 1993, the figure was 52 per cent. In 1996, this share increased to 64 per cent, and Mexico became the largest foreign U.S. textile and apparel supplier, a title held until then by China.[58] That same year, maquiladoras in the textile and apparel industries accounted for 18 per cent of total employment and 12 per cent of value added in the maquila sector as a whole – i.e., approximately 162,000 workers produced 4.68 billion pesos of goods.[59]

Government Intervention

*A Multilateral Special Regime
in Textiles and Apparel*

After the Second World War, new surges in cotton textile exports by developing countries, including Japan, prompted the United States and other industrialized economies to negotiate VERs and impose new protectionist measures. Although GATT rules offered numerous options to contracting parties for imposing restrictions, many developed countries chose to position themselves outside the GATT framework.[60] Shortly after Japan became a GATT contracting party in 1955, the United States convinced the Japanese government in January 1957 to announce a five-year VER on its exports of cotton textiles to the United States. It also negotiated VERs with other low-wage nations. Canada followed the U.S. initiative and held talks with Japan and other countries before concluding its own VERs in the late 1950s and early 1960s.

The Short-Term Arrangement (STA)

Market disruption caused by a rapid increase in developed countries' imports of cotton textiles became a central issue at the Fifteenth Session of the GATT Contracting Parties in November 1959. The working party created to study that issue reported in November 1960 that market disruption was indeed a problem. Following a suggestion made by the United States, the GATT Council of Representatives met in Geneva on 16 June 1961 and agreed to convene a conference to discuss a multilateral solution to market disruption in cotton textiles. Informal meetings to prepare work and consult on the issue took place in Washington, DC, on 21–3 June 1961, involving the United States, Canada, and six other textile-consuming countries. The conference, attended by sixteen GATT contracting parties and several observers, was convened in Geneva under the auspices of GATT in July 1961. It resulted in the one-year Short-Term Arrangement Regarding International Trade in Cotton Textiles (STA). This one-year arrangement was based essentially on U.S. proposals. It entered into force in October 1961. In addition to creating the Provisional Cotton Textile Committee to work towards a longer-term solution, the STA allowed importing countries to ask a participating exporting country to exercise restraint (i.e., quantitative restrictions) when unrestricted imports of cotton textiles were causing or threatening to cause disruption of its domestic market (article 1A). The STA also required importing countries to increase their quotas (article 1E).[61]

The Long-Term Arrangement (LTA)

The Long-Term Arrangement Regarding International Trade

(LTA), signed in February 1962 by nineteen governments, was very similar to the STA. It was originally to be in force for a period of five years, but it was extended for three years in 1967 and in 1970. To avoid market disruption, the LTA allowed quantitative restrictions by exporting countries at the request of importing countries (article 3) and provided for quota growth in importing countries (article 2). The LTA also permitted conclusion of 'mutually acceptable arrangements on other terms not inconsistent with the basic objectives of the Arrangements' (article 4).

Such arrangements rapidly became the preferred form of protection for Canada and the United States. The GATT textile study of 1984 noted that Canada 'negotiated a number of agreements for specific products (including non-cotton items). The United States at first resorted to many unilateral restraints, which were subsequently converted into bilateral agreements applying aggregate ceilings to the entire range of cotton textiles.'[62] By 1973, eighty-two countries had signed the LTA. But since the arrangement covered only cotton textiles, there was an incentive for exporting countries to shift to wool and man-made fibres. In fact, U.S. imports of man-made fibres increased from 31 million pounds in 1960 to 329 million in 1970.[63]

Although the United States also negotiated VERs on non-cotton products with Asian suppliers, pressure in Congress mounted, and the issue was brought before the GATT. GATT set up a working party in 1972 to study the textile industry and to propose a multilateral solution. The working party suggested negotiation of a new multilateral arrangement encompassing cotton, wool, and man-made fibre textiles. It also mentioned 'the need to refine the definition of market disruption, and the importance of an effective mechanism of international surveillance.'[64] These recommendations led to establishment of a negotiating group and the Multi-Fibre Arrangement (MFA), which entered into force on 1 January 1974.

The Multi-Fibre Arrangement (MFA)

The MFA covered textile products and apparel made of cotton, wool, and man-made fibres. Article 2 required that all existing unilateral quotas or quantitative restrictions negotiated under bilateral agreements be notified to the Textiles Surveillance Body (created under article 11) by the importing country, while article 3 allowed importing countries unilaterally to restrict imports that were disrupting markets if there was no agreement after consultations with the exporting country. But the governing principles of the MFA were article 4 and annex B. Article 4 dealt with 'situations involving a *real* risk of market disruption.'[65] Participating countries could conclude bilateral agreements on mutually acceptable terms without having to extend the terms of these agreements to other countries. Annex B governed the growth rates and base levels of article 4 and gave some flexibility to exporting countries in using part of a quota on one product against a quota on another (swing adjustments) or using part of a quota in the preceding year (carry-over adjustments) or the following year (carry-forward adjustments).

The MFA also created the GATT Textiles Committee (TC) and a multilateral Textiles Surveillance Body (TSB), to monitor the arrangement. Each MFA signatory was represented on the TC, while the TSB consisted of a chair and eight members, with equal representation for importing and exporting countries. The TSB had the mandate of reviewing unilateral actions under article 3 and bilateral agreements under article 4 and of making non-binding recommendations. Participating countries had to report their safeguard actions to the TSB, which also served as a forum for settling disputes. The arrangement was extended several times.[66] It was replaced on 1 January 1995 by the WTO Agreement on Textiles and Clothing (ATC).

Under the first MFA, Canada entered into several bilateral agreements for products not covered by (GATT) article XIX global quotas.[67] After these quotas were lifted, it negotiated more agreements with major suppliers such as Hong Kong, India, Korea, Macao, and Malaysia, under MFA II. It concluded other bilateral agreements under MFA III and MFA IV. Most of the quotas negotiated by Canada under the MFA framework, except for a few agreements under MFA II, grew at the target rate of 6 per cent per year.

The United States also concluded several bilateral agreements during the first MFA. Some covered aggregate levels of all MFA fibres, others restrained cotton products, and one targeted cotton and man-made fibre products. During MFA II, the United States negotiated seven agreements covering forty-six categories of products. Some of the aggregate restraints that went into force during MFA I were also liberalized. The main characteristic of the agreements concluded by the United States during MFA III was that they covered select clothing categories. Under MFA IV, the United States put together a new system of guaranteed access levels with set levels for categories of products assembled and cut in that country.[68] As of December 1993, it had signed bilateral agreements under the MFA with thirty economies and eleven other agreements with non-signatories.[69]

Mexico participated in both the LTA and the MFA. It negotiated bilateral agreements with the United States and the European Community. It set export quotas only with the United States.

The MFA undermined the multilateral system by allowing the violation of several GATT articles, such as articles I on MFN, XI on prohibition of quotas, and XIX, which requires that safeguard quotas be temporary and the result of a product-specific determination. It also did not stop erosion of domestic market shares in developed countries, because low-wage producers shifted their production to higher-value-added products, since restraints applied to volume, not to value of imports.

The WTO Agreement on Textiles and Clothing (ATC)

The launching of the Uruguay Round Multilateral Trade Negotiations in September 1986 marked the beginning of the end for the specific regime in textiles and apparel. GATT contracting parties stated that their goal was eventual integration of this sector into the GATT. After a ten-year transitional period ending on 31 December 2004, these two industries will be governed by GATT rules. The ATC, which applies to all WTO members, requires that unilateral quotas imposed under the MFA be notified to the Textiles Monitoring Body (TMB) and eliminated within a year of the WTO's entry into force. Quotas under bilateral agreements outside the MFA had also to be notified to the TMB and either eliminated within one year or phased out progressively over ten years, following a specific schedule notified to the TMB. MFA quotas imposed under bilateral agreements may continue as long as they were notified to the TMB within sixty days of the WTO's entry into force. Their phasing-out schedule was as follows. First, on 1 January 1995, WTO members had to remove quotas accounting for at least 16 per cent of their total volume of imports in 1990. Second, on 1 January 1998, they had to lift quantitative restrictions for another 17 per cent of their total 1990 volume of imports. Third, on 1 January 2002, they were to liberalize an additional 18 per cent of 1990 import volume. The remaining goods will be integrated into GATT on 1 January 2005. Moreover, during the transition period, quotas will increase progressively: 16 per cent in the first stage (1995–7), 25 per cent in stage 2 (1998–2001), and 27 per cent in stage 3.

The ATC (article 6) also provides for a transitional safeguard for products not yet integrated into GATT. However, the importing country must consult with the exporting country before applying a safeguard restraint and notify the TMB, which makes recommendations to the members concerned. Transitional safeguards are applied on a non-MFN basis when increased imports cause or threaten to cause serious damage to the domestic industry. These measures may not be imposed at a level below the actual level of imports from the country concerned during the year ending two months before the two countries consult. They may be maintained for up to three years or until quotas are liberalized and integrated into GATT. Multi-year safeguards must provide for quota growth of at least 6 per cent a year. Other measures, such as article XIX's safeguard measures for goods integrated into GATT and anti-dumping measures, are available to countries wishing to increase protection in the textile and apparel sectors.

Government Intervention in Canada: From Industrial Policy to Tariff Relief Measures

The Early Years: The National Policy and High Tariffs

The American Civil War provided an impetus for development of the cotton manufacturing industry in Canada, but it was the adoption of the National Policy by John A. Macdonald's Conservative government in 1879 that launched the rapid expansion of the textile industry. Canada had turned protectionist after failing on numerous occasions to convince the Americans to renew the Reciprocity Treaty of 1854 – a bilateral free trade agreement covering natural products abrogated by the United States in 1866.[70]

The Canadian tariff policy was no longer revenue-oriented but aimed at promoting import substitution. In fact, high protective tariffs on manufactured goods, including an increase from 17.5 per cent to somewhere between 20 and 30 per cent on cotton manufactures, resulted in substantial expansion of textile and apparel production and investment, as reported to Parliament in 1885. Over-capacity and -production led to a surge in exports to China and Africa by the end of the century. But Canada's decision in 1897 to establish imperial preference, lowering tariffs on British imported goods, devastated the domestic woollen textile industry. Output of woollen manufactures fell sharply to less than half their 1899 level by 1910. Cotton textiles were also affected, but to a lesser degree, since domestic producers were able to capture two-thirds of the market. The United Kingdom became the major foreign competitor for Canadian textile manufacturing goods, providing, for example, 90 per cent of Canadian wool imports in 1938 and 60 per cent of cotton imports.

Other measures served to increase protection for the textile industry during the Depression. Tariffs reached their peak in September 1930, when the tariff policy was changed so as to allow a significant increase in *ad valorem* rates, and tariffs were raised on a number of textile items. Some of these tariffs were later reduced under the Canada–United Kingdom Trade Agreements of 1932 and 1937 and the GATT negotiations. A special excise tax first applied on 2 June 1931 was also levied on imported goods, but not on domestic manufactured goods.[71]

VERs and the Interdepartmental Committee

The textile industry benefited from rapid growth during the Second World War, but the situation turned around in the 1950s because of intensified foreign competition. The Royal Commission on Canada's Economic Prospects, in its July 1956 report on the Canadian primary textile industry, stated that 'the industry's experience in the 1950–4 period can be described as defence of a declining share of a contracting market.' Other factors affecting the industry included inflation, appreciation of the Canadian dollar, the increasing range of textile goods being produced in a small market, rising prices and costs for Canadian-made products compared to those in competing countries, and contraction in the U.S. market.[72] In the later 1950s, imports of textiles and apparel from developing countries, especially from Japan, grew rapidly. These imports severely disrupted the market and convinced the Canadian government to request Japan to impose VERs on certain textile products. The results were mixed. Imports from other sources increased. For example, apparel imports from Hong Kong rose dramatically, capturing 0.5 per cent of total imports in 1955 and 23.8 per cent in 1960. Canada also concluded VERs with other countries and later formalized them in the STA and LTA.[73]

Overwhelmed by growing imports from Asia, Ottawa in early 1961 established the Interdepartmental Committee on Low Cost Import Policy to measure the impact of imports on manufacturers and to advise the government on the need to negotiate VERs with other countries. During the same year, Canada formalized the agreement with Japan and negotiated an agreement with Hong Kong. It finalized similar arrangements in 1963 with Israel, Macao, and Portugal. By 1970, it had concluded eighteen bilateral arrangements, following recommendations of the committee. These countries started exporting products not subject to restraints, and other nations began increasing their exports of goods covered in these bilateral arrangements.[74] The 'import' problem had thus been displaced. Moreover, Canadian tariffs after the Kennedy Round (23.6 per cent on all textiles, 33.7 per cent on knitted goods, and 25.5 per cent on apparel) were not shielding domestic producers from foreign competition. In fact, as underlined by Caroline Pestieau, 'imports increased more than a hundred-fold in man-made fibres, broad-woven man-made fabrics, and knitted fabrics between 1960 and 1969. Yet these were believed to be future growth areas and were the fields in which Canadian industry had made

the heaviest investment in the mid-1960s.'[75] As the situation dete-
riorated, domestic producers and trade unions urged Ottawa to
launch an initiative to protect production and investment.

Launching a Textile Policy: The 1970s

In 1970, Minister of Industry, Trade and Commerce Jean-Luc
Pepin announced a textile policy – the first comprehensive federal intervention in a particular industry, except for sectoral free
trade in automotive products. The goals of this new development strategy were 'to provide a sense of direction, a framework
and conditions within which the textile and clothing industries
can plan, invest and develop with a greater degree of confidence'
and 'to create conditions in which the Canadian textile and clothing industries continue to move progressively towards viable
lines of production on an increasingly competitive basis internationally.'[76]

The textile policy consisted of three types of measures – commercial, financial, and technical and promotional. Commercial
measures involved better investigation of dumped or subsidized
textile imports and establishment of the Textile and Clothing Board
(TCB) to advise the committee to implement specific measures
when 'low cost' imports were causing or threatening to cause
serious injury to domestic production and employment.[77] Moreover, Ottawa revised the Export and Import Permits Act so that it
could limit imports whenever VERs were not sufficient to protect
the domestic market. Financial support measures entailed adjustment assistance to primary textile and apparel firms under the
existing General Adjustment Assistance Program and a specific
program for textiles and apparel, the Adjustment Assistance Benefits Program (AAB), set up to compensate employees permanently laid off. Industrial incentives were provided to slow-growth
areas through the Department of Regional Economic Expansion.
Technical and promotional measures included establishment of
Development and Productivity Centres and creation of the export-oriented Fashion-Design Assistance Program. Other such
programs also aimed at fostering exports were the Program

for Export Market Development (PEMD) and the Promotional Project Program (PPP).

Free Trade in Textiles and Apparel?

A new National Textile Policy launched in 1981 led to establishment of the Canadian Industrial Renewal Board (CIRB), whose five-year mandate included helping the textile and apparel industries to restructure and modernize. Grants were authorized as long as firms agreed to evaluate their structures and marketing strategies. Although prospects seemed unlikely, the minister asked the TCB on 6 June 1983 to prepare a study on the economic impact of Canadian–U.S. sectoral free trade in textile and apparel products. The idea never became reality because of more comprehensive free trade negotiations that were about to begin.[78]

Policy Shift Away from Industrial Strategy

By the end of the 1980s, Canada's support for the textile and apparel industries underwent a profound transformation. The minister of finance, Michael Wilson, announced on 22 March 1988 a three-part program of tariff relief aimed at strengthening the competitiveness of the two industries. The program comprised immediate tariff reductions on specialty fabrics, duty remission programs, and a plan for future reductions to make Canadian tariffs on textiles and apparel comparable to those in other industrialized countries. To fulfill this third goal, the government created the Canadian International Trade Tribunal (CITT) on 31 December 1988 by amalgamating the Canadian Import Tribunal, the Tariff Board, and the Textile and Clothing Board. This independent body advises the minister of finance on the pace of tariff reductions and reports to Parliament through the minister. In addition to hearing appeals from rulings by Revenue Canada, CITT makes findings on whether or not dumped imported goods have caused or are threatening to cause material injury to the domestic industry. It also conducts inquiries and provides advice on economic, trade, and tariff matters as requested by the minister; conducts safeguard inquiries into complaints that increased imports are causing or threatening to cause serious injury to domestic producers; and investigates complaints by potential suppliers concerning procurement by the federal government.[79]

Ottawa's intervention in favour of domestic producers is therefore no longer about promoting an industrial strategy[80] but is primarily related to trade.[81] Protection afforded to Canadian producers comes from instruments such as tariffs, duty drawback schemes, anti-dumping and countervailing duties, and quantitative restrictions under the MFA. In early 1990, Canadian textile and apparel industries were protected by twenty-nine bilateral restraints, of which twenty-six covered clothing products, fifteen, primary textiles, and ten, household textile products.[82] Under the WTO Agreement on Textiles and Clothing, Canada notified the TMB about its quotas that were still in place when the WTO entered into force, including thirty-one restraints under the ATC. Canada also had twelve restraints with non-WTO members.[83]

Government Intervention in the United States:
The Pivotal Role of the Industry

Revenue Tariff Approach

Cotton manufacturing started when the United States banned imports from Britain under the Embargo and Non-Intercourse Acts of 1807–9. Following the end of the War of 1812, cotton imports from Britain were able to enter the U.S market with payment of the tariff of 25 per cent adopted by Congress in 1816 and imposed on all foreign cotton goods. The U.S. tariff structure did not impede export and import growth, but it encouraged investment in textiles and other import-competing industries. Strong support for free trade in the Democratic Party resulted in adoption of the Tariff Act of 1846, which lowered duties on all imports from an average of 29 per cent in 1845 to 23 per cent. Although the Democrats embraced a revenue tariff approach and promoted free trade, Franklin Pierce's administration rejected Britain's offer – after its repeal of the Corn Laws in 1846 – to roll back duties on goods such as cotton textiles and linens. In 1872 Congress ended the revenue tariff in favour of a tariff system aimed at protecting U.S. manufacturing.[84]

U.S. Trade Policy as a Tool of Foreign Policy

In the 1930s U.S. trade policy involved both tariff reductions as a foreign policy tool and implementation of quotas protecting the textile industry against low-cost exporting countries. The Trade Agreement of 1938 with Britain is a good example of how this new strategy affected the textile industry. In 1934 Congress had enacted Secretary of State Cordell Hull's Reciprocal Trade Agreements Program (RTAP), aimed at expanding and promoting U.S. exports abroad and at 'strengthening the foundations of world peace' by improving trade relations with key countries in a mutually and equally profitable manner. The main goal of the U.S. State Department in the negotiations with Britain was to offset the impact of the Canada–U.K. Trade Agreement of 1932, which, in the words of Alfred Eckes, 'had sharply reduced export opportunities for American fresh products.' The Americans proposed significant reductions of 40 to 50 per cent on duties on some labour-intensive manufactured goods such as cotton and woollen goods. They expected similar reductions on agricultural and automotive products in return. Britain refused these and cut down nominally its tariffs on products of great interest to the Americans. An agreement was finally struck in 1938. It carefully avoided the free-rider problem with labour-intensive textile-producing countries by 'breaking out tariff classifications,' thus excluding low-cost producing countries such as Japan.[85]

The other element of the new U.S. strategy was control of surges in imports through quotas imposed by the exporting country. Voluntary export restraints (VERs) were negotiated on Japanese rug exports following a determination by the Tariff Commission under section 3(e) of the National Industrial Recovery Act (NIRA). Moreover, the Japanese cotton industry negotiated a VER with the U.S. industry in January 1937 after the Tariff Commission had recommended a tariff increase for cotton cloth under section 336 of the Smoot–Hawley Act.

How the Industry Shaped Textile Trade Policy in the 1950s

The U.S. textile industry also helped shape trade policy in textiles and apparel in the 1950s. After the U.S. government championed Japan's entry to GATT, it negotiated a reciprocal agreement with that country. But the U.S. textile industry worried that tariff concessions to Japan would undermine its own position. Under the Trade Agreements Extension Act, as amended, it filed four escape-clause petitions with the Tariff Commission in 1956 to determine whether increased Japanese imports were causing or threatening to cause serious injury to the domestic industry. The commission recommended to the president a tariff increase for one product – cotton velveteens. But as Japan agreed to limit its exports of cotton goods, the president did not act on the recommendation.[86] Pressure on the State Department by the industry to impose quotas on Japanese textile goods had not succeeded because of the department's fervent support for GATT. J. Michael Finger and Ann Harrison note that the industry had informed the State Department that the Japanese were willing to impose quotas, but the department 'replied that they would vigorously oppose quotas, even negotiated quotas.' However, the industry convinced President Eisenhower's chief of staff, Sherman Adams, to discuss the matter with Japan. Shortly afterwards, the Japanese committee of industry and government members revealed that Japan would restrict exports of cotton cloth and blouses to the United States in 1956. It announced more restrictions and adjustments in 1956 and a five-year voluntary export restraint in January 1957.[87] Exports from Japan dropped as a percentage of total U.S. imports, but other economies, especially Hong Kong, saw their share of total imports increase substantially. This situation eventually led to more VERs.

The industry also favoured use of other instruments to protect textile products: section 204 of the Agriculture Act of 1956, granting the president authority to negotiate agreements limiting foreign exports to the United States or domestic imports of agricultural or textile products; and section 22 of the Agricultural Adjustment Act, authorizing the president to impose fees or quotas to limit imports of agricultural products.[88] Other forms of protection now available to the industry include the escape clause – i.e., sections 201–4 of the Trade Act of 1974, as amended – and anti-dumping and countervailing measures.[89]

The Industry Plays Presidential Politics: The Seven-Point Program

As imports kept rising, the U.S. industry turned to presidential politics in 1960 as a way to convince the White House that quotas were necessary to protect the domestic market. The Democratic candidate John F. Kennedy pledged 'to make a solution to the cotton textile import problem a top priority of his administration,' which gained him the support of both New England and the southern states.[90] After his election, Kennedy kept his promise and appointed on 16 February 1961 a cabinet committee, chaired by the secretary of commerce, to study the industry's problems.

Following recommendations of the committee, on 2 May 1961 he announced a seven-point program to help the textile industry. The president called on the Department of Commerce 'to launch an expanded program of research, covering new products, processes and markets ... in cooperation with both union and management groups'; on the Department of the Treasury 'to review the existing depreciation allowances on textile machinery'; on the Small Business Association 'to assist the cotton textile industry to obtain the necessary financing for modernization of its equipment'; and on the Department of Agriculture 'to explore and make recommendations to eliminate or offset the cost to United States mills of the adverse differential in raw cotton costs between domestic and foreign textile producers.' The president also said that he would 'send to the Congress a proposal to permit industries seriously injured or threatened with serious injury as a result of increased imports to be eligible for assistance from the Federal Government.' He directed the State Department 'to arrange for calling an early conference of the principal textile exporting and importing countries' in order to negotiate an international agreement on cotton textiles. Finally, the president reassured the industry that 'an application by the textiles industry for action under existing statutes, such as the [GATT] escape clause or the national security provision of the Trade Agreements Extension Act, [would] be carefully considered on its merits.'[91] This seven-point program led to the negotiations of the STA and the LTA.

Establishment of the CITA

The 1970s saw establishment in 1972 of the U.S. Committee for the Implementation of Textile Agreements (CITA) to oversee implementation of U.S. international textile agreements. CITA is chaired by the Department of Commerce, with representatives of the Office of the USTR, and the Departments of State, Labor, and Treasury as other members. CITA decides 'whether and when' the United States should impose quotas on textiles and apparel. It supervised implementation of the MFA from 1974 to 1994 and now performs the same task for the WTO Agreement on Textiles and Clothing. CITA is thus responsible for making determinations about invoking the WTO transitional safeguard mechanism.[92] It also participates, under the leadership of the USTR, in bilateral negotiations for quota agreements with non-WTO members.[93]

Special Access Programs for CBERA, Mexico, and ATPA

In order to allow textile and especially apparel producers to become more competitive, the United States permits these manufacturers to assemble articles in countries that are beneficiaries of the (U.S.) Caribbean Basin Economic Recovery Act (CBERA) under heading 9802.00.80 of the U.S. Harmonized Tariff Schedule (formerly known as item 807), provided that the components are made in whole or in part of U.S. fabric and that cutting takes place in the United States. Duty is paid on the value added when the product is re-exported to the United States. In 1986, the Reagan administration instituted the Special Access Program (also known as item 807A), which provides for 'guaranteed access levels' (GALs) to the U.S. market. This program covers apparel assembled in participating CBERA countries from 'fabric wholly formed and cut in the United States'; when it re-enters the United States, duty is paid on the value added off shore. The United States set up a similar program, the Special Regime, for Mexico, following the 1987 bilateral Framework Understanding. Products qualifying thereunder are allowed duty-free and quota-free access to the United States under NAFTA. In August 1995, the Americans created a Special Access Program for Colombia under the Andean Trade Preference Act (ATPA).[94]

Government Intervention in Mexico: From Import Substitution to Trade Liberalization

High Tariffs

Mexican government intervention in the textile industry began with the tariffs of 1821 and 1827 and with the 1829 list of prohibited cotton imports.[95] In 1830, Anastasio Bustamante's government established the Banco de Avio to provide low-interest loans for the modernization of the industry. The government hoped that the bank would operate with a fund of one million pesos, of which 20 per cent would come from diversion of customs revenue. Although the bank did not accumulate that much capital, it had invested approximately 650,000 pesos when it closed down in 1842. By the 1840s, opposition to tariff protection was rising. Two revolts, fomented by General Arista and by General de Avalos, occurred in 1841 and 1851, respectively, over this issue. Moreover, both artisans and merchants also complained, while the British, as holders of Mexican bonds, pressed the government to reduce tariffs. The British recommended that the Mexicans reduce their tariffs on manufactures and concentrate on producing raw materials.

Mexico lowered tariffs in the second half of the nineteenth century, but duties on foreign textiles remained very high, never being less than 100 per cent. Manufacturers were often torn between more and less protection. They demanded more protection on manufactured goods and lower tariffs on raw materials. But protection had a price – the government asked the industry to help finance the state, through levies such as the 5 per cent stamp tax of November 1893 on sales.

Sheltering the Domestic Industry and the
Maquiladora Program

After the Second World War, the industry suffered a severe down-
turn, which led the government of Miguel Alemán to adopt protectionist measures. Over the next forty years, high tariffs and
non-tariff barriers insulated the domestic industry. Restrictive
import licensing requirements kept out foreign competition. The
maquiladora industry program, established in the mid-1960s, has
fostered Mexican exports and created jobs along the U.S. border.
First, the Mexicans permitted duty-free importation of components to be assembled or processed as long as they were re-exported, and, second, the Americans agreed to impose duties only
on the value added once the product re-entered the United States.
Textiles and apparel are among the many sectors that have benefited from the program. In 1989, the government changed the
rules for the in-bond (maquiladora) industry. Duties paid on the
final good or on imported components allowed products to be
sold in the domestic market; imported parts had to meet certain
local content requirements.

On 24 December 1993, another decree modified the maquiladora
regime. As was noted in the WTO's 1997 Trade Policy Review of
Mexico, 'the decree introduced, inter alia, the maquiladora concept for services activities, allowed subcontracting between
maquiladoras and firms outside the maquiladora program, and
eliminated the authorization requirements for maquiladoras to
engage in domestic sales.'[96] On 23 October 1996, another decree
extended to two years the period for which imported inputs could
be in Mexico on a temporary basis. As of 1 January 2001, the program would apply only to non-NAFTA components when the finished product is exported to the United States or Canada and is
subject to import duties.

Dismantling Trade Barriers

In the mid-1980s, Mexico dismantled many trade barriers in textiles and apparel and greatly reduced credits and energy subsi-

dies. These new policies forced the rationalization of the textile and apparel industries. At the annual meeting of the Cámara Nacional de la Industria Textil (Textile Chamber of Commerce) in February 1994, the president, Enrique Aranzábal Lasagabaster, informed members that from 1987 to 1992 the industry had lost more than 10 per cent of its firms and 25,000 jobs.[97]

In order to increase the competitiveness of the private sector, the government has encouraged restructuring of the industry. For instance, the program PRONAMICE 1990–4 included support for technological development, export promotion, and financial assistance, as well as for training programs for workers. The Industrial Policy and Foreign Trade Program (PPICE) has been implemented under the National Development Plan 1995–2000. The development of textile cities such as Cuernavaca, which effort began in June 1996, is part of a strategy aimed at promoting vertical integration in the industry and increasing competitiveness. Funding comes from the state and federal governments and from the private sector.[98]

ISSUE-SPECIFIC POWER: STRINGENT RULES OF ORIGIN AND TEMPORARY TEXTILE TRQ

Despite having adopted over the years several measures to protect its textile and apparel industries, Canada did not have much issue-specific power at the outset of the NAFTA negotiations, in contrast to the United States. The U.S. government had also made use of numerous instruments and measures to protect and promote its industries, but its most single valuable resource was the FTA. The American textile and apparel industries had first opposed the FTA, which proved to be 'particularly onerous' for Canadian manufacturers. As underlined by Eric Barry of the Canadian Textiles Institute, the price that these manufacturers 'exacted from their government for their forced participation was a set of rules of origin designed to limit the use of third-country inputs in textiles and clothing that would qualify for FTA rates of duty.'[99] Since Canadian manufacturers use more foreign inputs than their American competitors, the FTA rules of origin were more disadvantageous from Canada's standpoint. As mentioned above, to partly offset this disadvantage, three tariff rate quotas were negotiated: in wool apparel, in non-wool apparel, and in non-wool fabrics and made-up articles.

On 24 October 1991, a few months after the beginning of the NAFTA negotiations, the two national trade associations for U.S. textiles and apparel, the American Textile Manufacturers Institute (ATMI) and the American Apparel Manufacturers Association (AAMA), called for stricter rules of origin in NAFTA. In their joint statement, they were demanding a 'yarn forward' rule[100] – a clear sign to the Canadians that textile rules of origin might once again become more restrictive.

However, one could assume that Canada, with the FTA provisions, had as much issue-specific power in textiles and apparel as it had in culture and could thus have achieved its objectives unilaterally by winning a freeze on the FTA rules of origin or at least full compensation for more restrictive rules. It could have pulled out of the NAFTA textile and apparel negotiations and the FTA. It could have negotiated a separate deal with Mexico. Although Canada thought about pulling out of the negotiations as we see below in the next section, it did not do so because it could not. Its tariff rate quota (TRQ) for non-wool fabrics and made-up articles was only temporary and due to expire on 31 December 1992. For Canada, to walk away from a trilateral deal meant saying goodbye to that TRQ, which would have damaged its textile industry. The Canadians were not willing to do that. The Americans had leverage with the 'fabric forward' rule of origin and the temporary TRQ, and they were prepared to use it. The TRQ for non-wool fabrics and made-up articles would not have been extended.

The U.S., Canadian, and Mexican textile and apparel industries have all attempted over the years to increase protection. But the Americans have undoubtedly been the most successful – first, with the VER vis-à-vis the Japanese cotton industry in the 1930s; second, by shaping U.S. trade policy in the 1950s and 1960s; and third, with the rules of origin negotiated in the FTA. Although the Canadians did not lack issue-specific power (for example, TRQs in non-wool apparel and wool apparel; geographical concentration of the apparel industry in Quebec; and the importance of these industries for Quebec and Manitoba), these resources were not sufficient to secure access to the U.S. market, on which Canada is highly dependent. Over 69 per cent of total Canadian textile exports and 86 per cent of total Canadian apparel exports went to that market in 1992.

TACTICS: INDUSTRY CONSENSUS IN THE UNITED STATES AND MEXICO

A Separate Working Group

When the NAFTA negotiations began in June 1991, there was no plan to have a working group dealing with textiles and apparel. However, it became clear very early that both Mexico and the United States felt that there should be such a group. For Mexico, it was a fundamental precondition for it to agree to sit at the table.[101] This sector is a major generator of jobs, and, as the rate of population growth had peaked in Mexico in the 1970s, young people born during that period were now looking for work. Moreover, the Mexicans were demanding elimination of U.S. quotas and high tariffs on the products in which they are very competitive. Access to the U.S. market was overall their single most important objective. The Americans, in contrast, wanted to renegotiate the FTA rules of origin. A working group devoted to textile and apparel issues would make their task easier. Both Mexico and the United States were thus using this tactic to achieve their preferred outcome. The Canadians initially opposed the idea but finally went along with it. *Inside U.S. Trade* wrote in July 1991 that the textile group had reportedly met in Washington, DC, on 22 July 1991.[102]

U.S. Industries Call for a 'Yarn Forward' Rule of Origin

As mentioned above, on 24 October 1991 ATMI and AAMA, the two trade associations for U.S. textiles and apparel, issued a statement calling for a 'yarn forward' rule of origin, a TRQ in non-wool apparel not exceeding 20 million SMEs, and one in wool apparel of two million SMEs. They also urged 'the U.S. government to take into account the extreme import sensitivity of the wool textile sector when negotiating the quota level.'[103] Other demands included a tariff snapback and a safeguard mechanism, customs co-operation and enforcement, no duty drawback, and the harmonization of labelling. As for tariff elimination, ATMI and AAMA were asking for a ten-year phase-out that could be accelerated to six years if acceptable rules of origin were adopted.

ATMI representatives had met with government officials at the Office of the USTR and at the Treasury. They were calling for a 'fibre forward' rule. Private-sector sources mentioned that USTR officials were 'very lukewarm but not adamantly opposed.' Treasury was more sympathetic, 'having no preconceived idea.' But it turned out that AAMA did not like the 'fibre forward' rule; it was satisfied with the FTA. Some of its members were even demanding more liberal rules of origin. ATMI and AAMA finally struck a compromise. They would ask for a 'yarn forward' rule, which upset the fibre people, who continued to lobby for their own objective. The next step was to convince the Mexicans to go along with a 'yarn forward' rule of origin.

Industry Consensus Makes U.S.–Mexican Government Alliance Possible

During the autumn of 1991, numerous meetings took place between representatives of the American and Mexican industries in Washington, DC, Greensboro, North Carolina, and Mexico City, with 'the blessing' of the U.S. government. NAFTA and GATT issues were discussed. The Mexicans wanted to forge an industrial alliance that would push for elimination of their quotas in NAFTA. They were prepared to ask their government to soften its stance on textile quotas at GATT, since Mexico was now importing textiles and would need some quotas to protect itself.

The Mexicans had felt that entering the NAFTA negotiations was like joining a poker game with no cards. They had already opened up their market and thought that they had nothing to offer. But when they saw that the Americans were interested in more restrictive rules of origin, American and Mexican manufacturers reached a compromise. The Mexicans would support a 'yarn forward' rule of origin in exchange for elimination of U.S. quotas on their exports. Both sides had also worked out a tariff phase-out and a customs position.

From that point on, the American manufacturers had to persuade the U.S. government that it was possible to strike a deal with the Mexican government. At that stage, there were some bilateral negotiations between the two governments. The Americans formally requested these negotiations and asked the Mexicans if they could consider a 'yarn forward' rule of origin. Mexico did not like the idea of more restrictive rules of origin. Commenting on the proposal, a senior Mexican trade official said: 'We did not like their rule of origin. But it was not too high a price to pay for the immediate elimination of the MFA quotas and the reduction of the Himalayas, the U.S. tariff peaks.' The United States was willing to trade the rules for the quotas but was much more reluctant to cut the 'peaks.' In any case, the two countries had struck a deal, and the Canadians were left out. Industry consensus had made a coalition possible at the governmental level.

In its NAFTA position paper on textiles, released in January 1992, SECOFI stated four arguments for elimination of U.S. quotas on Mexican textiles: first, they were incongruous vis-à-vis the MFA; second, Mexico was the only country among the three parties to face quotas; third, the quotas hurt investment; and fourth, Mexico was not a threat to the U.S. industry, since Mexican exports constituted only 3.2 per cent of all American textile imports in 1990. The Mexicans also stressed the need to reduce the U.S. and Canadian tariff peaks (57 per cent and 30 per cent, respectively), which applied on the products in which Mexico was very competitive. The Mexican position paper was calling for a rule of origin that would balance benefits for regional producers with greater competitiveness between the NAFTA region and other parts of the world.[104]

There was clearly a 'fit' between the two nations' priorities, and it did not take long for the U.S. government to cut a deal with the Mexicans. Both sides had engineered a *formula*: the textile provisions in NAFTA would benefit the producers of the region. The deal would favour the Americans and the Mexicans. Canada imports most of its yarns and fabrics from outside the region. It was the first turning point of the negotiations. Although the parties had exchanged offers and counteroffers since the autumn of 1991, the detail phase had started seriously for the Americans and Mexicans.

Canadians and Americans Clash over Rules of Origin

The 'yarn forward' rule is said to have been presented in early 1992 when the group on rules of origin held a joint meeting with the textile group.[105] In a letter to Democratic Senator Bill Bradley of New Jersey, Ambassador Carla Hills wrote that the rule was proposed jointly by the United States and Mexico.[106]

The Canadians immediately clashed with the Americans on rules of origin in textiles when they met near Ottawa before the fourth ministerial meeting. The meeting aimed at putting a final deal together, but many areas of disagreement remained. Sources told *Inside U.S. Trade* that 'Canada demanded that if a yarn forward rule of origin is adopted by the two other countries, existing tariff rate quotas on Canadian exports of textiles and apparel to the U.S. market would have to be substantially increased. Canada fears that the imposition of a rule that is more restrictive than one established under the U.S.–Canada bilateral free-trade agreement would have the effect of rolling back some of the benefits of that pact.'[107]

The U.S. industry consensus on rules of origin had made it easier for the Americans to show some flexibility to the Mexicans over early removal of quotas and tariffs. Their breakthrough deal had put the Canadians in an uncomfortable situation. 'We were the odd man out on the issue of rules of origin,' a Canadian trade official acknowledged in an interview. Also, Canada had no industry consensus on rules of origin. The textile sector had declared that it could live with the FTA 'fabric forward' rule, while the apparel industry was calling for single transformation. In order to try to convince its two counterparts that they should change their minds, the Canadian government decided to emphasize the need for more liberal rules of origin, arguing that such rules were more consistent with the kind of globalization taking place in the textile and apparel industries. The Canadians thought that they might be able to convince the Mexicans to soften their stance. The Mexicans should have been more interested than the Canadians in liberal rules, since their low-cost labour combined with low-cost off-shore fabric would have allowed their apparel industry to be even more successful in the U.S. market. The Canadians believed that 'it was counterintuitive for the Mexicans to push for stringent rules.' However, the Mexican position was driven by the 'textile people.'

Essential Character and the Substantial Transformation Test

By the Dallas Round in mid-February 1992, the Canadians were proposing to define the origin of textile and apparel products by their 'essential character.' The Americans opposed this notion, even if it describes the substantial transformation test – the general U.S. rule of origin. This rule is also set out in annex D.1 of the International Convention on the Simplification and Harmonization of Customs Procedures (Kyoto Customs Convention), to which the European Community/Union and most industrial countries subscribe, but not the United States.[108] The Americans proposed the following criterion: 'For the purpose of determining the origin of apparel in chapters 61 and 62, only the outershell and lining will be considered.'[109]

Leak of the Negotiating Text Raises Stakes

The leak of the Dallas Composite Text in March 1992 raised the visibility of what was at stake in the textile negotiations. That helped the Canadians. At the fifth ministerial meeting, held in Montreal in April 1992, the Canadian Apparel Manufacturers Institute dramatized the situation by saying it had 'identified four specific provisions in the draft that ... would destroy the Canadian industry.'[110] Besides the 'yarn forward' rule, which it opposed, the association charged that the United States was 'seeking a change in the current rules that would broaden the definition of woolen products, disqualify fabrics using a mix of foreign and North American yarns, and include the lining when the origin of a garment is being determined. Collectively these aspects of the text would harm the Canadian apparel industry.'

The U.S. definition of wool had been an unresolved issue inherited from the FTA. 'Under international tariff headings, woolen apparel is considered to be any garment with over 50 per cent chief weight wool.' In the Dallas draft, the Americans were offering four definitions. 'Collectively these definitions say that a garment with as little as 17 percent wool content, in the case of non-cotton vegetable fibers, will be defined as woolen apparel.' It meant that more products would fall under the definition of wool and, therefore, under the FTA TRQ.[111] With respect to fabrics of mixed origin, the Canadian apparel makers were also worried because the Dallas draft required that all the yarns in a fabric be from the NAFTA region. Moreover, the Canadian industry opposed counting for the first time the lining of a garment in determining its origin. This would mean 'that wholly Canadian-made outer shell could be disqualified for preferential duty treatment under NAFTA if the lining were imported.'[112]

The Quebec Card and the Triangular Approach in Textiles

The fact that the Canadian Apparel Manufacturers Institute chose Montreal – the capital of the Canadian apparel sector – to emphasize how the NAFTA draft could harm its industry was important. The industry is among the city's largest industrial employers. Montreal was also the political base of then Canadian Prime Minister Brian Mulroney. Although Canada adamantly opposed stricter rules of origin, it had very few cards in textiles and apparel. It was going to play up the Quebec card and the Canadian constitutional crisis, in conjunction with the possibility that Canada could opt out of a trilateral deal. In early April, *Women's Wear Daily* reported: 'Some Canadian officials have hinted Canada may have to exempt itself from the textile provisions of a trilateral pact.'[113] However, Canadian officials observed 'that their preference would be to work out a compromise within the parameters of the NAFTA first, and opting out [was] only a second best option.' They were concerned 'that such a dual system may hinder retailers from carrying Canadian product lines because of the difficulties involved.'[114]

In mid-April, after a federal–provincial meeting on the NAFTA negotiations, Quebec Minister of International Affairs John Ciaccia, member of the Liberal government, told the media that the NAFTA draft needed to be improved. Textiles and apparel were among the sectors that he singled out.[115] In early May, a Canadian trade official said 'that it would be possible to have a "triangular" rather than a trilateral deal in textiles, in which the U.S. and Mexico would negotiate a separate agreement, and Canada–U.S. textile trade would continue to be governed under the rules of the 1988 [FTA].'[116] The American Textile Manufacturers Institute had urged the U.S. government to support such an option. It was concerned that Washington would bow to Ottawa's demands and compensate the Canadians by increasing the TRQs.[117]

At the inaugural meeting of the Canadian Apparel Federation held in Montreal in mid-May, the industry told John Weekes, Canada's chief negotiator, that 'he should stick to his guns' and keep the FTA intact. Should the Americans disagree, the president of the Canadian Apparel Manufacturers Institute concluded, the Canadians should say 'Merci beaucoup, mais nous ne signons pas l'ALENA ...' (Thanks, but no thanks, we will not sign NAFTA).[118] In fact, knowing that such a move would be difficult, the apparel makers were calling for a triangular approach or at least no modifications to the FTA. A separate agreement was not a priority. 'Si aucune entente n'était signée avec le Mexique ... ça ne nous ferait ni chaud ni froid. Mais puisque [sic] qu'Ottawa croit de toute évidence qu'il en faut une, allons-y!' (We do not care whether or not an agreement is signed with Mexico. But since Ottawa wants one, let's do it!).[119]

The apparel industry tried to convince the governments of Quebec and Manitoba, two pro–free trade provinces where the industry is disproportionately important, to put more pressure on the federal government. It worked. In a press conference on 28 May 1992, Quebec's John Ciaccia announced that he was concerned about the impact of NAFTA on the Quebec apparel industry. He asked Ottawa to pull out of the textile negotiations if the Americans did not agree to change their position on rules of origin. He was calling on Ottawa to favour the triangular approach and to keep the FTA rules of origin.[120]

The Canadians took this approach to the table 'after they had come under intense pressure from the provincial government of Quebec and the Canadian apparel industry,' sources told *Inside U.S. Trade*.[121] Canada was playing its Quebec card. The Americans and Mexicans were upset. They complained to the Canadians that they were not negotiating in good faith and reportedly left the room. While the Mexicans were not prepared 'to pay the price of Canadian unity,'[122] the U.S. tactic was to threaten the Canadians quietly. The U.S. chief negotiator for textiles told his Canadian counterpart that if Canada was to opt out apparel, it would also have to remove textiles. This is exactly what the Canadian textile sector had feared. Its representatives had been shadowing the Canadian negotiators and were aware of what was at stake for them. The FTA TRQ for non-wool fabrics and made-ups was expiring at the end of 1992. The industry had used its TRQ heavily – 79 per cent in 1989, 98 per cent in 1990, and 81 per cent in 1991.[123] The TRQ had allowed the Canadians to export to the United States without having to meet the FTA rules of origin. Representatives of the Canadian textile industry met with ministers John Ciaccia of Quebec and Ed Philip of Ontario to try to persuade them that their industry would be hard hit without a TRQ. The triangular approach – not, with its three separate sets of rules of origin, very attractive to investors – was dead.

The United States and Mexico Reach a Deal

In the meantime, U.S. and Mexican negotiators had resolved their major problems at the Cancun meeting on 20 and 21 May. The Mexicans had almost broken off the negotiations a few days earlier, calling on the Americans to 'chop off their tariffs.' The

Americans were reluctant 'to cut those Himalayas.' A face-saving approach for both sides had emerged. But the two countries were still debating the A list (immediate liberalization) and the C list (more sensitive products). For the B-list goods – a large category of fabrics and apparel – each country would cut the tariff by the amount of the tariff 'and then phase out the remaining tariff in equal stages over five years. Mexico had been pressing the United States and Canada for an immediate cut of 50 percent on B list items, while proposing' to cut its tariffs by amounts that increased each year by 20 per cent. The United States had rejected this idea, proposing instead to phase out tariffs in increments of 20 per cent.[124]

Canada Seeks Compensation for More Restrictive Rules of Origin

The U.S.–Mexican accord was a turning point and the beginning of the end game for the Canadians, who again had been left out. From now on, their tactic was to focus on seeking compensation for the more restrictive rules of origin, issue by issue. The Americans had to offset the effects of the new rules on the Canadians. In an interview with the author in the autumn of 1993, a senior American trade official said: 'We already had an agreement with Canada and we were proposing to change this agreement. We were the *demandeur*. We sought to offset the Canadians.' By early 1992, the United States had 'apparently offered a small increase in the TRQ for exports of woolen products from Canada, and about a 50 percent increase – to just over 60 million SMEs – for non-woolen apparel.' The Canadian industry noted that these two TRQs were 'roughly equal to only 0.4 percent of the total U.S. market.'[125]

The Canadians knew what they wanted: first, a substantial increase in the wool TRQ, since Canadian exporters had been very successful in this sector; second, a permanent TRQ for non-wool fabrics and made-ups; third, a new TRQ for yarns; fourth, a *de minimis* rule of 15 per cent; fifth, the extension of duty drawbacks; sixth, a debit clause of 50 per cent for mixed-origin textiles; and seventh, a review clause for the rules of origin. They opposed the

U.S. definition of wool, inclusion of linings to determine the origin of a garment, the very brief list of 'short supply' category, and the so-called ample category (for example, denim, oxford cloth, jersey knit fabrics), whose products were not going to be allowed under the new TRQs.

A Canadian official told *Inside U.S. Trade* in early June that Canada was 'trying to enlarge and create new quotas.'[126] Trade Minister Michael Wilson confirmed to 'the House of Commons on June 8 that Canada was seeking greater access to the U.S. market through a tariff rate quota.'[127] In fact, the Canadians were trying to sidestep the rules of origin by increasing the quotas that would make these rules irrelevant. In a letter to Senator Bill Bradley of New Jersey at the end of May, U.S. Trade Representative Hills wrote that Canada had accepted the rule of origin for apparel.[128] The Canadians denied it: 'We never accepted it until the very end.'

In July, Canada increased the pressure on the United States. Following a 'secret' meeting with Hills on 19 July, Wilson emphasized 'that "the deal for our textile and clothing industries is still not what we need," and that NAFTA needs to "build on the access to the U.S. market that we achieved in the FTA."'[129] The Canadians kept up the pressure on the United States, which had agreed to more than double the TRQ for non-wool fabrics and made-ups – a major concession to the Canadian textile industry, which had hit its quota ceiling in 1990 and almost reached it in 1991. Canadian officials were confident. But the Mexicans were exasperated by the Canadians. A Mexican diplomat told Reuters that 'Mexico was ready to go with the U.S. alone' if Canada remained a barrier to reaching an agreement.[130]

The negotiations were deadlocked over textile issues in early August. Canada's tactics were to put a lot of pressure on the Americans. After the sixth ministerial meeting held in Mexico City on 25 and 26 July, Wilson wrote to his U.S. counterpart about textile issues. He identified 'the key remaining hurdle[s] to achieving a trilateral deal.' He focused on wool apparel and reminded Hills that the Americans had promised to compensate the Canadians: 'You had indicated that, in exchange for Canada accepting the proposed NAFTA rules, the U.S. would be prepared to offer TRQ adjustments where there was a clear impact on Canadian export interests. There is always room for debate on the level of impact which the NAFTA rules may have in a particular area. One cannot dispute, however, that there will be a significant impact with respect to wool apparel.' The new rules of origin 'would disqualify, from preferential duty treatment, a significant amount of Canadian wool apparel production that is currently eligible under the FTA.' In addition, 'our industry is concerned about Canada accepting the U.S. definition of wool, which is more restrictive than the "chief weight" definition which applies under the Harmonized System. While this U.S. definition is already being applied on an administrative basis, this approach has never been formally accepted by Canada and remains an important unresolved issue under the FTA.'

Before making his last offer on wool apparel, Wilson told Hills that Canada had been very reasonable and had already conceded a lot:

> 'Recognizing the U.S. sensitivities in this sector we have tried to be as moderate as possible. After considerable negotiation, we have revised our request to a 20 percent increase in the TRQ level (i.e. to move from 5 million to 6 million square meter equivalents) plus a 2 percent annual growth for the first five years of the NAFTA. As noted above, this increase is not out of line with the existing Canadian export levels which could be affected. It represents less than 0.5 percent of the U.S. market for wool apparel. The 2 percent annual growth rate is consistent with what has already been agreed for all other Canadian TRQ's into the U.S. under NAFTA. In an effort to address U.S. industry concerns about offshore fabric imports, we have also offered to limit the TRQ increase to wool garments which are produced from fabrics woven in the U.S., Canada or Mexico and where only the yarn has been imported. This approach targets the TRQ increase precisely to the impact of the 'yarn forward' rule.[131]

The letter also mentioned the debit clause of 50 per cent and the *de minimis* rule of 15 per cent. The United States made a concession on the debit clause but refused the *de minimis* provision. This clause would have allowed a good containing non-originating fibres or yarns in an amount not greater than 15 per cent of its weight to be considered originating and thus eligible for preferential duty. The Americans wanted 7 per cent, and they got it.

The End Game: The Watergate Hotel

At the Watergate Hotel in Washington, DC, where the chief negotiators met from 29 July to 12 August and the ministers from 2 to 12 August, the main issues were dealt with bilaterally between the United States and Canada. The lengthy discussions aimed at accommodating Canadian concerns. But on wool apparel, the Americans did not want to move at all. Canada thought that by making some concessions it would convince them to meet it halfway, but they refused – no concessions on the U.S. definition of wool, linings, and the TRQ (now TPL) for wool apparel. On wool apparel, the Americans were offering a freeze on the quantities available for the wool TRQ and wanted to add sub-limits. That stance angered the Canadians, since men's suits were 'the biggest success for the Canadian apparel industry under the free-trade agreement with the United States.' The two sides clashed over wool apparel until the very end. A Canadian official told the *Globe and Mail*: 'That deal is all about opening our sectors to greater competition. We're not about to accept a limit on one of our key exports now, and we're sticking to that.' Again, the Quebec card was in play. Wilson was 'clearly concerned about a potential political backlash in the province.' One of the most successful Canadian apparel manufacturers under the FTA had been Peerless Clothing of Montreal, which employed over 1,300 workers. Its president, Alvin Segal, had been on the front page of the most important newspapers in both countries. The $14-billion textile and apparel industries and their 160,000 workers were very much on the minds of the Canadian negotiators. The *Globe and Mail* wrote in early August: 'Indeed, only the auto negotiations ... are perceived by Canadian officials as being more important, as vehicles and auto parts are Canada's largest export to the United States.'[132]

A Canadian trade official who followed the negotiations very closely described the negotiations at the Watergate Hotel concerning wool apparel: 'Wool apparel was not settled until the very last day, the very last hour, the very last five minutes at the ministerial level.' The sub-limit in men's wool suits 'was the last matter to be resolved in the negotiations between Canada and the United States.'[133] That proves how crucial these negotiations were to the Canadians, who tried until the very end to get something out of the Americans. A member of the Canadian team told *Les Affaires*, a Quebec-based weekly business newspaper, that Canada had to freeze the TPL for wool apparel: 'C'était ça ou nous perdions tous les contingents tarifaires (It was that or we were losing all the quotas).'[134] After the handshake, the textile negotiators spent a few more months 'discussing and fine-tuning' the text.

CONCLUSION

Although Canada did not have issue-specific power and was limited in its choice of tactics after the U.S. and Mexican industries struck a deal on rules of origin, it performed fairly well in textiles and apparel. The lack of industry consensus at home made it more difficult for the Canadian government to develop a strong position. Ottawa used a contextual event – the Canadian constitutional crisis – to try to increase its leverage. The government of Quebec had asked it to keep the FTA intact in order not to harm its apparel industry, based in Montreal. But every sector could not be exempted from a trilateral free trade deal. Culture and agriculture were more politically sensitive and had to be exempted (culture) or negotiated bilaterally (agriculture). Thus pulling out of the trilateral negotiations in textiles and apparel was not an option, mainly because the textile industry would have suffered great losses had the Americans decided to retaliate against it and not extend the TRQ for non-wool fabrics and made-up articles. But Ottawa made sure that Quebec would not be totally unhappy with more stringent rules of origin in the apparel sector. Michael Wilson promised John Ciaccia compensation for the effects of the rules with the NAFTA TPLs. He also committed Ottawa, as soon as the NAFTA negotiations were over, to lowering the Canadian external tariff on fibres, yarns, and fabrics, as proposed by the Canadian International Trade Tribunal in 1990. Quebec went along with Wilson's promise, knowing that this change would benefit its apparel industry, which imports most of its raw materials from outside the NAFTA region. Quebec stopped asking for a change in the NAFTA rules of origin. It had pushed for a triangular approach, but its *sine qua non* was to prevent harm to textiles and apparel. Quebec knew that losing the TRQ for non-wool fabrics and made-up articles would hurt its textile industry.

The only other card left for the Canadians was to convince the Americans that they had to offer Canada a fair and balanced deal and that they could not renege on what they had agreed to in the FTA. In that respect, considering that they had almost no cards to play, the Canadians did well. In the short run, in non-wool apparel and non-wool fabrics and made-up articles, the TPLs offset the impact of the rules of origin and secured Canada's access to the U.S. market. But for wool apparel, the rules are more restrictive. Canada also won a concession from the United States, which accepted a clause requiring review of the rules of origin within five years of NAFTA's entry into force. This may eventually play in favour or against the Canadians, depending on their issue-specific power and choice of tactics at the time of the review.

At the end of the negotiations, Canada also used two other tactics to try to achieve its preferred outcome. Its negotiators thought that their conceding to the Americans on some issues would get the Americans to reciprocate, but the Americans did not have to. Canada had no leverage. The deadlock over textiles and apparel was the other tactic used by Canada. By slowing down negotiations, Canada hoped to obtain some concessions from the Americans, who were eager to have a deal before the beginning of the Republican convention in mid-August 1992.

Our interviews raised the issue of linkages with the negotiators. Most of them denied that there were any. Negotiators from all three countries agreed that the negotiations were pretty much self-contained in textiles and apparel. However, one of them added that 'maybe there were some other issues that were resolved that made it easier for Canada to accept the results in textiles.' In fact, the Americans had made a concession to Canada on the cultural exemption, but they were not prepared to move on textiles and apparel.

Chapter Five

The Automotive Sector:
Working with the Industry

The automotive sector has become one of the most integrated industries in North America. The Auto Pact of 1965 between Canada and the United States, which marked the first step towards a regional industry, has encouraged rationalization and specialization in the industry and has facilitated modernization of the auto sector in Canada. Automotive decrees by the Mexican government between 1962 and 1989 strengthened the relationship between U.S. and Mexican producers. But it is the opening of several in-bond, or maquila plants in Mexico by U.S. carmakers in the 1980s and the liberalization of the Mexican automotive regulations late in the decade that substantially integrated the industry.

At the outset of the NAFTA negotiations in 1991, U.S. automakers expressed serious concerns about Japanese competition. General Motors, Ford, and Chrysler – the Big Three, in descending order by size – were particularly worried that the Japanese transplants were using Canada as a platform to enter the U.S. market under the FTA's preferential treatment and wanted to ensure that Mexico would not be used for such a purpose. They supported the tightening of the rules of origin to be negotiated in NAFTA and demanded a higher content requirement for a manufacturer to benefit from preferential treatment.

Two events made these issues central to the negotiations. Most important, in early 1992 U.S. Customs ruled that Honda Civics assembled in Ontario between January 1989 and March 1990 did not meet the FTA rules of origin. In its own ruling, also published in early 1992, Revenue Canada held that, except for 1,500 engines, these same vehicles did satisfy the FTA rules of origin. The two decisions followed a *New York Times* article of 17 June 1991 outlining U.S. Customs's position, before the audit was completed and after a confidential memo was leaked to the newspaper. A month earlier, on 22 May, the United States had taken an administrative decision challenging the 1990 claim by CAMI on the application of the FTA rules of origin. The company, located in Ingersoll, Ontario, is a joint venture between General Motors and Suzuki. It maintained that non-mortgage interest had to be included in the 'direct cost of processing or direct cost of assembling' formula of the FTA's regional content requirement, whereas the United States argued that it should be excluded. The illustrative list in FTA 304 was silent with respect to including or excluding such cost from the definition.

After reviewing the main objectives of the parties and then looking at the outcome of the negotiations, this chapter discusses the main resources of the three state actors – first, market share and industry control and, second, government intervention and attempts at increasing such resources. It then assesses the role of issue-specific power, and it finally looks at tactics used in determining negotiation outcomes.

NEGOTIATORS' OBJECTIVES

The single most important Canadian objective in the auto negotiations was Honda-driven. U.S. Customs had ruled that the Honda Civics assembled in Alliston, Ontario, were Japanese and did not meet the FTA rules of origin. Canada wanted to resolve both the Honda and CAMI cases and to create a set of rules that would bring greater stability to the trading process and remove as much as possible the opportunities for unilateral actions on the part of any party; hence Canada sought transparent, predictable, stable, and less complex rules. It also wanted secure access to the U.S. market and to remain an attractive place to invest for automakers. Other objectives included not raising the threshold percentage of the regional value-content (RVC) requirement unless it could benefit the Canadian industry and increase its competitiveness; keeping the Auto Pact intact; and phasing out the Mexican auto decrees while allowing for a transition period during which Canadian-based automakers could export both vehicles and parts.

The United States wanted to raise the threshold percentage of the RVC first to 60 per cent and later to 65 per cent; simplify and tighten the rules of origin so as get rid of the FTA's 'roll-up/roll-down' (originating/non-originating) provisions; phase out the Mexican auto decrees (particularly the automotive decree covering automobiles and light trucks, and the autotransportation decree covering large trucks and buses) and all the trade barriers that inhibited regional integration; protect existing automakers in Mexico – namely, the Big Three – during the phasing out of the automotive decree; and eliminate Mexico's tariffs on U.S. automotive goods and its duty drawback programs.

Mexico's objectives focused on guaranteeing and improving the country's access to U.S. and Canadian markets with a view to expanding the region's auto market and taking advantage of economies of scale. Mexico also proposed the gradual elimination of all tariffs and all non-tariff barriers. It hoped to promote and attract foreign investment from the region as well as from other countries and to give special attention to vehicle and parts producers already installed in Mexico. Acknowledging that the auto industry was restructuring itself, the Mexicans pressed for rules that would benefit and increase the region's competitiveness. Other Mexican objectives included incorporation in the CAFE rules (to be explained in the following section) and retention of duty drawback as long as possible.

NEGOTIATION OUTCOME

Honda and CAMI: A Victory for Canada

Canada was successful in resolving both the Honda and CAMI disputes during the NAFTA negotiations. The U.S. implementing legislation provides that for certain vehicles exported from Canada to the United States on or after 1 January 1989 an importer may choose the NAFTA rule of origin to determine whether these vehicles are eligible for preferential duty treatment under the FTA.[1] As mentioned in chapter 1, U.S. Customs had found that Honda Civics assembled in Ontario between 1 January 1989 and 31 March 1990, with engines made in Ohio, did not meet the FTA value-content requirement. The binational panel formed under FTA chapter 18 agreed that CAMI could include non-mortgage interest payments in its calculation of its North American content, but this decision did not mean that CAMI vehicles would necessarily qualify under the FTA rule of origin. Canada won a special provision in NAFTA that allows CAMI to average the calculation of its regional value content over a class or a model line of vehicles with the corresponding class or model line at General Motors of Canada (GMC). This arrangement allows CAMI to have a better chance at qualifying for the NAFTA rule of origin, since its engines are available only offshore.[2]

Canada was determined to avoid the ambiguities that had arisen with the interpretation of the FTA rules of origin. Both the Honda and CAMI cases had convinced the Canadian government that the FTA rules needed to be improved. The first problem had to do with the definition of direct cost of processing – a concept used in the calculation of the North American value content. In the Honda decision,[3] U.S. Customs had ruled[4] that 'direct cost of processing' and 'direct cost of assembling' had distinctive meanings, even though the FTA states that 'direct cost of processing or direct cost of assembling means the costs directly incurred in, or that can reasonably be allocated to, the production of goods.' In the audit of CAMI vehicles, U.S. Customs had found 'that only interest costs paid in connection with a mortgage on real estate would be eligible in calculating the regional content of vehicles.'[5] Canada argued for inclusion of non-mortgage interest payments in 'direct cost of processing.' A binational panel under FTA chapter 18 later concluded unanimously in its favour.

Another problem with the Honda case was the ruling on intermediate materials.[6] Honda manufactured engines in Ohio from materials produced in both the United States and Japan. These engines were then shipped to Ontario to be used in the assembling of Honda Civics that were subsequently re-exported to the United States. Both Honda and U.S. Customs agreed that these engines contained more than the required 50 per cent North American content and thus, by virtue of the FTA's roll-up/roll-down rule, should have been treated as 100 per cent originating material. But since Honda Canada paid nothing for the engines, U.S. Customs 'disagreed with Honda's conclusion that 100 percent of their value qualified for inclusion in the value-added calculation,'[7] basing its ruling on the definition of 'value of materials originating' in FTA 304 – 'the price paid by the producer of an exported good for materials originating in the territory of either Party or both Parties or for materials imported from a third country used or consumed in the production of such originating materials.' If Honda *had bought* the engines from another North American supplier, the engines would have qualified as North American, and U.S. Customs would probably have ruled that the Honda Civics assembled in Ontario would have been eligible for the FTA preferential duty when exported to the United States.

The Net-Cost Method and Tracing

Specific rules of origin were negotiated in NAFTA to determine the regional value-content (RVC) requirement applying to automotive goods. As with other products, automotive goods qualify for preferential duty if they are wholly produced in North America. However, for automotive products not entirely manufactured in the NAFTA region, the rules of origin require variously a tariff shift in the Harmonized System of tariff classification alone (for example, windshields and tires), a tariff change and RVC, or just an RVC.[8] A 'net cost' method[9] determines whether these automotive goods satisfy the RVC requirement:

$$RVC = \frac{NC - VNM}{NC} \times 100,$$

where RVC = regional value content, NC = net cost of the good, and VNM = value of non-originating materials used by the producer in production of the good. Net cost is defined as total cost minus excluded costs – sales promotion, marketing and after-sales service costs, royalties, shipping and packing costs, and non-allowable interest costs.[10]

Both Canada and the United States were pleased with the results of the new rules of origin for the automotive sector. The 'net cost' method, which is based on a 'top-down approach,' differs sensibly from the 'bottom-up approach' of the FTA. The NAFTA method is more transparent and predictable, because it includes all costs except those specifically excluded and listed. The private sector was also satisfied with the results. Neil De Koker, president of the Automotive Parts Manufacturers' Association of Canada, told Parliament's Standing Committee on External Affairs and International Trade in February 1993 that the new rule of origin is 'simple, transparent, and enforceable.' David Worts, managing director of the Japan Automobile Manufacturers Association of Canada (JAMA Canada), concurred: 'We welcome the expected predictability, clarity and transparency of this formula in the hope that disputes such as Honda experienced will be satisfactorily resolved and that trade can be stabilized.'[11]

NAFTA requires tracing of automotive components and parts listed in annex 403.1 (passenger vehicles and small trucks) and annex 403.2 (other vehicles) when they are imported and incorporated into originating materials. The U.S. Department of Commerce writes that 'for cars and light trucks, the list of parts and components which must be traced when calculating regional value-content accounts for close to 80 percent of the total value of the vehicle.'[12] A less restrictive tracing rule applies to all other vehicles, such as larger trucks and buses, tractors, and specialty vehicles. Under NAFTA annex 403.2, only some engine and transmission materials have to be traced. Tracing signifies, as the Americans had hoped, the end of the FTA's roll-up/roll-down rule. Non-NAFTA materials do not count as fully originating (roll-up) or non-originating (roll-down) when the good is made of both originating and non-originating materials. A non-NAFTA component remains non-originating through the assembly process. Tracing certainly adds to the complexity of the NAFTA rules of origin in the automotive sector, but, as emphasized by Jon Johnson, 'this should not present a problem to parts producers in Canada because they provide similar information to assemblers ... which are entitled to Auto Pact benefits.'[13] The only difference here is that U.S. Customs is auditing this information, not Revenue Canada.

The Canadians also fought for uniform regulations 'regarding the interpretation, application and administration' of the rules of origin.[14] They also pushed for a Working Group on Rules of Origin, which, among other duties, helps to settle differences in interpreting, applying, and administering the rules of origin.

A Higher RVC: A U.S. Win

The threshold percentage for the regional value content (RVC) is higher in NAFTA than in the FTA. Because the 'net cost' method was found to 'increase the proportion of inputs treated as domestic by as much as seven percent,' according to the Americans, and by 1 to 2 per cent, according to the Canadians, Canada was willing to trade a more predictable rule of origin for slightly higher content – i.e., 60 per cent.[15] 'We would have preferred 60 percent phased in gradually over 10 years but at the end the Americans were asking for 65 percent, so we split the difference,' a senior Canadian trade official told the author in September 1993. The increase in the content level is being phased in over eight years, which gives the transplants time to adjust. For passenger vehicles, light trucks, and their engines and transmissions, the RVC increased from 50 to 56 per cent per year on the producer's fiscal year that starts on the day closest to 1 January 1998 and was to be raised to 62.5 per cent per year four years later, on the fiscal year's end closest to 1 January 2002. In the case of heavy trucks, buses, specialty vehicles, tractors, their engines and transmissions, and most vehicle parts, the threshold increased from 50 to 55 per cent starting on the first day of a producer's fiscal year closest to 1 January 1998 and was to rise to 60 per cent on the day closest to 1 January 2002.

Lower Threshold Percentage for New Plants and Refits: A Gain for Canada

Canada managed to win a concession from the Americans for new plants and major refits. The RVC is fixed at 50 per cent for the first five years in the case of a new vehicle prototype produced in a new plant (a new building with substantially new machinery). If the plant is a refit – i.e., it was closed for at least three consecutive months for plant conversion or retooling – a 50 per cent rule applies for the first two years only. This measure should help Canada to remain an attractive location for automakers, particularly for existing or future transplants.[16]

Averaging the RVC and the Special Provision for CAMI

NAFTA allows averaging in calculations of the RVC of an automotive good. During its fiscal year, a producer of motor vehicles has three ways to average its calculation – it may do so over the same model line within the same class produced in the same plant, or over the same class produced in the same plant, or over the same model line produced in the territory of a party.[17] As mentioned above, a special averaging rule was designed to allow CAMI to average its calculation over a class or a model line of vehicles manufactured during its fiscal year with the corresponding class or model line of vehicles produced in Canada by GMC, provided that at the beginning of CAMI's fiscal year GMC owns at least 50 per cent of the voting common stock of CAMI and that General Motors (GM)[18] buys a minimum of 75 per cent of the vehicles produced by CAMI.[19] Parts producers may also average the calculation of their RVC over any quarter or month or over their fiscal year if the good is sold as an after-market part. Producers of original equipment parts must calculate the average over the fiscal year of the motor vehicle to which the product is sold.[20]

Duty Elimination: Mexico Gets What It Had Hoped For

For goods entering Canada from the United States, the remaining duties were eliminated on 1 January 1998, according to the FTA schedule. Canadian tariffs on Mexican cars fell by 50 per cent immediately, and the remainder are being phased out by equal amounts over nine years. Tariffs on Mexican trucks dropped immediately by 50 per cent, with the rest to be eliminated in four equal annual stages. For other Mexican vehicles, tariffs are phased out over the ten-year transition period. Most Mexican parts already are entering Canada duty free under the Auto Pact. However, for those that are not, tariffs were eliminated immediately or after five years. Other tariffs (on buses, tractors, and trucks) are being phased out over a ten-year period.

The phasing out of U.S. tariffs on Canadian goods followed the schedule set forth in the FTA, with all remaining tariffs abolished on 1 January 1998. Tariffs on Mexican autos were eliminated immediately, which increased Mexico's access to the U.S. market. The tariff on light trucks was cut from 25 to 10 per cent and then phased out over four years. For heavy trucks, the 25 per cent tariff is being eliminated over a ten-year period. Most Mexican parts were already entering the United States duty free at the time of the NAFTA negotiations. In fact, almost 90 per cent of Mexican exports have entered the United States duty free since 1 January 1994. Mexican duties on Canadian and U.S. vehicles follow the same staging categories as the Canadian tariffs on Mexican automotive goods.

Canada Keeps the Auto Pact

The Auto Pact was not modified by NAFTA. In fact, Auto Pact firms that satisfy the Canadian safeguards under the pact 'do not have to meet the NAFTA rule of origin in order to be able to import duty free into Canada from anywhere.'[21] NAFTA keeps intact the two-tiered system created when the FTA eliminated the possibility of extending Auto Pact benefits to firms other than the Big Three, Volvo, and CAMI.[22]

Phasing Out of Mexico's Automotive Decrees: A Canadian Loss

Canada did not convince the Americans and the Mexicans to allow Canadian-based transplants to sell cars in Mexico during the phasing out of Mexico's automotive decree (covered in more detail below, on pages 181–5). NAFTA allows Mexico to phase out its decree over a long period ending 1 January 2004, by which time all provisions of the decree and of its implementing regulations will have to be consistent with NAFTA. During the transition period, only automakers (General Motors, Ford, Chrysler, Nissan, and Volkswagen) with existing assembly plants in Mexico at the time of the NAFTA negotiations have the right to import new vehicles into the country for sale there. NAFTA also allows Mexico to require import licensing during the phasing out of its auto decrees.[23] During the transition, the Mexican government cannot require that a firm reach a level of national value added higher than 20 per cent of its total sales in order to qualify as a national supplier or as an enterprise of the auto parts industry.[24] For assemblers, the 'national value added from suppliers' requirement (VANp) – i.e., value added that must come from Mexican domestic parts suppliers – was set at 36 per cent in the automotive decree of 1989. It is being eliminated gradually, dropping from 34 per cent during the five years after NAFTA's entry into force, to an annual reduction of 1 per cent during the following five years, to reach 29 per cent in 2003 and zero starting in 2004.[25] However, for manufacturers producing in Mexico prior to model year 1992, the requirement is less stringent. If they did not meet the 36 per cent rule in 1992, they are allowed to maintain the percentage reached during that year for as long as it does not exceed the percentage applicable under NAFTA.[26] To calculate the denominator for its content ratio of national value added from suppliers, a manufacturer producing in Mexico prior to model year

1992 should choose the greater of either its reference value or its total national value added (VANt).[27]

Mexico is gradually eliminating its trade balancing requirement to provide for the importation of more parts and components. The proportion of imports required in the calculation of the trade balance was to fall from 80 per cent in 1994 to 55 per cent in 2003, and finally to zero on 1 January 2004.[28] NAFTA also allows Mexican manufacturers with a surplus in their extended trade balance to divide that balance by the applicable proportion (for example, 63.3 per cent in 2000, 60.5 per cent in 2001, 57.7 per cent in 2002, and 55 per cent in 2003) in order to determine the total value of vehicles that they may import.[29] Quotas on imports of passenger vehicles have been eliminated.[30]

The autotransportation decree, covering large trucks and buses, has been eliminated as of 1 January 1994. However, from 1994 to 1 January 1999, Mexico was still able to restrict importation of these vehicles. During that period, a manufacturer was allowed to import 'a quantity of originating autotransportation vehicles equal to at least 50 percent of the number of vehicles of such type that the manufacturer produced in Mexico in that year.'[31]

CAFE Rules: Mexico Gets In

Appendix 300-A.3 of NAFTA requires that Mexican value added be counted as domestic with regard to the Corporate Average Fuel Economy (CAFE) regulations of the U.S. Energy Policy Conservation Act of 1975. Those rules divide vehicles destined for the U.S. market into two fleets – domestic and foreign. The objective of the CAFE rules is to stimulate production of small fuel-efficient cars in North America. Each fleet must meet a standard of 27.5 miles per gallon in order to avoid fines. Vehicles containing over 75 per cent of domestic (U.S., Canadian, or Mexican) value added are considered domestic, while those with less are classified as imported. With respect to the inclusion of Mexican value added as domestic, assemblers that have started production in Mexico after 1991 and non-NAFTA manufacturers had to comply with the new CAFE rules as early as 1 January 1994. Existing assemblers in Mexico, the United States, and Canada have been able to apply the new rule since 1997 but will be obliged to do so in 2004.

Other Provisions: Maquiladoras, Used Cars, and Standards Council

Sales from *maquiladoras* to the domestic market are going to become available gradually. In 1994, the proportion was no more than 55 per cent of the value of their 1993 exports. For the next six years, the allowed proportion was to increase by 5 per cent yearly. Seven years after the entry into force of NAFTA, restrictions on domestic sales were to be removed.[32] Other restrictions by Mexico and Canada on imports of used cars are being phased out over a ten-year period starting on 1 January 2009.[33] Finally, an Automotive Standards Council, with representation from each party, has the mandate of reviewing implementation of automotive standards and making recommendations to facilitate greater compatibility.[34]

Other provisions mentioned in the previous chapter also apply to automotive goods: a *de minimis* rule of 7 per cent, an acceleration clause, and elimination of full duty drawback by 1 January 1996 for Canada and by 1 January 2001 for Mexico.

RESOURCES

Trade policy instruments have helped increase the automotive resources of the three countries analysed in this book. From the very beginning, tariffs and domestic content requirements were at play in Canada and Mexico. The intention was to stimulate domestic production and encourage import substitution. In the United States, trade policy was also a major factor, but confidence in the industry's competitiveness in the first half of the twentieth century created pressure to eliminate tariffs on automotive products. The U.S. industry has influenced the distribution of resources in the auto sector by supporting the Auto Pact and certain measures to limit Japanese imports. It has also recently championed the opening of the Japanese auto market to its exports.

Market Share and Industry Control

The Canadian Automotive Industry

Although Henry Seth Taylor of Stanstead, Quebec, was the first person to build a horseless carriage – the popular early name for the automobile – in Canada in 1867, the country's automotive industry started in 1904, when Gordon A. McGregor, along with other Windsor businessmen, formed the Ford Motor Company of Canada. Since the early days, the industry has been dominated by U.S. motor vehicle manufacturers, General Motors, Ford, and Chrysler.

General Motors of Canada (GMC) came into being when Sam McLaughlin of Oshawa, Ontario, convinced William C. Durant – founder of General Motors – to supply Buick automobile engines to his company. McLaughlin had designed an automobile, but the high cost of producing engines led him to sign a fifteen-year contract with the Buick Motor Company of Flint, Michigan. In 1908 his firm produced 154 Buicks. In 1915 he also incorporated the Chevrolet Motor Car Company of Canada, and in 1918 he sold his two companies to General Motors Corporation, and they became General Motors of Canada. The other member of Canada's Big Three, the Chrysler Corporation of Canada, was incorporated on 17 June 1925. It succeeded the Maxwell-Chalmers Motor Company.[35] In November 1998, Chrysler merged with Daimler-Benz to become DaimlerChrysler. Among the Asian transplants, Honda was the first to build a plant in Canada. It started production of automobiles in Alliston, Ontario, in November 1986. Other companies, Toyota in 1986, and CAMI and Hyundai in 1989, joined Honda. The vehicle-assembly plant industry is thus foreign-owned.

General Motors, Ford, and Chrysler account for approximately 84 per cent of the production of passenger cars and light-duty trucks in Canada, while the Asian transplants produce the other

16 per cent. The Big Three also dominate sales, with 75 per cent, and employment, with 90 per cent. Most of the auto industry is located in Ontario, which has twelve assembly plants. At the time of the NAFTA negotiations, there were two plants in Quebec – GM's Boisbriand and Hyundai's Bromont (closed in the summer of 1993) – and Volvo had one plant in Nova Scotia (closed in 1998). Canada is also home to four truck producers: Freightliner, Navistar, Paccar, and Western Star. The first three have manufacturing facilities in both Canada and the United States, whereas Western Star produces only in Canada.

The Canadian auto parts sector is not as concentrated as the assembly industry. It is composed of captive parts producers – i.e., facilities owned by vehicle producers, foreign-owned independent producers of parts, and Canadian-owned parts producers – who manufacture 50 per cent of all the parts made in Canada. Although more than 500 establishments manufactured auto parts and accessories in 1992, a tiny proportion (slightly more than 3 per cent) dominated the industry, which can be divided into tier-one and tier-two suppliers. The former sell to assembly plants, and the latter to tier one. The parts sector is located in Ontario, with 75 per cent of the total, Quebec, with about 14 per cent, and British Columbia, with 6 per cent.

The automotive industry (parts and assembly) accounted for almost 10 per cent of total manufacturing GDP in 1992 and approximately 11.6 per cent in 1997. While Canada's share of the 'North American' market (Canada and United States combined) is only 9 per cent, its share of motor vehicle production was 17 per cent in 1992 and 17.5 per cent in 1997. Shipments reached approximately $45 billion in 1992 and more than $85 billion in 1997. The industry employed 137,000 workers in 1992, a slight increase after a drop during the recession of 1990–1. In 1997 direct employment fell from 152,000 to 143,000. While employment is generally fairly stable in vehicle assembly, it fluctuates more often in the parts sector, which accounts for more than 60 per cent of total employment.

Canada exports most of its production of motor vehicles – over 85 per cent. It is also overwhelmingly dependent on the United

States. In fact, exports there account for over 97 per cent of the total, and imports represent approximately 80 per cent of the total. Canada has had a surplus in the assembly industry for over thirty years and usually suffers a trade deficit in the parts sector. Exports to and imports from the United States account for approximately 90 per cent of Canada's total exports and imports of parts. Approximately 70 per cent of parts made in Canada are exported. Trade with Mexico is small in both motor vehicles and parts: exports represent no more than 1 per cent, while imports have increased significantly under NAFTA to reach over 10 per cent of total imports of vehicles in 1997 and around 5 per cent of total parts imported.

The U.S. Automotive Industry

The U.S. auto industry is over 100 years old. While General Motors, Ford, and Chrysler have been dominant since the very beginning, the first U.S. company set up to build and sell automobiles was the Duryea Motor Wagon Company of Springfield, Massachusetts; it sold four cars in 1895. After the establishment of Ford in 1903, General Motors in 1908, and Chrysler in the 1920s, production grew substantially. By 1929, over 5 million cars, trucks, and buses had been manufactured in the United States. In addition to the Big Three, there were several small automakers, but most of them ceased operations or were bought over the years by one of these three firms. Production of cars and light trucks is concentrated in a few states. Michigan, home of the Big Three, comes first, with 25 per cent of the total, followed by Ohio, with 16 per cent; Missouri, at 10 per cent; Kentucky, at 9 per cent; and Tennessee, at 6 per cent. There are also a few manufacturers of heavy-duty trucks and bus bodies – most notably, Ford, Freightliner, General Motors, Mack, Navistar, Paccar, and Volvo/GM.

In 1982 Honda became the first Japanese firm to manufacture cars in the United States. It is based in Ohio, where it has been making motorcycles since 1979. Other foreign firms have also entered in the U.S. market. Nissan started operating in Tennessee in 1983. New United Motor Manufacturing Inc. (NUMMI), a General Motors–Toyota joint venture, located in California in 1984. A Ford–Mazda joint venture – AutoAlliance International – has had a plant in Michigan since 1987. Diamond-Star Motor (now Mitsubishi Motor Manufacturing), first owned by Mitsubishi and Chrysler, arrived in Illinois in 1988, while Toyota has been in Kentucky also since 1988. Subaru-Isuzu has been installed in Indiana since 1989, BMW in South Carolina since 1994, and Mercedes Benz in Alabama since 1997. In general, transplants have been very successful. Their production went from zero in 1981 to 26.3 per cent of the cars made in the United States in 1993 and 34 per cent of those made in 1997. At the time of the NAFTA negotiations, the Japanese manufacturers held 30 per cent of the U.S. market (transplants and imports).

The U.S. auto parts industry is composed essentially of suppliers of original equipment (OE) and after-market firms for replacement parts. Approximately 5,000 firms serve these two markets, including 100 large businesses. Several foreign firms, particularly Japanese, European, and Canadian companies, have invested in the U.S. auto parts sector. By 1990, shortly before the NAFTA negotiations, these companies had captured 10 per cent of total industry shipments and 9 per cent of employment. Their share of production doubled between 1989 and 1993, to reach 14 per cent. While output of passenger cars and light trucks accounted for approximately 2.6 per cent of U.S. GDP in 1992, the auto parts industry contributed almost 2 per cent of GDP. The assembly industry employed about 263,000 people in 1992, and the parts sector, more than 600,000. In 1997, total employment reached over 1 million. As in Canada, the parts sector fluctuates between 60 and 70 per cent of total automotive employment. The value of shipments of motor vehicles, trucks, and bus bodies was U.S.$156 billion in 1992 and more than U.S.$200 billion in 1997. For parts and accessories, shipments totalled U.S.$106 billion in 1992 and close to U.S.$160 billion in 1997.

The United States has traditionally had a trade deficit in autos. The bulk of U.S. exports – i.e., approximately 90 per cent – used to go to Canada. But the United States has over the years become less dependent on its northern neighbour. Canada received 54 per cent of U.S. exports of motor vehicles in 1992 and 57.7 per cent in 1997. Other major buyers in 1997 included Mexico, with 8 per cent, and Japan, with 6.4 per cent. On the import side, Japan captured 46 per cent of the U.S. import market in 1992, Canada 33 per cent, and Mexico, 7 per cent. In 1997, Canada ranked first, at 38.5 per cent, followed by Japan, at 30 per cent; Mexico, at 13 per cent; and Germany, at 10.5 per cent. In the parts sector, Canada still gets more than 50 per cent of total U.S. exports (52 per cent in 1997), while Mexico's share has increased under NAFTA, to 20.5 per cent in 1997. Other buyers include Japan, at 5 per cent, and Germany and two trading blocs – the Andean Community (Bolivia, Colombia, Ecuador, Peru, and Venezuela) and MERCOSUR (Argentina, Brazil, Paraguay, and Uruguay) – each with approximately 2 per cent of the total. Canada, Mexico, and Japan share almost equally among themselves 75 per cent of the U.S. imports market.[36]

The Mexican Automotive Industry

It is widely believed that the automobile arrived in Mexico in 1908 – i.e., before the 1910 revolution. Ford opened the first automobile assembly plant in 1925. General Motors followed in 1935. Fábricas Automex, a privately owned Mexican firm and Chrysler licensee, was established in 1938 and started producing Chrysler cars in 1939. Chrysler bought 33 per cent of Fábricas Automex in 1962, increased its share to 45 per cent in 1968, and finally bought the company in 1972 after it had suffered major losses. Transplants arrived in Mexico in the 1960s. Nissan has been manufacturing cars in Aguascalientes since 1966 and in Cuernavaca since 1992. Volkswagen bought Promexa, a Mexican company, in the mid-1960s and has been based in Puebla since 1967. BMW, Honda, and Mercedes-Benz all started manufacturing vehicles in Mexico in the mid-1990s. After the merger between Chrysler and Daimler-Benz in November 1998, DaimlerChrysler announced that it would no longer assemble Mercedes-Benz cars in Mexico.

Production has traditionally been located in Mexico City, Cuernavaca, Puebla, Monterrey, and Ciudad Sahagún. The 1980s and the opening of in-bond maquiladoras took production to northern Mexico. New and very efficient facilities such as the Ford assembly plant set up in Hermosillo in 1986 marked the beginning of the modern Mexican auto industry, geared towards production for export. Mexico is also home to producers of medium-sized and heavy trucks and buses. Among those are the Big Three, Dina, Kenworth, Mexicana de Autobuses (MASA), Oshmex, Scania, Víctor Patrón, and Volvo (which bought Trailers de Monterrey in 1996). Mexico's automotive parts sector comprises approximately 700 firms, 70 per cent of them Mexican-owned. These are small companies with low technological content and little value added. But Mexico also has a flourishing auto parts sector made up of 750 maquiladoras located near the U.S. border and producing for export.[37]

The auto industry is fairly important to the economy of Mexico. It represented 9.5 per cent of manufacturing GDP in 1991 and 11 per cent in 1997. It also accounted during 1997 for 18 per cent of manufacturing employment and was the single largest source of foreign exchange revenues, ahead of oil and tourism. Production increased substantially in the 1990s, from 800,000 units in 1990 to over 1.2 million in 1996. Mexico accounted for only 2.5 per cent of total North American production of vehicles in 1986 but 10.5 per cent in 1997. Most of the growth took place in exports. In fact, during the peso crisis of 1994–5, export sales more than compensated for the slowdown in the domestic market. In 1996, for example, Mexico exported more than 970,000 units, compared to fewer than 280,000 in 1990. The parts sector has created most of the jobs in the auto industry, accounting for 80 per cent of the total. Assembly employed 60,000 people in 1992 and slightly more than 50,000 in 1996. The parts sector employed 285,000 people in 1992 and 226,000 in 1996, most of them in the maquila industry.[38]

Mexico is, like Canada, very dependent on the U.S. market for exports and imports of vehicles and automotive parts. Intra-firm trade has been very sizeable since establishment of maquiladoras in the early 1980s. It has increased significantly in the 1990s, which has made Mexico even more dependent on its North American neighbours, with which it has had a surplus for years. The United

States saw its share of Mexican exports grow from 73 per cent in 1991 to almost 86 per cent in 1996. Canada is also buying more cars and parts from Mexico – approximately 4 per cent of the total in 1996.

The data may be a bit difficult to analyse, since it is entirely possible that Mexican exports to the United States may be re-exported to Canada through intra-firm trade. Mexico's total auto industry exports amounted to U.S.$6.77 billion in 1991 and U.S.$20 billion in 1996. Imports also grew from U.S.$7.2 billion in 1991 to U.S.$10.4 billion in 1996. Excluding the in-bond industry, 80 per cent of Mexican vehicle exports went to the United States in 1997, about 9 per cent to Canada, 3 per cent to Chile, and 2 per cent to Brazil. The United States was also the main source of Mexican vehicle imports, sending 72 per cent, while Japan came next, with 20 per cent, and Germany third, with 8 per cent. In parts, excluding again the in-bond industry, the United States bought 70 per cent of Mexican output, and Brazil, Canada, and Germany, 3 per cent each. Imports of auto parts came from the United States, with 68 per cent; Germany, with 8 per cent; Japan, with 6 per cent; and Canada, with 1 per cent.

Government Intervention

Canada: Stimulating Domestic Production and Foreign Investment

Trade Policy as an Instrument to Limit Imports from
the United States[39]

At the beginning of the twentieth century, protection for the auto-mobile industry in Canada took the form of a 35 per cent general tariff rate applied almost exclusively to U.S. imports. The very few cars imported from Britain arrived under the British prefer-ential tariff, set at 22.5 per cent. Production grew substantially during the First World War, and by the early 1920s Canada had become the second-largest producer of motor vehicles in the world. However, cars were much more expensive in Canada than in the United States, partly because Canada did not enjoy the same economies of scale. As consumers started noticing the price differential, Canada put in place a new tariff policy in 1926. The duty on vehicles costing no more than $1,200 fell from 35 per cent to 20 per cent (and to 12.5 per cent under the British preferential tariff). For cars valued at over $1,200, the general tariff rate was 27.5 per cent (and 15 per cent under the preferential tariff). The 1926 policy also introduced the concept of duty drawback, intended to encourage Canadian content: the Canadian government refunded 25 per cent of the duty paid on imported components as long as auto parts from the British Empire – essentially Canadian parts, in this case – represented at least 50 per cent of the cost of the finished vehicle. The content rule also included exemption from the 5 per cent excise tax for cars with a retail price less than $1,200, as long as they qualified under imperial content.

In the early 1930s, the Canadian government sought to protect its auto industry. The Great Depression was devastating production of cars because of the severe decline in exports. In 1929, 263,000 cars were manufactured in Canada; by 1932, production had plummetted to 61,000. The first measure to be introduced was a tariff increase. In 1931, the general tariff was raised from 27.5 per cent to 30 per cent for cars priced at between $1,200 and $2,100 and to 40 per cent for cars valued at more than $2,100. Tariffs also went up on components, and a 1 per cent excise tax took effect on the duty-paid value of imported parts. This levy was raised to 3 per cent in 1932. R.B. Bennett's Conservative government also banned importation of used vehicles in 1931. All these measures proved successful in protecting the industry in the short run. Imports of vehicles dropped from 23 per cent of sales in 1929 to 3.5 per cent in 1931–3. And three U.S. carmakers (Graham-Paige, Hudson Motors, and Packard) started producing autos in Canada.[40]

Freer Trade amid Protection

While the Canadian government was trying to limit the number of U.S.-made cars entering the domestic market, it agreed without much concern unilaterally to grant duty-free treatment to British motor vehicles under the Canada–United Kingdom Free Trade Agreement of 1932. Closer to home, Canada's Tariff Board, in its 1936 report on the domestic automobile industry, reported doubts expressed by several people about the need to stimulate domestic production in view of higher prices for Canadian passenger cars. There was a 35 per cent price differential between Canadian and U.S. retail auto prices.

A few months later, the two countries signed a trade agreement. Effective 1 January 1936, U.S. imports would pay Canadian duties under the intermediate tariff (equivalent to what is now known as the most-favoured-nation treatment tariff). This meant a 17.5 per cent tariff on cars valued at less than $1,200 and 25 per cent for cars with a higher retail value. In May 1936, the recommendations of the Tariff Board were implemented. The rate of duty on all imported cars entering Canada under the intermediate tariff was set at 17.5 per cent, regardless of price. A safeguard provision allowed the government to increase the tariff to 22.5 per cent, should a surge in imports harm domestic production.[41]

The content rules established in 1926 were also revised in 1936. For example, the requirement for Commonwealth content, favouring Canadian production, was raised to 60 per cent. Imports of some auto parts such as bearings and compressors could enter free of duty, provided that these components were *not* made at all in Canada. Other auto parts such as chassis, frames, and locks also entered duty free if they were not manufactured in Canada and if they met an additional condition. Carmakers had to ensure 40 per cent Commonwealth content when their production was less than 10,000 vehicles, 50 per cent for 10,000 to 20,000 vehicles, and 60 per cent for more than 20,000 vehicles. Failure to meet these two conditions meant that the intermediate tariff of 17.5 per cent was applicable. While the largest carmakers established in Canada raised their Commonwealth content to meet these new requirements, others (Hudson Motors, Packard, and Studebaker) were unable to do so and shut down their Canadian operations.[42]

The Bladen Commission

Car production grew very strongly in Canada after 1945, but by the late 1950s imports were surging. European automakers took advantage of their low labour costs and modern plants to increase their exports substantially to both Canada and the United States. The British industry was particularly at an advantage in Canada: it could enter the market free of duty under the 1932 agreement.

By 1960, Canada's trade deficit in the auto sector was such that John Diefenbaker's Conservative government appointed Dean Vincent Bladen of the University of Toronto to head a royal commission to study its problems. The Bladen Report (April 1961) indicated that the industry's main problems stemmed from the absence of economies of scale – too many models were manufactured in low volume. While the United Auto Workers (UAW) union had proposed integration of the U.S. and Canadian industries and suggested negotiation of sectoral free trade, other groups, such as the Automotive Parts Manufacturers' Association, were asking for more protection. The Bladen Report 'recommended removal of the existing 7½ per cent excise tax, imposition of a 10 per cent rate of duty under the British Preferential Tariff, and changes in the formula for calculating the value for duty and sales taxes of vehicles to eliminate unfair discrimination against Canadian producers.' In June 1961, the government agreed to implement 'the removal of the excise tax and the change in the valuation basis for sales tax purposes.'[43]

The Bladen Commission had also suggested allowing importation of all vehicles and parts duty free, as long as they met the new requirements for Canadian content, 'calculated as a proportion of the total cost of manufacture of vehicles made in Canada, including the cost of imported components, together with the cost of imported vehicles and replacement parts.'[44] Therefore Bladen's formula would have required a carmaker manufacturing and importing more than 200,000 vehicles a year to demonstrate Canadian content of 65 per cent.

The Response from the Government

In October 1962, the Canadian government launched its new auto plan in response to the Bladen Report. It would enforce a 25 per cent tariff – waived during the previous ten years – to be paid on imported automatic transmissions. But it also set up a duty-remission program. Canadian automakers could recover the duty paid on a maximum of 10,000 engine blocks if they increased their exports of Canadian-made auto parts over the level reached during the base year – i.e., from 1 November 1961 to 31 October 1962. In 1963, the program was extended to imported vehicles and original equipment parts. Carmakers could recuperate the duty paid on vehicles and parts provided that they surpassed the level of Canadian content that they had reached in both products during the base year.

The industry and labour welcomed the new plan, but independent U.S. auto parts producers, who had the most to lose, opposed it. On 15 April 1964, the Modine Manufacturing Company, of Racine, Wisconsin – a producer of radiators – filed a countervailing duty petition under section 303 of the U.S. Customs Act of 1930, alleging that Canadian remission of duty was a 'bounty or grant.' The U.S. Treasury Department began a formal review. The U.S. and Canadian governments were worried. There was no injury test necessary at the time for a positive finding. Fearing that such a finding would seriously affect trade relations, and because U.S. automakers supported the Canadian scheme, the two governments sought to avoid a trade war and looked for an alternative solution. They finally negotiated sectoral free trade in the Canada–United States Automotive Products Trade Agreement, or the Auto Pact, signed on 16 January 1965 by Prime Minister Lester Pearson and President Lyndon Johnson. The U.S. Treasury terminated its review.

The Auto Pact

Under the Auto Pact, the United States agreed to allow duty-free entry to all vehicles with 50 per cent North American (i.e., Canadian and/or American) content. The Canadian requirements were much more demanding. First, only automakers manufacturing cars in Canada during the base year (1 August 1963–31 July 1964) could import auto products without duty. Producers had to maintain a ratio of production to sales at least equal to the ratio of the base year but not less than 75 per cent. They also had to maintain Canadian content in the production of vehicles in Canada at least equal to the base year. Ottawa wanted to ensure that domestic output would increase annually, but it failed to convince Washington to agree on such an arrangement. U.S. producers were more inclined to accept this idea and committed themselves in letters of undertaking to increase Canadian value added by at least 60 per cent of their expansion in their Canadian sales and by $260 million above the base year by the 1968 model.

The Auto Pact led to specialization in the North American industry and a significant increase in Canadian production. Only a few models are now produced in Canada, but since these vehicles are serving the entire North American market, manufacturers producing in Canada can now benefit from economies of scale. The Auto Pact was so beneficial to Canada that by the end of the 1960s it had a positive trade balance with the United States in automotive products. The Americans saw the Canadian requirements, also known as safeguards, as transitional.

Attracting Foreign Producers: Investment Incentives
and Tariff Rebates

When it became clear that foreign car producers, especially Japanese transplants, were ready to establish plants in North America to serve this vast market, the federal and provincial (particularly Ontario and Quebec) governments in Canada offered them investment incentives (also used by U.S. states), such as tax breaks, subsidies, and improvements to infrastructure.

Another instrument helped attract transplants to Canada. Starting in the mid-1980s, these manufacturers received duty rebates. Canada was hoping that these carmakers would eventually be covered under the Auto Pact. It offered three types of rebates. First, production-based duty-remission orders allowed a firm establishing a plant in Canada to import automotive products free of duty as long as it met the requirements set by the government in gradually meeting the Auto Pact safeguards. Second, export-based duty-remission orders permitted automakers to import automotive goods duty free provided that they could offset these imports with Canadian exports. The FTA eliminated the first type as of 1 January 1996 and the latter as of 1 January 1998. Third, and most interesting to the Japanese transplants, the duty drawback program reimbursed them for duty paid on imported materials for products destined for the export market. As mentioned above, under the FTA, this program was due to end on 1 January 1994; NAFTA extended it to 1 January 1996.

The 1990s: Staying Competitive

In addition to trade policy instruments and government incentives, programs related to innovation, human resources, and standards and regulations now serve the interests of automakers. Trade policy is improving the industry's competitiveness. Canada unilaterally eliminated the MFN tariff on original equipment parts on 1 January 1996. Vehicles and after-market parts also saw their tariffs decline substantially. In the Uruguay Round negotiations, Canada committed itself to reducing its MFN tariff on automotive goods from 9.2 per cent to 6.1 per cent by 1 January 1999. The U.S. MFN tariff on passenger cars is lower, at 2.5 per cent, but much higher, at 25 per cent, for light trucks and trucks of more than 20 tonnes, whereas the tariff on parts is 2.7 per cent. Mexico has a 20 per cent MFN tariff on vehicles and an average tariff of 15 per cent on parts.

During the two-year Automotive Competitiveness Review, launched in 1996 by the Canadian government, Japanese manufacturers lobbied for elimination of all duties on imported vehicles, while the Auto Pact firms pushed in the other direction. On 10 June 1998, the government announced its decision to keep its existing tariffs. On 11 February 2000, a WTO panel, set up at the request of Japan and the European Union, ruled that Canada's tariff system, favouring Auto Pact firms, violates the MFN and national treatment obligations under the GATT and the General Agreement on Trade in Services (GATS), as well as the provisions in the Agreement on Subsidies and Countervailing Measures prohibiting export subsidies.

*Government Intervention in the United States: Regulating
Japanese Competition*

Confidence in the Domestic Industry and Support
for Liberalization

The auto industry did not become a priority for U.S. trade policy
until the mid-1970s. In fact, the U.S. government had not attempted to shelter it from foreign competition until the first oil
shock of 1973. The Dingley Tariff Act of 1897, however, was the
exception. It classified auto goods as manufactured steel to
secure their protection with a 45 per cent tariff. Simon Reich, a
student of the U.S. auto industry, mentions that by the 1930s government protection had become unnecessary, because structural
constraints kept out foreign competition. Lacking the resources
and economies of scale that production for sale in the United
States required, European manufacturers were unable to challenge
their U.S. counterparts. Moreover, inexpensive gasoline in North
America allowed U.S. carmakers to manufacture large vehicles,
whereas Europe was producing smaller and more energy-efficient
automobiles.[45]

The Smoot–Hawley Tariff Act of 1930 raised most U.S. tariffs to
pre-1914 levels. In the case of auto products, the duty was unusu-
ally low after enactment of the new trade law – a meagre 10 per
cent. Nevertheless, the act affected U.S. automakers, who suffered
greatly when U.S. trading partners cross-retaliated and increased
their tariffs on autos – a luxury product in the 1930s. Exports of
motor vehicles and parts fell by 72.6 per cent between 1929 and
1931. A few years later, the United States attempted without great
success to cut foreign tariffs on U.S. auto products when negotiating bilateral trade agreements under the Reciprocal Trade Agreements Program (RTAP). The accession of Japan to GATT in 1955
gave it an opportunity to obtain duty reductions on automobiles
from both Japan and other countries.

After World War II, confidence in the U.S. auto industry was at
an all-time high. The industry was the most efficient in the world.
This situation led interagency committees of the government in

1947 and 1950 to suggest reducing the tariff on autos to 5 per cent. By 1953, the industry was so vigorous that a presidential report recommended elimination of tariffs on automobiles altogether.[46] The tariff was lowered to 8.5 per cent in 1956, to 6.5 per cent after GATT's Dillon Round (1960–1), and to 3 per cent after the Kennedy Round (1963–7). Offshore automakers posed no threat to the Big Three in the early 1960s; their share of the U.S. market was below 5 per cent in 1962 and rose above 10 per cent only by 1968. Over half of these imports came from West Germany.

The First Oil Shock and Growing Imports Lead to CAFE Rules

The first oil shock and the effects of the recession in the mid-1970s slower U.S. automobile sales. They also caused a shift in demand, away from fuel-inefficient American cars and towards more energy-efficient Japanese imports, whose share of the U.S. market rose from 15.2 per cent in 1973 to 18.2 per cent in 1975. To encourage the main U.S. assemblers to produce more fuel-efficient cars, Washington adopted the Corporate Average Fuel Economy (CAFE) regulations of the U.S. Energy Policy and Conservation Act of 1975. In 1970, it had also imposed severe restrictions on emissions under the Clean Air Act of that year.

The Auto Sector Becomes a Political Issue and a Trade Priority

A major change in U.S. policy and attitudes occurred during the first oil shock. Trade policy suddenly became a key instrument for protecting U.S. automakers against thriving Japanese imports. In 1974, the UAW raised the possibility of instituting quotas on imports. A year later, the UAW, until then an advocate of free trade, championed a dumping investigation against auto imports from seven countries, including Japan. Richard Nixon's administration was very concerned. Its European partners strongly voiced their objection and worried that the Tokyo Round negotiations of GATT could unravel. The Treasury Department dropped the investigation in 1976. By 1977, the UAW was once again proposing quotas on Japanese imports *unless* Japanese carmakers started operating plants in the United States.[47]

The effects of the second oil shock in 1979 were more dramatic. Production declined, and imports grew from 22.7 per cent of the U.S. auto market in 1979 to 28.2 per cent in 1980. The Big Three were losing money and seeing *their* market slipping away. Moreover, Chrysler was on the brink of bankruptcy and needed government assistance in the form of a loan guarantee of U.S. $1.5 billion. By 1980, pressure was very strong on Jimmy Carter's administration to provide relief to the industry. Instead of adopting protectionist measures, the government used other instruments, such as loan guarantees to auto dealers, to help the industry.

Ford and the UAW filed petitions in the summer of 1980 at the U.S. International Trade Commission (USITC) under section 201 of the Trade Act of 1974 asking for import relief. In November 1980, the USITC found that increased imports had not been a substantial cause of serious injury or threat thereof to the industry. Shortly after taking office, Ronald Reagan's new administration made public in the spring of 1981 a three-year program of voluntary export restraint (VER) negotiated with Japan. Japanese producers would limit their exports to the United States to 1.68 million cars per year. The VER was renewed several times and finally expired on 31 March 1994; it allowed Japanese manufacturers to increase the dollar value of their exports and to secure significant rent transfers.

Once the Japanese program ended, U.S. strategy aimed at seeking access for U.S. auto products to the Japanese market. On 1 October 1994, the office of the U.S. Trade Representative (USTR) initiated a section-301 investigation with respect to Japanese auto parts. On 10 May 1995, the USTR determined that Japanese policies and practices in this sector were 'unreasonable and discriminatory.' It also announced its intention to invoke the WTO dispute settlement mechanism. Consultations and negotiations with Japan led to the signing on 23 August 1995 of the U.S.–Japan Automotive Agreement, which had been reached on 28 June 1995 and come into effect for five years starting that day. Its main objective was to eliminate Japanese barriers to U.S. autos and auto parts, implemented on an MFN basis. A U.S. interagency enforcement team monitors the agreement and releases assessments semi-annually.

The Republic of Korea (South Korea) also signed a Memorandum of Understanding with the United States on 28 September 1995. It agreed to 'liberalize standards and certification procedures, reduces taxes that discriminate against imported vehicles, ... [and] allow foreign majority ownership of auto retail financing entities.' However, the USTR identified South Korea in its October 1997 'Super 301' report to Congress as being a priority foreign country.[48] U.S. concerns included tariff and tax disincentives affecting imports, auto standards and certification measures, and financing restrictions. On 20 October 1997, the USTR initiated a section-301 action, and, on 20 October 1998, a Memorandum of Understanding Regarding Foreign Motor Vehicles was concluded between the United States and South Korea. The section-301 action was dropped. Brazil and Indonesia also saw the USTR initiate an investigation of certain acts, policies, and practices affecting their auto sector. A WTO panel found, on 22 April 1998, that Indonesia had violated its WTO obligations by granting a conditional tax and tariff benefits intended to develop its auto sector. Indonesia agreed to comply with the panel's decision by 22 July 1999. With Brazil, the main issue was its granting of tariff-reduction benefits contingent on satisfying certain export performance and domestic content requirements, a practice the United States considered inconsistent with the WTO agreement on trade-related investment measures (TRIMs). Brazil and the United States reached an agreement on 16 March 1998, whereby Brazil undertook to comply with the WTO.

Government Intervention in Mexico: Decrees to Stimulate Domestic Production

After the Second World War, the auto sector quickly took centre stage in Mexico's new industrialization strategy. The government aimed at creating a strong auto industry with backward and forward linkages that would help develop the manufacturing base of the economy, stimulate investment, and create employment. The government also hoped to reduce significantly dependence on imports and the resulting burden on the balance of payments. For a short period, Mexico lifted its ban on imports of finished automobiles, but as imports surged, it reimposed the ban on auto imports and other luxury items in 1947. The ban was lifted again in 1951, but to little effect. Imports began pouring into the country, and the government felt that it had to adopt measures that would increase local production and reduce the trade deficit.

The 1962 Auto Decree: Import Substitution and Local Production

The first Mexican auto decree, signed on 23 August 1962, entered into force on 1 September 1964. Its objective was to reduce the number of automakers in Mexico, encourage economies of scale, and create a national industry. The decree required domestic content of 60 per cent from firms that had received permission to produce. This grado de integración (GIN), based on direct cost of production, had to include the engine and transmission. The decree was another step in the adoption of import-substitution policies put forward since the 1940s and aimed at increasing resources in the auto sector – more specifically, at creating local engine and transmission industries. The government offered fiscal incentives on imported components but prohibited imports of finished vehicles. It preserved price controls and production quotas introduced in the 1950s.

The state industrial development bank, Nacional Financiera, which had recommended the new auto policy, had suggested that no more than four or five firms be allowed to manufacture motor vehicles – one model each. Parts would have to be bought from independent firms. Automakers and parts producers would form joint ventures with majority Mexican ownership. The only two wholly foreign-owned car producers, Ford and General Motors, opposed most of these restrictions, but not the limiting of the number of automakers in the market, as long as *they* were included. These two multinationals and several other firms received permission to manufacture motor vehicles under the 1962 decree. Fábrica Automex was a Chrysler licensee, controlled, at 67 per cent, by Mexicans. Willys Mexicana, later known as VAM, was a Mexican firm, founded in 1946, assembling the Rambler (American Motors). Diesel Nacional (DINA) was the only government-owned company; set up in 1951, it was assembling Renault cars. Promexa, a Mexican company that applied to produce Volkswagens, had bought two of the first Mexican automakers – Automotriz O'Farrill, established in 1937, and Automóviles Ingleses, set up in 1946. When Volkswagen bought Promexa in 1964, its name was added to the list of producers. Two firms from 1955 were also allowed to produce: Representaciones Delta assembled, among other makers, the Mercedes-Benz, and Planta Reo de México, which had first assembled Ramblers, was then producing Toyopet (Toyota). The two firms ceased operations in 1963 and 1964, respectively. After the collapse of Planta Reo, Nissan was added to the list of producers. The last firm on the list was a Mexican company, Impulsora Mexicana Automotriz (later Fábrica Nacional de Automóviles). It started producing the German Borgward in 1967 but closed down in 1969. Therefore, by 1970, not only were there fewer automakers operating in Mexico, but the majority were wholly foreign-owned – Ford, GM, Nissan, and Volkswagen. Chrysler had increased its equity in Fábrica Automex to 45 per cent. VAM was now owned by American Motors (40 per cent) and the Mexican government (60 per cent), whereas DINA was still under the control of the government.[49]

The decree of 1962 convinced U.S. carmakers to become more integrated with the local industry in order to provide domestic content. Auto parts companies were set up with Mexican capital, since foreign ownership could not exceed 40 per cent. Although production of motor vehicles grew substantially, from 50,000 in 1960 to 190,000 in the 1970, the trade gap widened. Low-quality automotive goods were difficult to export, and imports kept rising. This difficulty prompted the government to reach agreements with automakers in 1969 on export requirements. Imports would need to be offset by exports.

The 1972 decree set similar requirements: the trade balance was very much on the mind of the government, which decided that 40 per cent of a firm's exports would have to be made of Mexican components manufactured by firms owned by domestic capital (a minimum of 60 per cent). The goal was that by 1975 exports should account for 50 per cent of imports. Moreover, the 1962 decree requirements were not only maintained but improved. Producers received additional production quotas when they exceeded the 60 per cent GIN requirement.

The 1977 Auto Decree: Export Promotion and Balance of Payments

The ever-growing trade deficit in autos, which was worsened by the devaluation of 1976, led to the promulgation of the 1977 decree. Fixing the balance of payments became the primary focus of the government, and the executive order required manufacturers to work steadily towards balancing trade within their own operations by 1982. The decree broadened the concept of imports to encompass interest payments, royalty, and dividend remittances. Moreover, export requirements meant that at least 50 per cent of a carmaker's exports had to come from local parts suppliers, which had to be majority Mexican-owned. The decree set foreign exchange quotas but abolished price controls and production quotas. Therefore firms could manufacture any number of vehicles, as long as they had sufficient domestic content and a trade balance in equilibrium. Failure to balance exports and imports was to be punished by a series of measures, including denial of subsidies and other fiscal benefits.

The decree encouraged multinationals to invest in Mexico by allowing up to 20 per cent of automakers' exports to be produced in maquiladoras. General Motors (GM) was the first to act. In November 1977, it announced expansion of a subsidiary – a maquila – manufacturing wiring systems in Ciudad Juárez. In February 1978, GM made it public that it was going to build four new plants near the U.S. border to produce vehicles, engines, and engine parts. Soon afterwards, Ford and Volkswagen followed with their own expansion, as did Chrysler and Nissan. Slowly, the auto industry in Mexico was becoming more integrated with its U.S. counterpart. There were more joint ventures between U.S. auto manufacturers and Mexican industrial groups.

The 1983 Decree: Increasing Domestic Content and Reducing the Trade Deficit

The auto industry in Mexico benefited from the oil boom. Production of passenger cars grew at an average annual rate of 25 per cent between 1977 and 1981. However, the trade deficit continued to increase and reached approximately U.S.$2 billion in 1981. The balance of payments crisis that followed in 1982 led to promulgation of yet another auto decree in 1983, aimed at cutting the trade deficit. To reduce the need for imports, the decree imposed a required GIN of 60 per cent for auto parts by 1985 and a global GIN of 80 per cent for each company. By 1987, the GIN for passenger vehicles had increased to 60 per cent, and firms could produce only one line and five models, unless they were able to be self-sufficient in terms of foreign exchange. Production fell sharply between 1981 and 1986, and manufacturers suffered major losses. This situation prompted Renault to stop assembling cars in Mexico in 1986. It had bought 40 per cent of DINA's equity in 1978, and DINA and VAM had merged in 1983. Government policies appeared to show results vis-à-vis the trade balance, but the trade surplus did not originate from higher vehicle exports but rather from the collapse of domestic demand and, to a lesser extent, from increased exports of engines.[50]

The 1989 Decrees: Liberalization with Protection

The new administration of Carlos Salinas de Gortari consulted with all parties before issuing its three new decrees of 1989. The president was about to start dismantling the import-substitution program that his father, Raúl Salinas Lozano, had implemented when he was secretary of industry and commerce under President Adolfo López Mateos (1958–64). The autotransportation de-

cree of 1989 dealt with production of buses, trucks, and other vehicles and expired on 1 January 1994. The other two decrees are
still in force. The *Auto Popular* decree is aimed at providing consumers with a reasonably priced car. Only Volkswagen (and its
Beetle) and, to a lesser extent, General Motors (Chevy Corsair)
are taking part in this program. Manufacturers have to meet certain requirements, such as the use of low-lead fuel, a maximum
price set by SECOFI, and production of at least 40,000 units, as
well as adequate domestic content and balanced trade. In exchange, these companies receive tax exemptions.

The automotive decree of 1989 is being phased out by NAFTA
over a long period, ending on 1 January 2004. It had the objective
of liberalizing the auto industry, strengthening the parts sector,
generating a trade surplus, and bringing in foreign investment. It
eliminated restrictions on lines and models. While it removed rules
for specific domestic content, it introduced a more general rule:
36 per cent of a car's parts had to come from domestic suppliers.
Moreover, for the first time in years, imports of vehicles were allowed, though in limited numbers. For instance, imports could
not exceed 15 per cent of domestic sales for the 1991 and 1992
models and 20 per cent for 1993 and 1994. To be considered for
these quotas, a manufacturer needed to show a positive trade balance and offset these imports with specified exports. For example, in 1991, firms had to generate U.S.$2.50 in exports for each
dollar of imported vehicles. The required ratio was two to one in
1992 and 1993 and 1.75 to one in 1994.

ISSUE-SPECIFIC POWER: PROTECTION VIA THE FTA

Once again, the sections in this chapter on government intervention have demonstrated that all three countries – Canada, Mexico,
and most recently the United States – have attempted over the
years to increase their resources in the auto sector. But in the case
of Canada, it appeared that these resources were not sufficient to
provide the Canadians with issue-specific power at the beginning
of the NAFTA negotiations. The Honda and CAMI cases, exam-

ined briefly in the introduction to this book, were at the heart of the problem in the auto sector. On 17 June 1991, the *New York Times* reported that 'after a year long audit, the United States Customs Service has concluded that Honda took improper advantage of the ... [Canadian–U.S.] free-trade agreement to avoid paying millions of dollars in duties on cars imported into the United States from its Alliston, Ontario, plant.' In a confidential memorandum to the U.S. Treasury Department on the preliminary results of the Honda audit, Customs Commissioner Carol B. Hallet wrote: 'We have determined that Honda has failed to meet the requirements for free-tariff treatment.'[51] What was troublesome to the Canadians was that it was widely believed that Hondas made in North America generally had a higher domestic content than cars produced by other Japanese carmakers. On June 18, six Democratic representatives sent a letter to President George Bush urging him to undertake 'an across-the-board examination of all "transplants" and all their models imported from Canada' to determine whether they were in compliance with the FTA.[52] U.S. Customs had already begun to audit the CAMI plant in Ingersoll, Ontario. As mentioned above, an administrative decision had been made by the United States on 22 May 1991 to exclude non-mortgage interest from the 'direct cost of processing' formula of the FTA's rule-of-origin requirement, but CAMI was claiming that such costs should be counted.

Industry specialists in Canada were concerned that the leak to the *New York Times* about the Honda audit, the letter from members of Congress – including House Majority Leader Richard Gephardt – the CAMI investigation, and the call to raise the North American value-content requirement were sending a powerful message to the transplants: do not locate future investments in Canada. The results of the final Honda audit, released on 2 March 1992, meant that the Honda Civics assembled in Ontario and exported to the United States from 1 January 1989 to 31 March 1990 did not satisfy the North American content required by the FTA. Therefore Honda had to pay U.S.$17 million in duties. To the Canadian automotive industry, this decision signalled that 'the United States ... [was] using its muscle to try to win back a more favourable balance of production,' according to Toronto-based automotive analyst Dennis DesRosiers.[53] Canada had been very successful since the beginning of the Auto Pact. The industry had been rationalized. It had captured a larger share of North American production – 17 per cent in 1992, compared with 7 per cent in 1965 – whereas its share of the North American market was approximately 9 per cent.

Although Canada did not appear to have issue-specific power in the NAFTA negotiations, in fact it did. The FTA was protecting Canada. The unanimous decision of the binational panel under the FTA's chapter 18 in favour of CAMI showed that Canada was right in its interpretation of non-mortgage interest payments. Moreover, Canada had also invoked chapter 18 in the Honda dispute and was confident about winning the case, especially with regard to the distinction made by U.S. Customs between 'direct cost of processing' and 'direct cost of assembling.' The FTA had also preserved – even though it weakened – the Auto Pact, which remained 'very important to the Big Three.' Canada's large shares of North American production and employment resulted from the Auto Pact. Therefore Canada had resources in the auto sector but was very dependent on its exports to the U.S. market. The Canadians had everything to gain by joining the NAFTA negotiations. It was an opportunity to clarify the rules of origin, resolve the Honda and CAMI investigations, and make sure that a bilateral Mexican–U.S. agreement would not isolate the Canadian industry.

The United States and Mexico also had key resources at the outset of the negotiations. For example, the United States could count on Canada and Mexico's increasing trade dependence. Also, the economic importance of the Big Three, headquartered in the United States, for the auto production of each party would help the Americans realize their objectives of raising the level of regional value content and protecting existing automakers in Mexico. The Mexicans had the advantage of being the growing market to which both U.S.- and Canadian-based carmakers wanted access.

TACTICS: WORKING WITH THE INDUSTRY AND BUILDING A CONSENSUS

Most issues related to the automotive sector in the NAFTA negotiations were dealt with by the automotive working group and the working group on rules of origin. Each had its own dynamics.

Auto Working Group: Phasing Out of the Mexican Decrees

The first trilateral meeting to address automotive issues took place in Washington, DC, on 19 December 1990, during the pre-negotiation phase, seven weeks before Canada formally joined the NAFTA talks. The Americans, who took the chair, tried to initiate an irritant-based discussion. According to participants, their message to their counterparts was the following: 'We will discuss all the things we do not like about Mexico. We will add a couple of issues that have not been settled in the FTA and we will proceed from there.' The Mexicans did not favour that approach at all. But they added a few issues of their own: the CAFE rules and the U.S. truck tariff, which the Americans said they were not in a position to discuss.

After Canada entered the negotiations, it took a very, very long time for the automotive working group to sit down and really start discussions. The first formal meeting was held in Ottawa in the spring of 1991, well before the talks were launched. However, it was not until early summer that the group met again to get into substance. Then there was 'an enormously long break' before the next meeting, in the autumn of 1991. Negotiations started moving only in early 1992. The first full year was not very substantive. But there were reasons for that long delay. The most important challenge involved the future status of the Mexican decrees. Canada and the United States had 'an enormously steep learning curve' to understand how the decrees worked and how the Mexican industry was structured. It took them a very long time to sort it all out. 'The only way we could get into serious negotiations was to be able to meet the Mexicans on an even footing,' a Canadian trade official stated in an interview.

The Big Three Call the Shots

Another reason for the delay was that the United States was waiting to hear from Congress, parts manufacturers, the UAW, and especially the Big Three before making any serious move. On 9 September 1991, the chairmen of Chrysler, Ford, and General Motors wrote to U.S. Trade Representative Carla Hills, Secretary of Commerce Robert Mosbacher, and Secretary of the Treasury Nicholas Brady. Their objective was to urge the administration to work for a fifteen-year transition period before complete elimination of the automotive decree: 'U.S. negotiators must ensure that the evolving competitive environment under a NAFTA does not disadvantage the position of existing investors in Mexico relative to those who may wish to enter.'[54] The Big Three were proposing a two-tiered structure, with two separate transitional rules. Tariffs and other trade barriers would be phased out more rapidly for tier-one producers – i.e., the Big Three, Nissan, and Volkswagen, the major assemblers of passenger vehicles and light trucks in Mexico as of 1 January 1991.

Searching for a Formula: The Canadians Keep Quiet

When they first went into the negotiations, the Mexicans made it clear that their automotive decree was not negotiable. But in fact the three countries sought to engineer a *formula* that 'would allow Mexico to become fully integrated into the North American auto industry,' as explained by a Mexican trade official. Different regional models, such as free trade and semi-free trade, were looked at. The *Financial Post* reported that the Canadians 'proposed creating a North American trade pact, similar to the ... Auto Pact. It would [have] ... create[d] the type of manufacturing industry among the three countries that would capitalize on each other's strengths in order to compete with European and Asian manufacturers.'[55] But the 'regional model' did not succeed. There was an impasse. The negotiators then chose to focus on each country, which meant going back to what the Americans had suggested in the beginning: an irritant-based discussion.

The Americans and Canadians were eager to phase out the Mexican automotive decree. A *formula* had to be found to determine how fast to do so. The Mexicans wanted to be included in the CAFE rules, even though the Big Three had shown no interest in such a proposal. The Canadians were in complete agreement with the Americans: the Mexican decree was highly protectionist and distorted investment patterns. However, even though the 'decree had to go,' the Mexicans needed a transitional period to create an adequate infrastructure and become a partner within the integrated system. Canada's point of principle in the auto negotiations was that the integration of Mexico would strengthen the North American industry. 'We started with a positive point of view, we did not see Mexico as a threat. We thought that NAFTA offered more opportunities than threats,' a Canadian trade official recalled. But the Americans were doing much of the work to convince the Mexicans to phase out their decrees. The Canadians were on the sidelines. Because of the Auto Pact, the Canadian tactic was to be quiet. 'We were not involved as much as the Americans. We did not have a decree. We had been in that position in the FTA with the Auto Pact,' a Canadian trade official acknowledged during an interview for this book.

The Auto Pact: Support from the Big Three

The only Canadian issue that became contentious during the negotiations was the Auto Pact. The Mexicans started drawing parallels between the Auto Pact and their automotive decree. The Americans at that point had a dilemma. They had agreed to keeping the Auto Pact in the FTA. And with respect to Mexico, they were saying: 'No post-transitional programs.' The Canadians had repeated over and over again that the FTA and the Auto Pact were not renegotiable. That constituted one of their overall objectives in NAFTA. The Canadians played their cards well. Although the American negotiators also called for elimination of the Auto Pact, 'they were never utterly convincing in the negotiations that they wanted to eliminate this agreement because clearly the Big Three were interested in keeping it,' a Canadian trade official suggested. The Americans 'had done their driving' on the Auto Pact in the FTA. NAFTA did no damage to the Auto Pact because Canada had the support of the Big Three. The discussions centred not on whether or not to open up the Auto Pact but on whether to maintain it or eliminate it.

The Canadian Transplants: No Access while Mexico Phases Out Its Automotive Decree

Although they concurred on most issues, the Canadians and the Americans did not agree on the role of transplants in a liberalizing Mexican auto market. The Canadians wanted access as quickly as possible for their exports. However, a Canadian trade official acknowledged that 'it was apparent from day one that the Americans were not interested in our point of view. Nor were the Mexicans. They did not wish to take on the United States and the Big Three over this issue. They could see some economic benefits in fostering a happier situation for the Big Three along with Nissan and Volkswagen.' The Americans and Mexicans finally cut a deal. The Japanese (except for Nissan) and others would have to fit under a different set of rules during the transition period. The Canadian-based transplants would not benefit from the opening of the Mexican market during the phasing out of the automotive decree. Lacking industry support, Canada 'lost' on this issue.

Slow Pace of Negotiations

The pace of the negotiations had accelerated in early 1992, but it slowed down after the Dallas 'jamboree' in February. The Americans and the Canadians had gained the impression from the Mexicans that they were going to make some considerable moves. But when the group met again, the Mexicans were apparently not prepared to become as forthcoming as the United States and Canada had thought. On 1 April 1992, a senior Canadian official confirmed to *Inside U.S. Trade* that the negotiations on the Mexican decrees were still at an early stage: 'I think the negotiation on opening up the Mexican market is more about the transition of how it will be opened up and about whether it's going to be opened up, but given the complexity of their decrees, that negotiation is still very much in the stage of a lot of detail being left open.'[56]

Stalemates happened all the time. One negotiator said: 'We would just make a tiny incremental gain in the discussions, and there would be a roadblock. No movement. What to do? We would try to get a slot with the chief negotiators, which involved much more waiting. It also meant that the chief negotiators had to be trained up to these very complex issues.'

In May 1992, the detail phase had already begun. *Inside U.S. Trade* reported that the U.S. industry had proposed that Mexico immediately reduce its trade-balancing requirement from a ratio of 2.5 to 1 to 2 to 1 – i.e., a Mexican auto assembler would have to export twice the value of its imports. The requirement would then be phased out over the transition period. But the Mexicans were trying to buy time. *Inside U.S. Trade* reported that they were offering 'an initial drop in this export-import ratio, but it ... [remained] unclear whether the trade balance requirement would be evenly phased out over the transition period in the Mexican proposal, or whether it will be done in discrete steps. Early last month Mexico had offered to ease the requirement to a 1:1 ratio immediately, but at that time left unclear how long it would take before lifting the requirement completely.'[57]

The working group met in May, and 'things started moving,' albeit very slowly. The Mexican newspaper *El Financiero* wrote that the Americans had shown some flexibility over national value added from suppliers – a key issue for the Mexicans.[58]

The Big Three had followed the negotiations closely and were frustrated with the many roadblocks in the auto working group. In June 1992, in a meeting with the three countries, the Big Three announced that they were not satisfied with the opening up of the Mexican market. They told the American and Mexican negotiators: 'If we do not get access to the Mexican market during the transition period, we will not support NAFTA.' That was a turning point. Politically, neither the U.S. nor the Mexican government could afford to lose the support of the Big Three, which had been very active in each country, shadowing the negotiators.

The talks had been really bogged down. The critical issue was how fast the Mexicans would open up their market. The negotiations had reached a point of political sensitivity, where they could no longer be done at the working group level. The dialogue had shut down between the United States and Mexico. Again, because of the Auto Pact, the Canadians felt that 'it would have been inappropriate to become engaged.' The chief negotiators got involved once more and started politicizing the issues. The Americans wanted a NAFTA deal before the election of November 1992.

In early July, several issues had been resolved. There was an agreement in principle on national value added from suppliers, quotas for heavy trucks, phasing out of restrictions on used cars, and application of the CAFE rules to Mexico.[59] However, all these issues were linked to the trade-balancing requirement, the key Mexican issue, on which there was no agreement. Mexico had acquiesced in a ten-year transition period and was proposing a very slow phasing out. The United States was 'insisting that a growing market ... [could] accommodate both Mexican domestic producers and a rising import share.'[60] Sources told *Inside U.S. Trade* in late July that 'Mexico is proposing that approximately 25 percent of market growth be opened for imports, while the U.S. is pushing for a figure closer to 60 percent.' The industry called the approach faulty, telling the negotiators that they had lost sight of the *formula* that had been agreed on early in the negotiations: to make the North American auto industry globally more competitive by integrating Mexico and eliminating its decrees.[61] The remaining auto issues had been politicized, and only the ministers could resolve them. The sixth ministerial meeting, in Mexico City on 25 and 26 July, reached a tentative agreement on trade balancing.[62]

A Canadian close to the negotiations summarized the last few weeks at the Watergate Hotel: 'In the context of opening up the Mexican market to imports, the Ministers discussed the trade-balancing requirement, the lowering of the national value-added in local parts procurement, the broadening of the definition of what could be included within the national value-added provision. All that was done in the context of knowing that the Mexicans were essentially trying to grow their auto parts industry. It was acutely sensitive for them.'

The Big Three were willing to let Mexico strengthen its auto parts industry, provided that they could have 'a privileged situation vis-à-vis the new entrants – and here read the Japanese for new entrants,' commented a Canadian official. He added: 'The political interests of the companies, their support for the U.S. and Mexican governments had to be played at the political level. It could not have been done in any other way.' A negotiator remarked: 'We knew from the very first day we sat down that those issues would have to go to the ministers.'

There was no complete text in the automotive sector on 12 August. This forced the auto working group to stay in Washington, DC, a little longer. The negotiators had tried to write a text, but it had too many brackets – three sets on virtually every clause. The detail phase had been engaged but not completed by 12 August. The negotiators had to come up with a series of definitions about the decrees. A negotiator close to the talks acknowledged that 'it was by itself a bit of a negotiation because where a term existed in the decrees, the Mexicans would not allow any variation of it because of the legal nature of the definition.'

Working Group on Rules of Origin

One of the major reasons why it took so long for the automotive working group to move on many issues was that it was waiting for the working group on rules of origin to make some progress of its own. Many issues in both groups were linked. The dynamics in rules of origin were very different from those in autos. First, the group had to come up with rules of origin for almost all sectors, except textiles. Second, the meetings were much more continuous. Reminiscing about his experience, a negotiator said: 'We had long, intensive sessions where everyone got to know each other very well. It was a very comfortable relationship. The negotiators never blew up together or very rarely.' The method of the group was to do everything it could at the negotiator level, so as to avoid going to the chief negotiators.

Honda and CAMI Cases

The Honda and CAMI investigations had politicized rules of origin for the Canadians. The Canadians believed that these two cases were 'undermining the spirit of the FTA and that the whole idea of free trade was at stake in Canada,' as a trade official commented a few months later. The cases were especially sensitive in southern Ontario – the 'cradle' of the Canadian auto sector. Canada faced two alternatives: to invoke chapter 18 of the FTA, the dispute settlement mechanism – or to use NAFTA to rewrite and clarify the rules of origin in autos. It chose to do both.

Negotiations Driven by the Number

In the United States, the main issue was regional value content (RVC). With respect to the auto sector, the role of the working group on rules of origin was thus paramount. One of the negotiators acknowledged this fact: 'The auto sector is so important to the three countries that symbolically we knew the success of NAFTA would be judged by what each country got in autos. And in autos, we knew it would be judged by the rule itself and the regional value content, the number.'

While the Canadians were preparing their strategy for the NAFTA negotiations, the Americans kept pressing publicly for a higher RVC. John Simpson, the Department of Treasury's deputy assistant secretary for regulatory, tariff, and trade enforcement, told the Senate Finance Committee in the summer of 1991 that the United States wanted a higher threshold going into the NAFTA negotiations. Simpson, the U.S. negotiator on rules of origin in NAFTA, also said that in light of the Honda case it was 'likely' that the rule of origin for autos would be tightened.[63]

During a meeting of the Canada–U.S. Trade Commission, held on 18 August 1991 in Seattle, Washington, on the eve of the second ministerial meeting, Carla Hills and Michael Wilson agreed to address the RVC for autos in the NAFTA talks. But they disagreed over whether non-mortgage interest – the key issue in the CAMI audit by U.S. Customs – should be included in the calculation. The *Toronto Star* wrote that the United States was seeking to increase the level to 75 per cent but would settle for 60 per cent.[64]

In September and October 1991, the U.S. and Canadian automotive industries made public their views on rules of origin. These recommendations would become a determining factor in the negotiations. The Big Three proposed that the new rules of origin meet the following objectives:

1. EXPAND employment and increase the international competitiveness of the North American automotive industry.
2. ASSURE that the benefits of the full NAFTA only accrue to companies that have made meaningful manufacturing and research and development commitments in North America. There should be no opportunity to inflate content levels or manipulate compliance through accounting, cost allocation, or pricing practices.
3. FACILITATE trade throughout North America with a simplified approach that will reduce the complexity of data gathering, calculations, audits, and cost allocations. Cost elements must be easily obtainable from normal cost accounting sources.
4. HARMONIZE the requirements of the rule to be compatible with existing GATT valuation and Generally Accepted Accounting Principles (GAAP).
5. CREATE a stable rule that will not significantly change the way in which business transactions are accounted and reported in each of the three countries.[65]

They favoured a rule that would provide for company-wide averaging and avoid the roll-up/roll-down approach. But they could not agree on the level of regional content. Chrysler and Ford supported a 70 per cent requirement, and General Motors did not want to go above 60 per cent.

The U.S. parts industry proposed a 75 per cent content provision, whereas the UAW recommended 85 per cent. Moreover, five Democratic Congressmen close to the U.S. auto industry wrote to Ambassador Hills on 23 October 1991 expressing their concerns about the negotiations.[66] They urged the Bush administration to raise the regional content level and to replace roll-up/roll-down with tracing requirements – a suggestion that would become an important attribute of the NAFTA rule of origin.

On 20 September 1991, the recommendations of the Motor Vehicle Manufacturers' Association (MVMA) to the Canadian government 'mirrored' those of the Big Three to the Bush administration. As expected, the Japan Automobile Manufacturers Association of Canada and the Association of International Automobile Manufacturers of Canada held different views. In the context of NAFTA, they were calling on the Canadian government not to increase the RVC. The main demand of the Automotive Parts Manufacturers' Association (APMA) was an RVC of 75 per cent and a Canadian value-added requirement of 50 per cent. The province of Ontario was also seeking a Canadian content requirement. APMA supported calculation of the FTA rule of origin, but with elimination of roll-up/roll-down. It proposed a system of averaging based on a company's country content. APMA also recommended what would become the most valuable card in Canada's negotiating tactics: to form a group with representatives from the industry 'to develop a satisfactory system of definitions and measurements.'[67]

During these few first months, the working group on rules of origin had been meeting regularly. Each side was trying to find a method that it could employ – a *formula* that would establish the framework of how products would be traded. Change in tariff heading was the first preference of the governments involved. It is a simple rule, easy to administer. But because of the Auto Pact and the CAFE rules, the Big Three wanted a regional value content. A negotiator remembered having argued with the Big Three against that model: 'We told them that an industry as savvy as textiles did not want a regional content because the government could not enforce it. But it did not matter, they wanted a regional value-content requirement, and they got it.'

Canada: Building an Industry Consensus

The Canadians were determined to improve the rules of origin and to strike a balance between the different positions of the industry. Canada wanted to keep the Big Three happy and also remain an attractive place to invest for Asian and European automakers. To build an industry consensus, the Canadian government created a NAFTA subcommittee within the Automotive Advisory Committee to the Minister of Industry, Science and Technology. Members included the Big Three, the transplants, MVMA, JAMA Canada, the dealers, the parts industry, the Canadian Auto Workers (CAW), and the provinces. This subcommittee met monthly during the first half of the negotiations and much more regularly afterwards. It proved invaluable to Canada. Representatives of the auto industry and of the Canadian government spent countless hours trying to create a *formula* that would be predictable, transparent, easy to understand and to audit. Canada's objectives were two-fold: to come up with a good formula that would avoid other Honda-like cases and then to use the Canadian industry to convince its U.S. counterparts, particularly the Big Three, to support this formula. The next step was to have the U.S. industry persuade its negotiators to adopt this formula. A Canadian negotiator summarized this tactic: 'We had to convince the U.S. government. So we told our industry that to the extent what they wanted could also be helpful to the U.S. industry, they should cast what they wanted in those terms. Ring up the U.S. industry and say: "You think there's nothing in this for you, see ..." Then you get the U.S. industry telling the U.S. government that this may be useful.'

Although in autos the Big Three were very integrated and 'the shots were called by headquarters,' this tactic helped the Canadians get what they were hoping for: a good formula. While the United States was focusing almost exclusively on the Big Three, the Canadians made an effort to include everyone, especially the transplants. Canada became known as 'the voice of the transplants' during the negotiations.

Searching for a Formula: The Net-Cost Method

Between the 'direct cost of processing' approach of the FTA and the 'net cost' formula of NAFTA, there were different attempts made to establish a method. For instance, in January 1992, *Inside U.S. Trade* wrote: 'Canada is expected to raise a complex proposal in rules of origin that will affect trade in cars between the three countries to ensure that the NAFTA did not disproportionately benefit one country. Under the proposal as it is now understood, Canada is expected to recommend that 70 percent of the trade in products that have more than 70 percent North American content be allocated among the three countries ... based on current trade flows, private-sector sources said.'[68] But because that particular proposal could have meant the end of the Auto Pact, it did not survive.

A Canadian negotiator acknowledged that 'it was really at the plenary session in Dallas in February 1992 that the "net cost" method started to gel as an acceptable concept.' However, chapter 3 of the Dallas Composite Text, which does not mention autos at all, shows that the negotiators were still far from having found a formula.[69] The Canadians used as their key concept 'cost of processing or assembly, or both,' defined as labour, non-labour, and research and development costs. This would later become 'cost of inputs' and then the 'net cost' method. The Americans chose to keep the FTA wording, 'direct cost of processing or assembly, or both,' but to define it differently. They included only inventoriable and period costs.[70] The United States was searching for a method easy to audit.

The Mexicans based the calculation of their regional content on the difference between the value of the exported good and the non-regional value of materials used or consumed in the production of that good, then divided the difference by the value of the exported good. To determine the non-regional value of materials, Mexico listed four categories: wholly originating materials, imported materials, regionally processed materials, and fungible materials. 'Regionally-processed materials' is a concept that could apply to autos. It means that the regional value content of a vehicle would be based 'on the critical processes used in its production.' Many problems could arise with such an approach. If applied on a model-by-model basis, it 'would make it administratively burdensome for companies with several product lines,' an industry source told *Inside U.S. Trade*. The Mexicans were concerned that a value-content test based on labour costs would be discriminatory. 'Mexico's low wages would mean that the threshold for duty-free treatment could only be met with the heavy use of North American parts.'[71]

After Dallas, negotiations slowed. By late February and early March, the Honda audit was complete. U.S. Customs had found that the Honda Civics assembled in Alliston, Ontario, did not qualify for duty-free treatment under the FTA, because the engines manufactured in Ohio from both North American and foreign parts did not meet the FTA's 50 per cent requirement. In its ruling in February 1992, the Customs and Excise Branch of Revenue Canada held that the same engines did qualify for duty-free treatment. According to Revenue Canada, only 1,500 engines manufactured in November 1989 did not satisfy the FTA requirement. The fact that the two Customs services, using the same rules, could reach such different conclusions demonstrated to the NAFTA negotiators that the rules of origin had to be well-defined and easy to understand. For Canada, it also meant that it needed to push for customs co-operation, uniform regulations, and a working group on rules of origin that would, among other things, help implement and administer the rules of origin and the uniform regulations. Canada wanted to ensure that there would not be many interpretations of the same case. In the FTA, there was an informal administrative agreement between U.S. Customs and Revenue Canada dealing with uniform regulations. It was called 'the consensus.' But since that document had no legal base, U.S. Customs did not recognize it as binding.

What really angered the Canadians in the Honda case was that U.S. Customs had made its regulations public only on 22 January 1992, well after the June 1991 leak to the *New York Times*. Prime Minister Mulroney referred to the U.S. Customs action as 'low-level politics.' For Canada, 'it was an attempt by the Americans to attack the Japanese where they could get them, not in Japan but in Canada,' a Canadian trade official said. Michael Wilson announced on 2 March 1992 that 'rules of origin disputes, like that involving Canadian-made Honda Civics, will have to be resolved before a free trade deal is concluded.'[72] Canada's tactic was to stay firm on that point until the very end. The U.S. government was divided over the issue. Some at the Treasury thought that 'the U.S. had shown bad faith'; others argued that 'the Canadians were hysterical to think that it was politically motivated.' At the Office of the USTR, senior officials favoured renegotiation of the rules over litigation.

The Canadian negotiators continued to consult, test, and improve their formula with the auto industry. In mid-April 1992, the detail phase had begun. *Inside U.S. Trade* reported that Canada had already been proposing a version of the net-cost method: 'The Canadians have ... recommended netting out the value of non-originating labor and materials in the numerator. In the denominator, Canada suggests taking the total cost of labor and materials from a company's financial statement, excluding such items as expenditures on sales promotion and royalties, for example.'[73]

Mexico had not changed its mind. 'The Mexican proposal would place the selling price of the vehicle in the denominator, and in the numerator it would net out the value of product not originating.' This formula, known as the transaction value method, was seen as 'unstable because it is based on fluctuating prices.'[74] Mexico wanted to give automakers the choice between its formula and the Canadian proposal. The Americans, who had held to their position, opposed the Mexican proposal for the auto sector. 'What if one company qualifies under one method and does not under the other? They'll crucify us,' an American negotiator reportedly told the Mexicans. That led Mexico to abandon this concept for the auto sector.

The Canadians and the Americans were both using the cost of inputs to determine the RVC. However, Canada was pressing the United States to accept a 'top-down approach.' Canada's tactic of working with the industry produced results. The Canadian industry convinced its negotiators that different companies define costs differently. Representatives of the industry had spent hours comparing their ledgers. So rather than starting with nothing and building up, as the Americans were proposing, the Canadians finally persuaded their counterparts at the end of May to adopt the top-down approach. Sources told *Inside U.S. Trade* that 'the new "net cost" approach was accepted by the U.S. ... after Mexico and Canada refused to go along with the "direct cost of processing" approach favored by the Administration and by the U.S. auto and auto parts industry.'[75]

The Number, Again

On 28 May 1992 John Simpson, the U.S. chief negotiator for rules of origin, said that 'he expected Canada would be willing to accept a threshold content higher than the 50 percent negotiated in the 1988 U.S.–Canada Free Trade Agreement because of the flexibility the U.S. has shown in accepting a new formula. Industry sources said this week that negotiators for the three sides are now discussing a threshold in the 60 to 65 percent range.'[76]

A few days later, after a meeting in which Michael Wilson had briefed the provinces on the NAFTA talks, Ontario Industry Minister Ed Philip confirmed that Wilson was thinking about accepting a 60 per cent RVC, phased in.[77] For the Canadians, this trade-off was worthwhile if it meant a clearer and simpler rule. But the Canadians did not want to go over 60 per cent. A senior Canadian trade official explained why Canada was holding back: 'It was because of our policy perspective. We wanted to be able to attract as much productive investment as possible. The clearer the rules, the easier it is to attract investment. But if the hurdle is much higher to jump over, however clear it may be, why live on this side of the hurdle and have to jump it all the time if I can live on the other side of the hurdle and stay in bed?'

In June 1992, Simpson told the American Association of Exporters and Importers that the United States was seeking a 65 per cent threshold. That corresponded to the consensus level on which the Big Three had agreed. The Americans were determined to convince the Canadians that the rule allowed for more foreign inputs treated as domestic (6 or 7 per cent) so that they should be compensated with a higher content requirement. Canada denied that the new 'net cost' method would increase the content requirement by more than 1 or 2 per cent. But the Canadians told the

Americans that they could be willing to accept a 60 per cent level 'phased in over a period equivalent to the time it takes to develop two new model lines, or roughly 10 years,' a source told *Inside U.S. Trade*.[78] Canada wanted to make sure that the transplants would have time to adjust, whereas U.S. administration officials were calling for a six-year transition period.

Canada had been talking to the transplants. They were not monolithic on regional value content. Some, like Honda, told the government that 65 per cent was acceptable if there were more transparent and predictable rules. Others, like Toyota, were much more worried.

Going into the Watergate session in late July, several issues remained unresolved. The RVC was tied to almost every issue. The negotiators prepared matrices that followed a 'domino theory,' according to some participating trade officials. The 'number,' as it was known, drove all the other issues. The ministers were thus able to choose among different scenarios. One of the issues linked to the RVC was tracing. Canada had never been very interested in tracing, but since the Big Three and the parts industry favoured it, Canada went along. The Americans had been pushing very hard to eliminate the roll-up/roll-down of the FTA. For the Canadians, a higher number meant less tracing. Another issue – albeit not negotiated by the working group on rules of origin – also tied to the number was the extension of duty drawbacks. The Canadian government, General Motors, and Ford all pressed for an extension of the program.

Two of the most important Canadian demands were a special provision that would allow a 50 per cent RVC during the first five years for a new plant and the first two years for a refit. The other demand involved the 'CAMI clause.' The United States and Canada had agreed on a company-wide averaging approach. John Simpson told *Inside U.S. Trade* that this provision was intended to allow CAMI to average its production with that of GMC.[79] The Mexicans totally opposed such an approach. They told the Americans that they were prepared to make a deal. They would accept a 65 per cent RVC without the CAMI provision. They also told the Americans that *they* should pay for CAMI.

Mexico won. The averaging approach in NAFTA is based on a class or model line.

The negotiations were well into the detail phase, with offers and counteroffers. The United States was asking for 65 per cent regional value content, and Canada had repeated that it did not want to go over 60 per cent. Finally, both accepted a 62.5 per cent RVC phased in over eight years, with a special provision for CAMI. The transplants would have preferred a general affiliation rule. Canada wanted 60 per cent and could not go over 65 per cent. A U.S. trade official who followed the negotiations closely said: 'The Canadians could not be seen as capitulating to the Americans, so a 65 per cent level was out of the question. We ended up with 62.5 per cent.'

CONCLUSION

The Canadians were happy with the results. They had a new rule of origin, special provisions for CAMI and the new plants and refits, an extension to the duty drawback program, and a working group on rules of origin that would facilitate the implementation and administration of the rules. All parties had also agreed to negotiate uniform regulations. Moreover, the United States had agreed to a provision in its implementing legislation that allows Honda to apply the NAFTA rules of origin retroactively. Resolving the Honda case was essential before Canada would agree to the handshake. But a lot needed to be negotiated after 12 August 1992, according to one of the negotiators. Although the text was being written as the negotiations progressed, there were many details that had to be 'discussed.'

Canada performed well in the auto sector. Its single most valuable negotiating tactic was enlisting the support of the Canadian industry. The Big Three wanted to maintain the Auto Pact, and so both the Americans and the Mexicans did not attack Canada seriously on this issue. The negotiators and the industry worked as a team to develop a transparent, predictable, and easy-to-audit rule of origin. The Canadian industry was also instrumental in convincing the U.S. industry to support the new rule of origin. Working with the industry – not just the Big Three, but the whole spectrum – helped Canada. The Canadians knew how far they could go on each issue. They were able to look at each issue from everyone's perspective. They wanted to strengthen their industry. To do so, they chose to strike a balance between the different positions espoused by industry members. Their ideal was to keep everyone happy. That led, for instance, to a special provision for CAMI which pleased General Motors. Tracing, favoured by Ford and the parts industry, became acceptable to Canada. Honda had also informed the negotiators that it did not object to tracing if it meant having a more transparent rule. The provisions for new plants and refits were aimed at existing and future transplants. The industry also supported uniform regulations and the mini-dispute settlement mechanism of chapter 5 – i.e., the Working Group on Rules of Origin. Ford and General Motors pushed for extension of duty drawbacks.

The close relationship between the industry and the government also let the Canadian negotiators 'educate' themselves in the first half of the negotiations. They were then better prepared technically to make whatever point they wanted. Another tactic used by the Canadians was to do most of the drafting, whenever possible. By doing that, Canada was obviously trying to achieve its preferred outcome. 'The wording is everything,' a Canadian trade official commented.

Without the support of the domestic industry in developing the 'net cost' method, it would have been more difficult for the Canadian negotiators to come up with a formula that would have satisfied the industry and won the approval of both the Americans and the Mexicans. A new rule was crucial for the Canadian automobile industry. Without a clear and predictable rule, there was less hope of attracting more investment from Asia. However, to convince the Americans, Canada needed more than just tactics. A binational panel created under chapter 18 of the FTA had sided with the Canadians in their definition of the FTA rule of origin in the CAMI dispute. Another binational panel might have favoured the Canadian point of view in the Honda case, because the U.S. Customs ruling made the point that 'direct cost of processing' and 'direct cost of assembling' had distinct meanings, whereas article 304 of the FTA states that these two expressions have the same definition. The Americans understood that it made more sense to renegotiate the rules of origin.

Moreover, Canada was also successful in preserving the Auto Pact because it secured the support of the Big Three. Once again, issue-specific power would not have been sufficient to produce a 'win' for Canada. In fact, Canada failed to convince the Americans and the Mexicans to allow Canadian-based automakers to export vehicles and parts to Mexico during the phasing-out period of the Mexican automotive decree because it did not have the backing of the Big Three. Canada had neither issue-specific power nor strong tactics in this case. Canadian-based companies were not present in Mexico, and Canada did not have the support of the industry. The Big Three championed the 'no' side, whereas the transplants were more preoccupied with engineering a new rule of origin.

CHAPTER SIX

The Pharmaceutical Industry: Ending Canada's Compulsory Licensing Regime

The pharmaceutical sector in North America mirrors the world pharmaceutical industry. While resisting the trend towards strong patent protection until the late 1980s, Canada and Mexico have now adopted a patent regime aimed at striking a balance between encouraging innovation via development of new drugs and reducing health care costs through production of generic drugs. The United States, in contrast, the largest producer and consumer of pharmaceutical products in the world, had long before Canada and Mexico espoused the idea of a friendly environment and policy framework for research and development (R&D) spending in pharmaceuticals.

Canada and Mexico used tariffs in the past as a policy tool to shield their home markets from imported drugs. However, at the beginning of the NAFTA negotiations, the main issue at the bargaining table was not tariffs but Canada's patent regime, specifically its system of compulsory licensing for pharmaceuticals. In 1987, Canada had increased its protection for brand-name drugs, but the compulsory licensing system was still at the centre of its policy on pharmaceuticals. Generic firms were able to apply for a licence to manufacture a pharmaceutical product provided that they paid a royalty of 4 per cent. The Canadians had been able to keep their system in the FTA because this agreement did not cover intellectual property, but the Americans were prepared not to let this happen again. They wanted Canada to abolish its system.

This chapter examines, first, the objectives of the negotiators and, second, the outcome of the negotiations. It then reviews, third, the resources of industry and of government and, fourth, the tactics of the negotiators in an attempt to explain the main outcome of the negotiations.

NEGOTIATORS' OBJECTIVES

At the outset of the negotiations, Canada still favoured the system of compulsory licensing[1] for pharmaceuticals in both NAFTA and the Uruguay Round. However, as we see below, external pressure and a government review of the industry convinced the government to change its objective during the negotiations. In January 1992, Canada endorsed full patent protection for pharmaceuticals and threw its support behind the Dunkel Text – the GATT package proposed on 20 December 1991 by Arthur Dunkel, GATT's director-general. The main Canadian objective in pharmaceuticals became having NAFTA reflect the consensus of the Dunkel Text.

As noted in chapter 3, the Americans had made elimination of Canada's compulsory licensing one of their two chief objectives with respect to NAFTA's intellectual property chapter. They aimed at prohibiting discrimination among fields of technology so as to ensure that pharmaceutical products are not under a special regime. They were also determined to narrow down the conditions for allowing compulsory licensing and to provide for 'pipeline protection' for pharmaceuticals, i.e., to provide protection for existing inventions before a patent is formally granted. Moreover, according to the U.S. General Accounting Office, the U.S. negotiators 'wanted to lock in the intellectual property protection the Mexican government had passed in 1991' with its new industrial property law.[2]

Mexican objectives were also geared towards ensuring that government procurement provisions would not apply to Mexico with respect to pharmaceutical products.

NEGOTIATION OUTCOME

Several chapters in NAFTA cover issues related to pharmaceutical goods. This section examines provisions on intellectual property, rules of origin, tariffs and safeguards, standards, and government procurement, which all directly affect the pharmaceutical industry of each NAFTA party.

Intellectual Property

National treatment (article 1703) is the cornerstone of the NAFTA provisions on intellectual property. It requires that nationals of another party will not be discriminated against with respect to protection and enforcement of all the intellectual property rights that a party accords to its own nationals. Enforcement provisions (articles 1714–18) allow a party to obtain compensation for infringement of rights protected in the chapter on intellectual property. Parties must adhere to the substantive provisions of four conventions, one of which, the Convention for the Protection of Industrial Property (Paris Convention, 1967), is directly relevant to pharmaceutical goods (article 1701).

Patent Protection, Patentability, and Basic Rights

Obligations relating to patent protection in article 1709 apply to pharmaceutical products. Paragraph 1 of that article requires each party to make patents available for any inventions, whether products or processes, in all fields of technology, provided that these inventions are new, result from an inventive step, and are capable of industrial application. Paragraph 2 allows exclusions from patentability to protect *ordre public* or morality, including protecting human, animal, or plant life or health or to avoid serious prejudice to nature or the environment, provided that the exclusion is not based solely on the ground that the party prohibits commercial exploitation in its territory of the subject matter of the patent. Paragraph 3 excludes from patentability diagnostic, therapeutic, and surgical methods for treatment of humans or animals; plants and animals other than microorganisms, although parties have to provide for protection of plant varieties; and biological processes for production of plants or animals.

Article 1709 of NAFTA provides also for protection of both product and process patents. In the case of a product (subparagraph 5[a]), the patent owner has the right to prevent other persons from making, using, or selling the subject matter of the patent without the consent of the right holder. In the case of a process patent (subparagraph 5[b]), the patent holder has the right to prevent others from using that process and from using, selling, or importing at least the product obtained directly by that process without the consent of the right holder.[3] Paragraph 6 permits exceptions to these exclusive rights as long as they do not unreasonably conflict with normal exploitation of the patent and do not unreasonably prejudice the legitimate interests of the patent owner, taking into account the legitimate interests of other persons.

Non-Discrimination among Fields of Technology: A U.S. Win

The United States succeeded in prohibiting discrimination among fields of technology (article 1709[7]) within a party's patent regime. The U.S. government and the brand-name pharmaceutical industry wanted Canadian compulsory licensing for pharmaceuticals abolished. Compulsory licensing is still allowed under strict conditions, but a party can no longer discriminate against certain products such as pharmaceuticals.[4] This clause required removal of special provisions under the Canadian Patent Act. Although Canada continues to have compulsory licensing provisions in its patent law, it cannot have a regime that applies *only* to the pharmaceutical industry.

Article 1709(7) also requires that patents be available and patent rights enjoyable without discrimination against imported products. Prior to NAFTA, failure to exploit a patent in Canada during the first three years after patent grant could have led to the government's giving licences to applicants to use that patent. The Americans and Mexicans convinced their Canadian partners to do away with this requirement.[5]

Article 1709(7) also prevents parties from discriminating with respect to the territory where an invention was made. Essentially,

Canada and Mexico won over the United States in this case. They successfully made the point that the United States needed to change its practice and ensure that inventive activity within their territories be considered.[6]

Compulsory Licensing: Stringent Conditions

Article 1709(10) strictly disciplines compulsory licensing, including government use. Applications must be considered on their individual merits (subparagraph a). There is no automatic authorization. The applicant for a licence must have been unsuccessful in his or her efforts to obtain authorization from the right holder on reasonable commercial terms and conditions within a reasonable period. However, this requirement can be waived by a party in the case of a national emergency or other circumstances of extreme urgency or in cases of public non-commercial use (subparagraph b). Therefore the United States, which has allowed for years the use of compulsory licensing for defence and national security purposes, may still do so.

Subparagraph c limits the scope and duration of the compulsory licence to the purpose for which it was authorized. Moreover, subparagraphs d–f make use of the licence non-exclusive, non-assignable, and authorized predominantly for the supply of the party's domestic market. Subparagraph h requires that its right holder be paid adequate compensation. Subparagraphs g, i, and j render any decision relating to authorization of the licence, as well as remuneration provided in respect of such use, subject to judicial or other independent review. Finally, according to subparagraph l, a compulsory licence cannot be authorized for the right to use a dependent patent – i.e., a patent that cannot be used without the use of another patent – except as a remedy for an adjudicated violation of domestic laws regarding anti-competitive practices. In fact, in some cases, according to subparagraph 10(k), the use of compulsory licensing is allowed to correct anti-competitive practices; in such instances, requirements relating to subparagraphs b–f of paragraph 10 may be waived.

Pipeline Protection: A U.S. Victory

Another key U.S. objective – pipeline protection – was reached in NAFTA with respect to pharmaceutical and agricultural chemicals. For example, article 1709(4) requires that patents for such products granted in the territory of one party must be given patent protection in the territory of another party for the unexpired term of the patent granted in the first party, provided that the product has not been marketed in the party providing protection and that the person seeking such protection makes a timely request.

Patent Duration, Assignment, and Revocation

Article 1709(12) of NAFTA provides for a term of protection for patents of either a minimum of twenty years from the date of filing or seventeen years from the date of grant. A party may also extend the term of protection to compensate for delays caused by regulatory approval processes. Article 1709(9) permits patent holders to assign, transfer, or license their patents. Article 1709(8) provides for revocation of a patent when grounds exist that would justify a refusal to grant the patent or when the grant of a compulsory licence has not remedied the lack of exploitation of the patent.

Trade Secrets and Pharmaceutical Products

Article 1711(5) of NAFTA protects data for pharmaceutical and agricultural chemicals using new chemical entities in the event that submission of the data is a condition for approving marketing of these products. Article 1711(6) also protects them against 'me-too' products by ensuring that no person other than the person who submitted them may, without the latter's permission, rely on such data in support of an application for product approval during a reasonable period of time of not less than five years after their submission.

Rules of Origin

Pharmaceutical goods are deemed to be originating if they are wholly produced in the NAFTA region. But they have to undergo processing in that same region if they are partly made of foreign inputs. A change in the Harmonized System (HS) of tariff classification at the chapter or heading level is necessary. Regional content is also often essential. Pharmaceutical producers can generally choose either the 'transaction value' method, which requires regional content of 60 per cent, or the 'net cost' method, requiring 50 per cent.

Tariffs and Safeguards

For originating goods, NAFTA phases out tariffs on pharmaceuticals within ten years of the date of its entry into force, although some duties were eliminated immediately. All remaining tariffs between the United States and Canada were abolished following the schedule set forth in the FTA. Canadian tariffs on pharmaceuticals were phased out under NAFTA and the WTO. NAFTA trade ministers agreed in April 1998 to accelerate tariff cuts for some products, including certain pharmaceuticals.

NAFTA has eliminated several non-tariff barriers. For example, it prohibits most import licences, such as those required under Mexico's Inventions and Trademarks Law of 1976. However, it allows drug-related import licences in the case of opiates needed for health and safety reasons.[7] Other non-tariff barriers are still significant between NAFTA parties. For example, pharmaceutical products cannot be traded between the United States and Canada, unless they have been approved for sale by each country's regulatory body.

The NAFTA safeguard mechanism (article 801) applies to pharmaceutical products. During the transition period, this mechanism allows Canada and Mexico, and the United States and Mexico, to suspend their tariff reductions should a surge in imports constitute a substantial cause of injury, or threat thereof, to their domestic industry. A country may increase the tariff to the MFN rate for a period of up to three years, but only once for any particular product. After the transition period, a party cannot take emergency action against another party in cases of serious injury unless it has that party's consent.

Standards

Standards and technical regulations are major issues for the pharmaceutical industry. Article 904(1) of NAFTA leaves each party free to adopt, maintain, or apply any standards-related measure. However, paragraph 3 requires each party to grant national treatment and MFN treatment to goods (or services) of another party in respect of its standards-related measures. Articles 906 and 908 encourage parties to make compatible their respective standards-related measures. Finally, article 909(1)(a) requires parties to notify the other parties in writing sixty days before adopting or modifying a technical regulation so as to enable interested persons to become acquainted with the proposed measure.[8]

Government Procurement

NAFTA opens government procurement to suppliers of other parties for contracts equal to or exceeding U.S.$50,000 for government entities and U.S.$250,000 for government enterprises, adjusted according to the U.S. inflation rate as set out in annex 1001.1c (article 1001). A lower threshold of U.S.$25,000 has been established (annex 1001.2c) for goods contracts between Canada and the United States. In Mexico, the government is a major buyer of pharmaceutical products. However, until 1 January 2002, the NAFTA provisions on government procurement do not apply to the Secretaría de Salud (Health Department), IMSS (Mexican Social Security Institute), ISSSTE (Social Security and Services Institute for Government Workers), Secretaría Defensa Nacional (National Defense Department), and the Secretaría de Marina (Navy Department) for drugs that are not patented in Mexico or whose Mexican patents have expired. In Canada, provinces are major purchasers of pharmaceuticals. Although the government procurement provisions of NAFTA do not apply to provinces or states, article 1024 requires that prior to review of these provisions the parties must attempt to consult with their state and provincial governments with a view to obtaining commitments, on a voluntary and reciprocal basis, to include within NAFTA procurement by state and provincial government entities and enterprises. The parties had to begin reviewing these provisions no later than 31 December 1998.

RESOURCES

The patent regime has been the single most important instrument used by all three countries to increase their resources in the pharmaceutical sector. It has served to promote innovation and stimulate domestic production. In the United States, patent protection has aimed at encouraging R&D activities and therefore at enhancing development of new drugs. Until the late 1980s and early 1990s, the main objective of the Canadian and Mexican patent regimes was to foster production of low-priced pharmaceutical products. Compulsory licensing was the main vehicle in Canada, whereas lack of patent protection for pharmaceutical products was the primary tool in Mexico. Trade liberalization in Mexico led to enactment of a modern industrial property law in 1991. Pressure to attract investment and research spending and the new international consensus on intellectual property developing at GATT convinced Canada to provide a more competitive environment for pharmaceutical products by amending its patent law in 1993.

Market Share and Industry Control

The Canadian Pharmaceutical Industry

The Canadian pharmaceutical industry traces its roots back to the nineteenth century, when E.B. Shuttleworth set up a pharmaceutical firm in Toronto in 1879. Foreign companies soon followed, but, as Myron Gordon and David Fowler mention, they 'engaged in secondary manufacturing and sales since there was no incentive for backward integration into the manufacture of fine chemicals, or for undertaking R&D.'[9] Notable domestic firms included Charles E. Frosst and Company, founded in Montreal in 1899, as well as Ayerst, Connaught Laboratories, McKenna and Harrison, and Mowatt and Moore, which began operations during the interwar period. All these firms eventually fell under foreign control. For example, Merck Sharp and Dohme bought Charles E. Frosst in 1965, and Connaught Laboratories, owned by the University of Toronto, was the last major Canadian pharmaceutical company sold to foreign interests – Pasteur Mérieux Sérum et Vaccins of France, in 1989.

The domestic industry comprises three sectors: the brand-name producers, which are subsidiaries of U.S.- and European-based multinational pharmaceutical corporations; the generic drug industry, mostly Canadian-owned; and the new bio-pharmaceutical sector. The brand-name and the bio-pharmaceutical firms engage in R&D, whereas most generic firms manufacture and sell drugs that are either no longer protected by the patent regime or are under compulsory licence. However, a few large generic drug firms such as Apotex and Novopharm have also invested substantially in R&D.

The industry is concentrated in Montreal and Toronto. Its share of manufacturing GDP is small, at 1 per cent of the total. By 1997, Canada had 164 pharmaceutical manufacturers. Value of shipments increased from $4.5 billion in 1994 to $5.4 billion in 1997, and employment went up from 20,000 in 1994 to more than 23,000 in 1997. The brand-name firms account for approximately 75 per cent of these employees. Sales reached $6.62 billion in 1997 and $7.46 billion in 1998. Canada is the ninth-largest pharmaceutical market in the world, according to IMS Health, representing 2 per cent of worldwide sales and 7 per cent of combined Canadian and U.S. sales. Non-patented drugs captured 40 per cent of the Canadian market in 1997, a significant drop from the early 1990s, when these drugs accounted for 50 per cent of the total. But R&D increased significantly in the 1990s. The ratio of R&D to sales rose from 6.9 per cent to 15.7 per cent between 1988 and 1997.

Canada traditionally runs a trade deficit in pharmaceutical products, in which it is essentially an importer. In 1998, exports and imports amounted to $1.5 billion and $4.15 billion, respectively. The United States is Canada's main trading partner, buying two-thirds of its exports. Imports from the United States represent close to 60 per cent of the total. Intra-firm trade between U.S. multinationals and their Canadian subsidiaries accounts for most of this trade. Mexico ranked well behind other countries as a purchaser of Canadian pharmaceutical products.

The U.S. Pharmaceutical Industry

The U.S. pharmaceutical industry started in Philadelphia between 1818 and 1822 with a few manufacturers of fine chemicals. After the War of 1812 with Britain, it was less costly to produce some drugs at home than to buy British imports and pay high tariffs. In fact, it was relatively easy for pharmacists to manufacture drugs because it involved very rudimentary processes. But imports from London did not stop altogether, and the British were still providing most drugs sold in the country. By the 1840s, Philadelphia and New York were the main U.S. centres for the sale of drugs. Some U.S. firms had become very successful. For example, Smith Kline and Company sold quinine to American troops during the Mexican–American War of 1846–8. But since price changes and prohibitive tariffs generated uncertainty in the market, the Philadelphia Drug Exchange was created in 1861, just before the start of the Civil War. It became the primary location for the sale of drugs by manufacturers, importers, and wholesalers.[10]

Until the late 1940s, the industry performed very little research. Pharmaceutical firms were basically manufacturers until the early 1940s. Most products were sold without prescription, and most drugs that 'worked' were prescribed for almost everything. Very few basic medicines (such as aspirin, codeine, insulin, morphine, and quinine) were offered. The industry relied mainly on natural or known substances, which were patentable and patented. After the Second World War, research technology brought new products to innovative firms. The industry became vertically integrated, and patent licensing to other firms made room for patent monopoly.[11]

The U.S. drugs sector encompasses four sub-sectors: pharmaceutical preparations, diagnostic substances, medicinals and botanicals, and biological products. Shipments reached U.S.$71 billion in 1993 and over U.S.$91 billion in 1997. The United States produces one-third of all drugs sold in the world. Total employment increased over the period from 200,000 in 1993 to 215,000 in 1997. Production workers account for half of those totals. The industry is primarily located on the east coast. Brand-name firms generally perform a high level of R&D, spending 20.3 per cent of their combined domestic sales and exports on such activities in 1997. As the world's leader in R&D expenditures, with 36 per cent of the total, the United States is the main discovery centre, accounting for two-thirds of all new drugs between 1940 and 1988.[12]

Sales of prescription drugs amounted to U.S.$82 billion in 1997. The share of the generic industry represented 40 per cent of the units sold but less than 10 per cent of the revenue. The United States is by far the largest market for drugs, with 40 per cent of world sales. It became a net importer of pharmaceutical products in 1997. Total imports increased from U.S.$6 billion in 1993 to U.S.$14.2 billion in 1997. The main U.S. trading partners are the United Kingdom, with 18.2 per cent of total imports; Germany, with 16.7 per cent; Ireland, with 13.3 per cent; Switzerland, with 9.1 per cent; and Japan, with 8.5 per cent. Canada and Mexico's combined share has not fluctuated much under NAFTA, standing at 5.6 per cent in 1997. Total exports also increased during that period from U.S.$7.2 billion in 1993 to U.S.$14.2 billion in 1997. Canada remains the primary export market for U.S. products, receiving 13.5 per cent of total exports in 1997. The other sizeable markets are Japan, at 11.2 per cent; Germany, at 11 per cent; the Netherlands, at 9.6 per cent; and the United Kingdom, at 8.3 per cent. Mexico took only 2.3 per cent of all U.S. pharmaceutical exports in 1997.[13]

The Mexican Pharmaceutical Industry

Two major events launched the Mexican pharmaceutical industry in the 1940s. First, the recent arrival of Spanish and Czech refugees contributed to the development of this incipient sector. Second, the American chemist Russell Marker discovered that Mexican *barbasco*, unlike other plants elsewhere, contains a high level of the substance necessary to manufacture steroid hormones. This breakthrough led to establishment of a major Mexican pharmaceutical firm, Syntex, and other smaller companies. They started synthesizing hormones. Mexico soon became the main supplier of steroids in the world, and Syntex among the first suppliers of oral contraceptives. Foreign laboratories represented by local salesmen saw these new developments as a business opportunity and set up manufacturing firms in the 1950s. In fact, multinationals put pressure on the Mexican government to eliminate the domestic monopoly on barbasco. Most of the initial local firms, including Syntex (owned by Roche of Switzerland since 1994), have either been bought by multinationals or ceased to exist.[14]

The industry has three sectors. In 1996, pharmochemicals, or primary products, accounted for 4 per cent of production. Medicines for both human and animal consumption captured 60 per cent and 16.5 per cent, respectively, of production, and auxiliary products less than 20 per cent. At the time of the NAFTA negotiations in 1992, there were approximately 350 laboratories producing pharmaceutical products in Mexico. By 1997, the number had dropped to 218, of which roughly forty were subsidiaries of multinationals. Firms with fewer than fifty employees accounted for 44 per cent of the total in 1997, and those with more than 250, 20 per cent. Total employment increased from 22,000 in 1994 to 40,000 in 1997, largely through the hiring of more managerial and sales personnel. The manufacturing segment was rather stable during that period, at 16,000 employees.

The Mexican industry is concentrated in Mexico City (Federal District), which has close to 70 per cent of the labs. Other major locations include the states of Jalisco and Mexico, each with approximately 10 per cent. The industry has a very small ratio of R&D to sales – only 1 per cent. Its share of GDP is also small, at 0.4 per cent. Production reached 44 billion pesos in 1997, and sales amounted to U.S.$3.6 billion in 1993 and U.S.$4.4 billion in 1997, according to statistics from Canifarma, the National Chamber of the Pharmaceutical Industry. Mexico is the fifteenth-largest pharmaceutical market in the world. Although sales to the public sector represented 52 per cent of all units sold in 1997, they accounted for only 18 per cent of the total market, because prices of pharmaceuticals sold to government-run enterprises under the National Health System are very low. Government procurement by IMSS, ISSSTE, the Ministry of Health, and other institutions goes back to the 1940s. It is restricted to suppliers established in Mexico. Most of the products (83 per cent) sold to the public sector are manufactured by domestic firms. These companies control 28 per cent of the total market, whereas foreign multinationals are the dominating force, at 72 per cent.

Like Canada, Mexico is an importer of pharmaceutical products, primarily of chemicals and active ingredients. Exports amounted to U.S.$1.2 billion and imports to U.S.$1.53 billion in 1997. Intra-firm trade between multinationals and their Mexican subsidiaries constitutes 80 per cent of this trade. The United States and European countries are Mexico's main trading partners. Canada's share is fairly small (0.5 per cent in 1994). Latin America and Asia purchase 30 per cent of Mexican pharmaceutical exports.

Government Intervention

Canada: Controlling Innovation and Prices

Two types of government policies have shaped the pharmaceutical industry in Canada: drug regulations and the patent regime. Provincial formularies have also played a major role, with their choice of medicines to be made available freely (or with co-payments) to senior citizens and people on welfare.

Regulating Drugs: A Historical Perspective[15]

Government intervention in the drug industry began in 1875. The Inland Revenue Act of that year, inspired by the British legislation enacted in 1860 and revised in 1872, aimed at controlling manufacture and sale of adulterated food and drugs. The Adulteration Act of 1884 improved on the Canadian law of 1875. It defined the terms 'drug' and 'adulteration' and recognized British and U.S. pharmacopeias. A few amendments followed. For example, in 1890, standards for food and drugs were established by order-in-council. In 1899, an amendment gave priority to British pharmacopeia over U.S., in cases where these two standards differed. In 1909 the Proprietary or Patent Medicine Act required registration of all secret-formula non-pharmacopoeial drugs. This law was revoked in 1977, and drugs listed under the 1909 act are now covered by the Food and Drugs Act.

The Food and Drugs Act of 1920 replaced the 1884 Adulteration law. Administration of the drug legislation had been transferred from the Department of Customs and Inland Revenue to the Department of Trade and Commerce in 1919 and to the Department of Health (now Health Canada) in 1920. Parliament amended the 1920 act several times. In 1934, it banned advertisement of certain drugs (for cancer, diabetes, and so on), and in 1941 some drugs became available by prescription only. The government adopted regulations on sale and distribution of new drugs in 1951, requiring that a new drug submission be filed before the drug was sold on the market. Once a drug was determined to be safe, a notice of compliance was issued.

In 1963, the regulations of the Food and Drugs Act of 1953 were revised, following the scandal over thalidomide – a new sleeping pill found to have caused birth defects in thousands of babies born in Europe. The regulations were influenced by amendments to the (U.S.) Food, Drug and Cosmetic Act made in 1962. New drugs must now be approved by Health Canada before clinical testing takes place. Evidence of safety and effectiveness must also be presented before drugs are marketed. Authorization is granted through a notice of compliance. Drugs are manufactured according to standards included in publications such as the *Canadian Formulary*.

Patent Regime: From Compulsory Licensing to Bill C-91

Patent protection has a long history in Canada. The first statute –

a copy of the (U.S). Patent Act of 1793 – was adopted by the legislature of Lower Canada (Quebec) in 1824. Shortly after Confederation in 1867, Canada's first Patent Act was promulgated in 1869.[16] More than fifty years later, the patent law enacted in 1923 aimed at increasing resources in the pharmaceutical industry by favouring the entry of new Canadian firms. The Patent Act allowed compulsory licensing of food and drug patents. Until 1969, compulsory licences were granted for the manufacture, use, and sale of patented processes. However, since the Patent Act allowed the licensee to use the patented process but not the active chemical ingredients, which had to be imported in most cases, very few firms applied for a licence. In fact, from 1935 to 1969, only forty-nine applications were made, and twenty-two were granted.[17]

In the late 1950s as well as in the 1960s, several government-sponsored studies concluded that drug prices were higher in Canada than in other countries. Two options were put before the Canadian government: to abolish patents altogether or to amend the Patent Act in order to introduce compulsory licensing to import. In 1960, the Royal Commission on Patents, Copyrights and Industrial Designs (Ilsley Commission), recommended compulsory licensing for product patents. In 1963, the Restrictive Trade Practices Commission called for abolition of drug patents, while the Royal Commission on Health Services in 1964 recommended compulsory licensing to import. A few years later, in 1967, the House of Commons Special Committee on Drug Costs and Prices (Harley Committee) reported that drug prices were 75 per cent higher in Canada than elsewhere because chemical ingredients had to be imported. The committee recommended compulsory licensing to import drug products.[18]

In 1969, Bill C-102 amended section 41 of the Patent Act to allow compulsory licensing to import medicines. The intention was to increase the industry's resources by creating a domestic generic industry and to lower prices by increasing competition. The royal commissioner of patents had to issue compulsory licences, when requested, unless there were significant reasons not to do so. Royalty rates were set at 4 per cent of the net selling price of a drug. The brand-name firms opposed the law and challenged it in court, questioning the quality of these new 'generic' products. They also cut prices. But as cheaper drugs became available to Canadians because of new generic products, the government grew concerned about the low level of R&D in the industry. In 1983, the Liberal minister of consumer and corporate affairs recommended variable royalty rates based on R&D activities, a period of market exclusivity, and an exemption from compulsory licences for firms willing to commit themselves to price and performance levels. A year later, the Royal Commission of Inquiry on the Pharmaceutical Industry, chaired by University of Toronto Professor Harry C. Eastman, was created to analyse issues relating to patent protection in the industry. Its report, tabled in May 1985, stated that compulsory licensing did not have 'a substantial negative effect on the profitability of Canadian innovations in pharmaceuticals because such research activities are undertaken to develop new products for sale on the world market and not simply in Canada. The Present [Patent] Act, therefore, does not present a financial barrier to research or to collaboration between small research-intensive firms and multinational pharmaceutical firms.'[19] The commission recommended a four-year period of market exclusivity for brand-name drugs and creation of a pharmaceutical royalty fund to be financed 'by payments made by firms holding compulsory licences, the payments to be determined by the value of the licensee's sales of compulsory licensed products in Canada multiplied by the pharmaceutical industry's world-wide ratio of research and development to sales ..., plus 4 per cent.'[20] The incoming Mulroney government did not implement the recommendations; the Progressive Conservative party had promised during the 1984 election campaign to review the patent law to encourage R&D activities without increasing significantly the prices of patented medicines.

Bill C-22 was enacted in 1987 after having been returned twice to the House of Commons by a Liberal-led Senate. The bill amended the Patent Act and changed the compulsory licensing regime for pharmaceuticals.[21] For drugs approved after 27 June 1986, it gave patent holders ten years of protection against compulsory licences to import and seven years of market exclusivity against compulsory licensing to manufacture. It granted a full twenty years of protection to drugs researched and produced in Canada. In exchange, the brand-name industry, represented by the Pharmaceutical Manufacturers Association of Canada (PMAC), pledged to increase its ratio of R&D to sales to 8 per cent in 1991 and 10 per cent in 1996. To monitor this promise by patentees and to ensure that prices of patented medicines were not excessive, the government set up the Patented Medicine Prices Review Board (PMPRB) under the 1987 amendments to the Patent Act. Canada is the only country that regulates drug prices through its Patent Act.[22] By 1991, the R&D-to-sales ratio for PMAC patentees had reached 9.8 per cent, and by 1996 it was 12.3 per cent. In fact, as reported by the PMPRB in its annual report for 1997, the ratio increased every year between 1988 and 1997, rising from 6.5 per cent to 12.9 per cent.[23] The PMPRB is also 'responsible for regulating the maximum prices that patentees may charge for prescription and non-prescription patented drugs sold in Canada for human and veterinary use.'[24] Failure to comply with price-reduction orders could result in fines or imprisonment.

Although Canada was offering more protection to its brand-name industry, a 1991 Pharmaceutical Review by the government found that other countries were increasing the protection given to patentees. These actions were putting Canada at a disadvantage. Moreover, the set of proposals released in December 1991 by Arthur Dunkel was a clear sign that an international consensus was emerging within the context of the Uruguay Round of multilateral trade negotiations and that Canada would have to change its Patent Act eventually. Therefore, in January 1992 the government announced that it was endorsing the Dunkel Text and full patent protection for pharmaceuticals. In June of the same year, it introduced legislation to that effect; Bill C-91 received royal assent on 4 February 1993 and was reviewed in 1997, as required by the law. It abolished the special regime for compulsory licensing for pharmaceuticals. Licences granted before 20 December 1991 continue in effect. The new law provides for full patent protection – a patent term of twenty years for applications with a Canadian filing date on or after 1 October 1989. For applications filed before then, the patent term is seventeen years from the date of grant. In May

2000, a WTO panel found Canada's term of protection for pre-October 1989 patents inconsistent with the Agreement on Trade-Related Aspects of Intellectual Property Rights (TRIPS), which requires a patent term of twenty years from the date of filing.

Two other provisions of Canada's Patent Act are contentious. The early working exception allows third parties to use a patented invention during its term of protection when such use is to obtain the regulatory approval for the marketing of an equivalent product upon expiry of the patent. The other provision permits manufacturing for stockpiling during the last six months of the patent. On 17 March 2000, a WTO panel set up at the request of the European Union ruled in favour of Canada in the case of the early working exception. The stockpiling provision was found to be inconsistent with the TRIPS agreement.

Bill C-91 also gave the PMPRB the power to order fines and to lower prices of patented medicines. As the WTO noted in its Trade Policy Review of Canada for 1998, 'the guidelines issued by the PMPRB limit prices of most new patented drugs to the range of prices for existing drugs used in the treatment of the same disease; to the median of the prices charged for the drug in other industrialized countries (currently France, Germany, Italy, Sweden, Switzerland, the United Kingdom, and the United States); and to increases in the consumer price index (for patented drugs already on the market).'[25]

Mutual Recognition Agreement with the European Union

On 14 May 1998, Canada and the European Union signed a Mutual Recognition Agreement (MRA) covering several sectors, including pharmaceuticals. The previous Good Manufacturing Practices Guidelines had required the testing in Canada of imported European drugs.

Government Intervention in the United States: Reluctance to Regulate

Adulterated Drugs

Government regulation in the pharmaceutical sector began in 1848 when Congress enacted the Drug Importation Act. Signed by President James K. Polk one week prior to the proclamation ending the Mexican–American War, the act was the direct result of numerous complaints concerning the harmful effect of adulterated drugs during that conflict. Although poor drug quality was responsible for only a few deaths in the war, this issue had been a concern of American pharmacists and physicians for a long time. It was the motivation behind publication of the first *United States Pharmacopoeia* (*USP*) in 1820 and establishment of pharmacy colleges in Philadelphia in 1820 and New York City in 1828. Secretary of the Treasury Robert J. Walker, a free-trade supporter and the real force behind the lowering of tariffs in 1846, had championed the idea of the act. The customs service, in charge of enforcing the new law, fell under his responsibility. In addition to protecting the infant pharmaceutical industry, the act was aimed at gaining support for the president in the west and south, where drug adulteration was most prevalent. The act gave powers to examiners to refuse entry to imported drugs that did not meet the standards set in the United States, Britain, France, and Germany. But a negative decision by examiners did not necessarily lead to elimination of the drug. The importer, who could appeal the decision, was allowed to try to re-export the drug within six months of the final decision. In fact, poor-quality drugs did not disappear. Lax enforcement left imported adulterated drugs still available. Moreover, the law did not address issues related to domestic drugs.[26]

Tragedies in Camden, New Jersey, and St Louis persuaded Congress to pass the Biologics Control Act of 1902. Contaminated vaccines were blamed for an outbreak of tetanus cases and the deaths of several children in 1901. The objective of the law was to regulate production and sale of biological products, vaccines, serums, and other similar products. Producers had to be licensed by the secretary of the treasury through the Hygienic Laboratory of the Public Health Service. On-site inspections and strict enforcement ensured that producers unable to meet the standards were denied a licence.

After several unsuccessful attempts to regulate the quality of domestic drugs in the 1890s, Congress adopted the Pure Food and Drugs Act in 1906. It aimed at enforcing standards of quality and purity for both processed foods and drugs. It included all drugs covered in the *USP* and the *National Formulary* (*NF*), the latter first published by pharmacists in 1888. These two publications became the official standards for pharmaceutical products. The act of 1906 defined drugs as 'any substance or mixture of substances intended to be used for the cure, mitigation, or prevention of disease of either man or animals.' Adulterated drugs deviating from the official standards without any indication as such and misbranded as drugs – i.e., drugs sold under a false name or without any mention of addicting substances – could be seized after inspections by the Department of Agriculture and its Bureau of Chemistry, which administered the new law. Adulterated and misbranded drugs were prohibited in interstate commerce. But the 1906 act did not cover false or misleading therapeutic claims.

The Sherley Amendment of 1912 prohibited 'labeling medicines with false therapeutic claims intended to defraud the purchaser.'[27] It followed a 1911 Supreme Court judgment in *U.S. v. Johnson*, which stated that the 1906 act prohibited not 'false therapeutic claims but only false and misleading statements about the ingredients or identity of a drug.'[28]

Effective drug regulation was difficult until the early 1940s. Although there were only a few drugs that 'worked,' the technology and knowledge of the time did not allow researchers to show why a drug was or was not working. Therefore it was next to impossible to win a case because of a false therapeutic claim.[29] The Bureau of Chemistry, set up when President Abraham Lincoln hired a chemist in 1862, was the main agency responsible for enforcing the 1912 amendment. The Bureau became the Food, Drug, and Insecticide Administration in 1927 and the Food and Drug Administration (FDA) in 1930.

Another tragedy led to enactment of the Food, Drug, and Cosmetic Act of 1938. The Massengill Company had introduced the Elixir Sulfanilamide on the market in September 1937. The sulfanilamide was already available in capsules and tablets, but the company wanted to sell a liquid form of it. To do so, it used a solvent, diethylene glycol, which proved very toxic. Over a hundred deaths, many of them of children, occurred, but no prosecution was possible under the 1906 act. The company ended up paying U.S.$26,100 in fines for mislabeling its product.[30]

Dividing Up the Market: Prescription-only versus Over-the-Counter Drugs

The 1938 law required that a drug application be filed with the federal secretary of agriculture (under whose jurisdiction the FDA was operating) before a new drug became available for interstate commerce. The application had to state the content and uses of the drug and show that it was safe under the recommended conditions. The application was automatically approved after sixty days unless the secretary of agriculture objected. Reasons for rejecting an application included insufficient evidence that the drug was safe. The FDA regulations that accompany the 1938 act ensured that drug packaging contained information on uses and dangers. Such a requirement was unnecessary for drugs sold by prescription, as long as they had a label indicating instructions 'not likely to be understood by the ordinary individual' and as long as their shipment was made exclusively by or on the prescription of the medical profession. This new regulation divided the pharmaceutical market into two categories: prescription drugs and over-the-counter products. But the law did not identify which drugs had to be sold by prescription. The Durham–Humphrey Amendment in 1951 clarified which drugs could not be safely used without medical supervision and limited them to prescription.[31]

Post-War Regulations: Beyond Safety to Efficacy

At the end of 1959, Democratic Senator Estes Kefauver of the Antitrust and Monopoly Subcommittee of the Judiciary Committee held hearings on the drug industry. He was very concerned about the vast profits made by pharmaceutical companies because of the high prices of patented drugs. In 1961 he introduced a bill aimed at fostering competition in the industry by banning separate brand names for prescription drugs. His legislation included a compulsory licensing provision requiring firms to license their patented drugs after three years for a maximum royalty of 8 per cent of sales. Lacking support, the second version of the bill almost died in July 1962, but the story of the drug thalidomide broke and helped garner support for drug legislation. Although the FDA had delayed thalidomide's introduction into the United States on grounds of insufficient information (the FDA returned the application to the company every sixty days), the drug had been distributed to doctors for clinical testing, and a few cases of babies with serious birth defects had emerged. The Kefauver–Harris Amendments were later drafted and passed by Congress and signed into law in October 1962. The FDA was now required to approve a drug before marketing could begin. Companies had to show not only a drug's safety but also its effectiveness. The FDA received the mandate to control clinical testing of new drugs for humans. Without its formal approval, no new drug could reach the U.S. market. The amendments also required an overall review of all the drugs under the 1938 act. The FDA removed from the market those that did not meet the efficacy requirements.[32]

Balancing Innovation and Price Competition

The stringent control of the 1962 amendments increased the cost of having a drug approved by the FDA. To counterbalance these effects, Congress enacted in 1984 the Drug Price Competition and Patent Restoration Act (Waxman–Hatch Act) to stimulate both innovation and price competition. It provided partial patent restoration to brand-name drugs to compensate for the time (frequently up to eight years) and money lost during the wait for FDA approval. The act permitted extension of the life of a patent for a maximum of five years, as long as the extension did not last for more than fourteen years after FDA approval. Only one product per patent and one patent per product are eligible for extension. In order to stimulate price competition, the act also created the Abbreviated New Drug Application (ANDA), under which a company can request FDA approval of a generic product as long as the drug is shown to be bioequivalent to the brand-name product. In such circumstances, clinical testing is not necessary. The applicant must meet one of the following requirements: the original patent has expired or will expire on a specified date, the patent is invalid, or the patent information on the drug has not been filed. On approval, the generic drug receives a 180-day exclusivity period. The law also established a provision by which generic drugs cannot file applications for brand-name products for a period of five years, creating a five-year exclusivity period for data.

The 1980s also saw adoption of the Orphan Drug Act to encourage firms to develop new drugs for rare diseases. A seven-year market exclusivity, a 50 per cent tax credit for some clinical research expenses, direct subsidies, and streamlined FDA procedures are among the incentives offered to companies for doing research on diseases affecting fewer than 200,000 persons.[33]

Speeding Approval and Encouraging Innovation

The Prescription Drug User Fee Act of 1992 required the industry to pay user fees to help the FDA hire 600 additional reviewers in order to speed up drug approval. The FDA spent more than U.S.$327 million during 1993–7 on hiring personnel and improving procedures. In 1997, the FDA Modernization Act (FDAMA) extended the 1992 law. It is estimated that U.S.$600 million will be spent in user fees (except for orphan drugs) during the five-year period of the new law. Approval times should be reduced from an average of twelve months to ten. The FDAMA also extends the patent life of a drug for an additional six months when research-based companies conduct clinical trials in children so as to determine the effects of the drug on them. Another important provision concerns fast-track approval of drugs for patients with life-threatening diseases. Other incentives to do more research include an R&D tax credit. First enacted under the Economic Recovery Act of 1981, the R&D tax credit has been renewed sporadically ever since for short periods.[34]

Government Procurement: Rebate Programs

Federal and state governments are major purchasers of pharmaceutical products. Medicaid, for instance, accounts for 15 per cent of U.S. pharmaceutical business. In 1990, as part of the federal budget, Congress passed a drug-rebate package requiring pharmaceutical companies to pay a rebate on products that they sell to Medicaid. In 1992, the Veterans Health Care Act mandated another discount program for Medicaid. The Department of Defense also has a discount program, but a voluntary one. Moreover, several states have rebate systems. Other government programs include the AIDS Drug Assistance Program, enacted in 1987 to help AIDS patients who do no have insurance or are underinsured, and the Vaccines for Children Program, established in 1994, which increased the government's involvement, dating back to 1962, in purchasing childhood vaccines.[35]

Mutual Recognition Agreement with the European Union

The United States and the European Union negotiated a pharmaceutical Mutual Recognition Agreement (MRA) in 1997. The parties have agreed to recognize each other's inspections of facilities for the manufacturing of drugs and biologics.

Patent Regime

The patent regime has encouraged R&D in the pharmaceutical industry. U.S. patent laws trace their origins back to English-inspired colonial laws of the seventeenth century.[36] The U.S. constitution gives the federal government jurisdiction to enact patent laws. Article 1, section 8, states: 'The Congress shall have the power ... to promote the progress of science and useful arts, by securing for limited time to authors and inventors the exclusive right to their respective writings and discoveries.' The first patent statute was enacted in 1790; another in 1793 provided patents for 'any useful art, machine, manufacture, or composition of matter, or any new and useful improvement ... not known or used

before the application.' This definition is still used today to identify patentable subject matter, although the term 'process' replaced
the word 'art' in 1952. In 1836, the patent law was revised. The
1836 act created the Patent Office and a system to examine applications. Another revision was passed in 1870.

The main U.S. patent law in force today was adopted in 1952.
Its provisions are accompanied by a large body of court decisions.
Patents are available for any inventions that meet the tests of nov-
elty, non-obviousness, and usefulness. Amendments were enacted
in the 1980s and 1990s, including those required under NAFTA
and the WTO Agreement on Trade-Related Aspects of Intellectual Property Rights (TRIPS).

*Government Intervention in Mexico: Promoting and
Protecting the Industry*

The Patent Regime: The Early Years

One of the first laws to affect the nascent Mexican pharmaceutical
industry was the Industrial Property Law (Ley de Propiedad Industrial) of 1942, allowing for patent protection for a period of
fifteen years. Government intervention in industrial property was
nothing new. Early attempts at protecting Mexican inventions include the decree by the Spanish courts in 1820 to guarantee, for
ten years, the right to property to inventors. A year later, in 1821,
Mexico gained its independence from Spain. Over the next 100
years, four major laws would address patent protection. The first
was enacted in 1832. The second, adopted in 1890, granted patent
protection for twenty years, renewable for five years. The Patent
Law (Ley de Patentes de Invención) of 1903 had similar provisions for patent duration, whereas that of 1929 allowed a maximum term of twenty years.[37]

Import Substitution: Mexicanizing the Industry

Starting in the 1960s, government intervention in the pharmaceutical and chemical industries sought to reduce and limit the im-

ported inputs necessary for the manufacture of pharmaceutical products. This policy stimulated development of a sizeable chemical industry and licensing of technologies to manufacture drugs. The 1970s brought more resolute favouring of the local industry, to the detriment of foreign subsidiaries. Efforts were directed at 'Mexicanizing' the industry. In 1973, the new Law to Promote Foreign Investment (Ley Para Promover la Inversión Extranjera) made it impossible for wholly foreign-owned pharmaceutical multinationals to build new factories and facilities. Existing companies were, however, 'grandfathered.' In 1976 the Inventions and Trademarks Law (Ley de Invenciones y Marcas) replaced the Industrial Property Law of 1942 and eliminated protection for pharmaceutical product and process patents, as well as for chemical compounds, agricultural chemicals, and beverages and food for human and animal consumption. The term of protection for patents was now ten years. Pharmaceutical multinationals opposed without success the new law, arguing that patent protection was necessary to allow them to recuperate their R&D investments.

The lack of patent protection led to the growth of a substantial domestic industry in pharmochemical and pharmaceutical products. In the absence of patent protection, it became much easier to copy drugs produced by multinationals. Process patents were often imported from countries that had no patent law.

The Mexican government in the 1970s and 1980s sought to regulate transfer of technologies. Laws of 1972, 1982, and 1990 addressed this issue. For example, the Law on the Transfer of Technology and the Use and Exploitation of Patents and Trademarks (Ley sobre el Control y Registro de la Transferencia de Tecnología y el Uso y Explotación de Patentes y Marcas) of 1982 legislated regulatory review of transfers of technologies, such as patent and trademark licences.

The Pharmaceutical Decree

During the debt crisis of the mid-1980s, the government decided on more government intervention in the pharmaceutical industry and in 1984 issued a decree. The Comprehensive Program for the

Development of the Pharmaceutical Industry 1984–88 fostered the development of Mexican laboratories and promoted domestic production. It also aimed at expanding exports. In its Trade Policy Review of Mexico of 1993, GATT found that 'protection of the industry was assured by prior import permits which were to be maintained for at least five years under the condition to assign investment equivalent to 4 per cent of annual sales to research and development.' Special programs encouraged production of certain products, and incentives such as five-year protection from imports were offered to domestic manufacturers. The decree also required that drug prices be set by SECOFI and that exports be increased to at least 30 per cent of total sales. Local content requirements and rigorous quality controls for imports became mandatory.[38]

Restoration of Patent Protection

Mexico amended its Inventions and Trademarks Law of 1976 in December 1986, after joining GATT. It restored process patent protection to a number of inventions, including pharmaceuticals and chemicals, for a period of fourteen years. The law also granted compulsory licences for reasons of public health and national defence or when the patent was not worked in Mexico. Patents lapsed after five years if not worked. A few years later, Mexico extended protection to product patents for pharmaceuticals. In fact, on 27 June 1991, fifteen days after the beginning of the NAFTA negotiations, Mexico adopted a comprehensive industrial property law affording protection comparable to what is offered in industrialized countries. It amended the 1991 law in 1994 to comply with NAFTA and the TRIPS agreement. The new legislation repealed the Transfer of Technology Law and added, among other things, patent protection for pharmaceutical, chemical, and biotechnological products and processes for a non-renewable period of twenty years. The industrial property law also grants pipeline protection. It is administered by the Mexican Institute of Industrial Property (IMPI), an independent organization created by

SECOFI to register patents and trademarks. IMPI also handles administrative disputes related to issues covered in the law.

Fostering a Generic Industry

On 7 May 1997, a new Health Law (Ley General de Salud) was published in Mexico's Official Gazette (Diario Oficial). Regulating health matters has a long history in Mexico. It goes back to 1527 when Protomedicato, the first health regulatory body, began operations.[39] One of the key objectives of the new law of 1997 was to open the domestic market to generic pharmaceutical drugs. But the law, which entered into force sixty days later, created a major controversy. Pharmaceutical multinationals opposed it for two reasons: it did not define the term 'generics,' yet it made generic identification mandatory for a prescription (article 225). On 4 February 1998 the government issued regulations to implement the new law; the multinationals had won their case. There was now a clear definition of generics, and brand-name drugs were not automatically excluded from prescriptions written by doctors. The regulations define an interchangeable generic medicine as a drug containing the same active ingredients, components, and dosage forms as the brand-name drug (test of bioequivalence and bioavailability). This definition is similar to the one used by the World Health Organization. A generic drug must also be included in the Ministry of Health's *Catalogue of Interchangeable Generic Medicines*. Regulatory approval of the drug is necessary, as it is for all drugs sold in Mexico. It must be obtained from the Ministry of Health (Dirección General de Control de Insumos para la Salud).

The multinationals were also successful in ensuring that physicians be allowed to prescribe brand-name drugs. In fact, the mandatory prescription of generic medicines is necessary only for medicines listed in the catalogue. A brand-name drug may also be added to the prescription in this case. Article 31 of the regulations, which entered into force in August 1999, also states that when the prescription specifically mentions the brand-name drug, substitution is allowed only when permitted by the doctor who has written the prescription. Article 231 clearly indicates that violation of this regulation entails a fine ranging from 6,000 to 10,000 days at the minimum salary.

Finally, the new regulations require that all pharmaceutical-related goods to be imported be registered and authorized by the Ministry of Health, as is the case for all drugs. An importer must have an establishment in Mexico and a 'sanitary licence' in order to be able to import such goods and guarantee quality control.

ISSUE-SPECIFIC POWER: WEAK PATENT REGIME
PUTS CANADA AT A DISADVANTAGE

Canada appeared to have issue-specific power in pharmaceuticals at the beginning of the NAFTA negotiations. The FTA had not dealt with intellectual property, although parties had agreed to 'cooperate in the Uruguay Round of multilateral trade negotiations and in other international forums to improve protection of intellectual property.'[40] Moreover, the Canadian government was convinced that the increased patent protection afforded by Bill C-22 would encourage investment and R&D in the pharmaceutical industry. The provision on compulsory licensing had been weakened but not eliminated, despite very intense U.S. pressure.

In fact, Canada did not have issue-specific power. As we saw above, it began once again to feel pressure to amend its patent law in the early 1990s. The authors of the Pharmaceutical Review of 1991 had concluded that Bill C-22 was strengthening patent protection for pharmaceuticals, but not enough to attract investment: 'Competing economies (U.S., France, Italy and Japan) have implemented or are actively considering the implementation of legislation to provide increased periods of market exclusivity for drug products in response to concerns about the erosion of effective patent protection due to lengthy R&D and regulatory approval periods.'[41] Countries were using their patent regimes to attract investment and R&D spending. The governmental review concluded that 'competitive patent protection is a necessary but not a sufficient condition for foreign direct investment in the pharmaceutical sector.'[42] Therefore there was a need to amend the Canadian patent law to offer more protection to brand-name drugs. Moreover, the Canadians were also faced with having the Mexicans at the NAFTA table. Mexico enacted a new and very modern industrial property law in June 1991 providing for full patent protection (twenty years from filing) as well as pipeline protection for pharmaceutical and chemical products. Canada could not achieve its objective of keeping its compulsory licensing system for pharmaceuticals without having to pay a price. The Pharmaceutical Manufacturers Association (PMA), now known as PhRMA, representing the research-based pharmaceutical industry in the United States, 'had even begun to insinuate that US-based pharmaceutical companies would tend to favor Mexico, which had higher levels of protection than Canada.'[43] These factors weighed in favour of the United States. Mexico had already decided to change its law in order to be able to negotiate NAFTA.

TACTICS: CANADA CHAMPIONS THE DUNKEL TEXT

U.S. Pressure

As mentioned above, prior to the beginning of the negotiations, in March 1991 the Mexican government introduced a new industrial property law, which took effect in June. Several private-sector sources in Mexico have indicated that this law was a pre-condition ('el boleto de entrada') put to the government by the United States for negotiating NAFTA. Mexican trade officials denied such a link. For them, the main reason for a new patent law was the Mexican pharmaceutical industry's lack of competitiveness vis-à-vis the rest of the world. But they acknowledged that the Americans were expecting them to change their law: 'We went far beyond the U.S. expectations,' commented one Mexican trade official.

In July 1991, PMA President Gerald J. Mossinghoff took Mexico as an example to show how weak the Canadian patent regime was. He told a U.S. House of Representatives technology subcommittee that Canada's patent law was 'the weakest by far of any major industrialized country, and weaker than laws adopted in some developing areas such as Mexico, Korea, and Eastern Europe.' U.S. Trade Representative (USTR) Carla Hills had assured the PMA that 'decent improvement' would be achieved with Canada in intellectual property protection in NAFTA.[44]

In November 1991, Robert Sherwood, a U.S. expert on intellectual property law, told a free trade conference organized by the University of Toronto's Centre for International Studies that the PMA was 'pushing the Bush Administration to achieve in the North American talks what it failed to achieve in' the FTA. Sherwood emphasized that the issue was not so much Canada but the fact that developing countries were 'using Canada as an example to justify compulsory licensing as a means to achieve lower prescription-drug prices.'[45] The Pharmaceutical Review (1991) stressed the same reasons: 'The pressure in the GATT and NAFTA negotiations to remove the compulsory licensing provisions from our Patent Act is coming from many countries. The demand is based on both economics and politics. These countries see Canada's current intellectual property regime as a threat to their economic prosperity in that many developing countries are considering Canada's system for themselves. Obviously, this would provide a lower cap on the revenues of pharmaceutical companies than would be the case if compulsory licensing were completely eliminated.'[46]

The Geneva Factor

Developments in the Uruguay Round of multilateral trade negotiations in Geneva was crucial to NAFTA. In early December 1991, the *Toronto Star* wrote that Germain Denis, Canada's senior GATT negotiator, had confirmed that 'significant progress has been made toward an agreement on intellectual property and patent protection.' But Canada was insisting 'on the right to use ... a licensing plan ... [taking into account] the trade-offs between more research and investment versus lower prices.'[47] On 20 December, there was a major breakthrough in the GATT negotiations. As we saw above in this chapter, Arthur Dunkel, GATT's director-general, made public a set of proposals. The Dunkel Text provided for full patent protection and non-discrimination among fields of technology within a country's patent regime. Canada was falling short on both issues.

Although the Dunkel Text was 'just a draft,' the Canadians were about to make an important decision, signalling a turning point in the NAFTA negotiations. The Pharmaceutical Review of 1991 had shown that competitive patent protection was a necessary condition for attracting new investment and R&D. Moreover, the emerging international consensus over pharmaceuticals in the Dunkel Text and U.S. pressure on Canada in GATT and NAFTA to abolish the Canadian system of compulsory licensing for pharmaceuticals convinced Canada that it should do so. The *New York Times* wrote in November 1992 that the Bush administration had 'made eliminating the Canadian law a condition for concluding the [NAFTA].'[48] A Canadian trade official acknowledged that Canada had to take a stand because 'the Dunkel Text was going to create a great deal of uncertainty since it had implications on Canadian law. It was neither beneficial for the innovative side nor for the generic side of the industry not to know what would the patent regime of Canada be. In addition, there was a global restructuring going on in the pharmaceutical industry with the rationalization of community production and research. If Canada wanted to attract part of those investments, there was a need to change the patent regime.'

The Canadians had basically two options: to endorse unilaterally the Dunkel Text by amending their Patent Act or to negotiate changes to the act within the NAFTA negotiations, since it was difficult at the time to forecast when the Uruguay Round would end. The first option appealed more to the Canadian government. It was politically easier – indeed, industry sources told *Inside U.S. Trade* 'that changing the system would be politically easier if it were forced by the GATT rather than appearing as a Canadian concession to the U.S., which would cause political difficulties in Canada.'[49]

Therefore, on 14 January 1992 Trade Minister Michael Wilson announced that Canada was endorsing the Dunkel Text. The government introduced legislation on 23 June giving full-term patent protection to pharmaceuticals and eliminating the special compulsory licensing system. The law was retroactive to 20 December 1991. But a Canadian trade official explained that the decision on compulsory licensing had to be balanced with increased health care costs: 'How do you ensure that the gains made on the intellectual property side are not wiped out by losses on health care?' It was in that dynamic that Canada made up its mind – to counterbalance the rise in health care costs, the government enhanced the powers of the Patented Medicine Prices Review Board.

Although Canada had agreed to eliminate its special regime, the U.S. industry kept increasing the leverage of the Bush administration vis-à-vis the Canadian government. In a letter to Hills on 26 February 1992, the Intellectual Property Committee, a coalition of thirteen U.S. companies, wrote: 'In clear straightforward language, the NAFTA must require Canada to dismantle its discriminatory compulsory licensing regime for pharmaceutical products and to suspend the granting of any compulsory licenses from 20 December 1991 and onward.'[50]

Searching for a Formula: The Dunkel Text

The NAFTA working group on intellectual property had met regularly – once a month, since the first meeting held in Washington, DC, on 19 July 1991 – when the substantive discussions began in January 1992. The Canadians had found their formula, the Dunkel Text. They told their counterparts that the three countries had just spent five years negotiating the same issues in GATT and thus that NAFTA should reflect the consensus reached in the Dunkel Text. It took Canada a few months to convince its colleagues to use that formula. A trade official close to the talks observed that 'relatively quickly, we had a lot easier time in intellectual property than the other groups because we had in front of us a compromise text that everybody, at least 95 per cent, could agree to.' The official added: 'By March/April 1992, we had a pretty good idea that we were going to end up with the Dunkel Text. This does not mean that people could not play games. But with respect to the form of the text, its structure and content which a lot of the other groups struggled with, we reached a consensus very quickly. If you look at NAFTA and the Dunkel Text, you will see that not only the language is pretty much the same but the structure is also the same.'

Compulsory Licensing

With regard to patent, the main contentious issue in the NAFTA negotiations had to do with the U.S. proposal in the Dallas Composite Text to restrict use of compulsory licences '(a) to remedy an adjudicated violation of competitive level; and (b) to address, only during its existence, a declared national emergency.'[51] The Americans were pushing for more stringent language than that of the Dunkel Text. As reported by *Inside U.S. Trade*, Canada and Mexico disagreed and were proposing to use 'the TRIPS language on compulsory licensing as the standard for the NAFTA, which allows for compulsory licensing in a wider range of circumstances, and calls only for "adequate" compensation to the patent holder.'[52]

According to Canadian sources, the U.S. starting position in the GATT TRIPS negotiations, more than in NAFTA, was to call for total elimination of compulsory licensing. But the Americans could not live with that, because they have compulsory licensing in their own laws for anti-trust purposes. Nevertheless, the Canadians were concerned. The Americans wanted to make a distinction between compulsory licensing and government use. A Canadian trade official remarked: 'The United States has government use provisions which state that the government can absolve anyone from infringing a patent as long as that individual or company sells the product to the government or lets the government use the patent. For Canada, there is no difference between government use and compulsory licensing. A rose by another name is still a rose.'

All three parties finally agreed to import most of the TRIPS language on compulsory licensing into NAFTA. However, NAFTA goes further, because it prohibits compulsory licensing of a patent to allow use of another patent. But this use is permitted to remedy a practice determined after judicial or administrative process to be anti-competitive. TRIPS does not require such a condition. It allows compulsory licensing when the second patent involves an important technical advance of considerable economic significance. The owner of the first patent is entitled in this case to get a cross-licence on reasonable terms to use the second patent.[53]

Pipeline Protection and Parallel Importation

The United States was also eager to include a provision that would allow for pipeline patent protection. Parallel imports constituted another outstanding issue. In the Dallas Composite Text, Mexico had proposed that 'once goods have been placed on the market of a Party by or with the consent of the holder of the intellectual property rights associated therewith, such goods may be legitimately imported from, or exported to, the territory of any Party. Moreover, any person may legitimately use, sell or distribute such goods within the territory of any Party.' *Inside U.S. Trade* wrote in May 1992 that the U.S. pharmaceutical industry feared 'that such a provision could lead to a flood of low-cost imports from Mexico.'[54] NAFTA ignores the issue and leaves it to the parties to ban parallel imports.

Detail Phase

As most issues got resolved 'pretty quickly,' the working group became anxious not to get too far ahead of the pace of the negotiations, the chief negotiators, and the other groups. The negotiators met less frequently. The detail phase, which began in the spring of 1992, and 'legal scrubbing' benefited from the fact that the negotiators were using the Dunkel Text. A negotiators acknowledged that 'it was much easier for us than for a number of other groups.'

CONCLUSION

Once it became clear, because of the Dunkel Text and the Pharmaceutical Review, that Canada's issue-specific power was low, the government chose to make a concession and eliminate its compulsory licensing system for pharmaceuticals. Canada decided to make the concession at the multilateral level because its tactic was to hold on to the GATT package in NAFTA and make sure that the Americans would not ask for more. The Canadians had few options. The status quo could have jeopardized their presence in NAFTA or could have obliged them to make concessions in other, more sensitive sectors where the Americans were also pushing hard. The Americans, in contrast, had strong tactics. The administration relied heavily on the consensus among brand-name firms in both the United States and Canada.

The United States clearly met its objective in pharmaceuticals. Canada abolished its system of compulsory licensing. The arguments in favour of doing so were so compelling that Canada decided to change its objective during the negotiations. For the Mulroney government, the results of the GATT and NAFTA negotiations with respect to pharmaceuticals were not a loss, when compared to its initial goal, because the change in the Canadian patent regime was going to lead to an improved investment climate and more R&D. In fact, Canada met its *new* objective on pharmaceuticals in NAFTA. Chapter 17, on intellectual property, is almost identical to the TRIPS agreement, although NAFTA goes beyond TRIPS on a few issues, as we saw above.

Conclusion

This book has attempted to provide a theoretical framework to explain the outcome of a negotiation in the field of international trade, using as case studies four issues negotiated in NAFTA. The main argument put forward here is that negotiation outcome has two characteristics: structure and process. Structure is made up of the resources that a state brings to the table in a given issue area. Process, in contrast, refers to the state's behaviour as expressed by its tactics during negotiation. But neither resources nor tactics alone can predict the outcome of a negotiation. The key message conveyed in this book is that it is the right mix of resources and tactics that explains negotiation outcome.

A number of questions raised in chapter 1 have guided the analysis throughout the case studies. How does one define 'winning' and 'losing' in a given issue area? What are the resources of a state as it enters a trade negotiation? Are all resources equally important? Which tactics should a negotiator choose in order to achieve his of her objectives? Is the utility of some tactics linked to certain resources? How does one take advantage of contextual factors? In addition to reflecting on the importance of the negotiating team, this chapter addresses other issues that influence negotiation theory and the framework used in this book.

WINNING AND LOSING

A country engages in a trade negotiation because it assumes that its citizens will be better off with a signed agreement than with no agreement. This book has determined winning and losing by measuring the outcome of the agreement against the goals of the parties. It has determined victory by comparing the outcome with the objectives of a state actor, not by ranking negotiators among themselves.

The use of a framework based on both structure and process implies that objectives may change throughout a process. Therefore comparing the outcome of an agreement with a state's initial objectives may at times be misleading. The pharmaceutical case shows that contextual events may force a party to modify its objectives during a negotiation. The Dunkel Text of December 1991 clearly summarizes the new consensus that was emerging on the international front at GATT. It convinced the Canadian negotiators that their original NAFTA goal had become unsustainable. An internal study prepared by the government had reached the same conclusion. The new objective became endorsing the GATT package. But when measured against Canada's initial objective, the NAFTA agreement is a loss, since it requires non-discrimination among fields of technology within a country's patent regime and imposes stringent conditions for use of compulsory licensing. However, a correct assessment of the case commands that the new objective be the one against which the evaluation is made. What the framework may lose in analytical refinement it gains in empirical usefulness. In this instance, the outcome is a win for Canada.

RESOURCES

Assessing the Parties' Resources

As we saw in this book, issue-specific power is based on the relationship between the parties to a negotiation. Resources that lessen the dependence of a state vis-à-vis its negotiating partners increase its issue-specific power. The FTA played such a role for Canada in culture. Conversely, resources that augment the dependence of a state actor lower its issue-specific power. For example, the large share of Canada's exports and imports in textiles and autos and of the Canadian cultural market captured by the United States raised Canada's dependence vis-à-vis that country and lowered its issue-specific power. So did the expiration of Canada's TRQ for non-wool fabrics and made-up articles negotiated in the FTA.

Each party must be aware of its issue-specific power when entering a negotiation. Although resources are usually static in the short run, they may vary during the negotiation process. A negotiator must be able to assess his or her own resources and those of his or her counterparts at any given time. This is an essential condition to be met before negotiators identify the tactics to achieve their state's preferred outcome. Again, the pharmaceutical case illustrates this point quite well. A re-evaluation of Canada's resources in the fall of 1991 indicated that its patent regime was weak and needed to be modernized in order to attract foreign investment and R&D. Competing economies, including Mexico's, had already or were in the process of increasing the market exclusivity afforded to brand-name drugs. Canada had to take a stand. It did not have issue-specific power. After deciding unilaterally to endorse the Dunkel Text by amending its Patent Act, Canada selected a new tactic for the NAFTA negotiations, championing the GATT package.

All Resources Are Not Created Equal

It is worth repeating that resources can compensate for one another, but not all resources have the same weight. Canada's cultural exemption is a prime example of how one resource can significantly reduce a country's high level of dependence. The exemption strengthened government intervention in this sector and more than offset Canada's small share of its own cultural market.

It is difficult to determine a priori which resource will be key in any negotiation. But it is evident from the cases examined above that a trade agreement binding some of the parties involved in a given negotiation constitutes the most important component of issue-specific power when it allows a party to opt out of the negotiation and use the previous agreement as a fall-back position. It serves as an alternative to the negotiation. The more alternatives a resource provides to a country in reaching its objectives and reducing its dependence vis-à-vis other negotiating partners, the more issue-specific power this country has.

In culture, the FTA provided Canada with the option of walking away from a NAFTA deal without compromising its main objective, whereas in textiles it gave leverage to the United States, because Canada's TRQ for non-wool fabrics and made-up articles was expiring. Canada did not have a fall-back position in textiles. Walking away from NAFTA would have hurt its industry. In autos, the FTA was also a valuable asset to Canada. It had preserved the Auto Pact and protected the country in the CAMI case. However, it was clear that the negotiation was presenting an opportunity to clarify the FTA rules of origin, which were at the heart of the Honda and CAMI disputes. In pharmaceuticals, the FTA did not address issues of intellectual property. Although Canada could have used that agreement as an alternative to NAFTA and withdrawn from the negotiations, in fact, as we saw, a contextual factor – the GATT package – had changed the issue power for Canada. The FTA was no longer an option.

Other international agreements covering issues on the negotiating table can also prove to be critical resources. The same applies to domestics laws and government intervention. For example, Mexico's adherence to the Rome Convention increased its leverage when it was demanding an exception to national treatment for secondary uses of sound recordings. The carve-out provision for moral rights in the Berne Convention Implementation Act of the United States became a major asset for the Americans. It helped them achieve their objective of ensuring that NAFTA does not impose any obligations on the United States as to implementation of Berne article 6*bis* on moral rights.

TACTICS

Selecting Tactics

Tactics are used to reveal the state's preferences and persuade other parties. The choice of tactics must take into account both the objectives and the resources of a state. Once the objectives have been identified and the resources measured, tactics are selected to achieve the state's desired outcome. As suggested in this book, these tactics have to be credible, to increase the leverage of the negotiator, and to lead the country closer to its objectives. Each state must be able to identify the domain of tactics that it may need to attain its objectives. Contextual factors may increase or reduce such a domain.

When a country has issue-specific power, it uses tactics to produce a 'win.' For example, although Canada could have walked away from NAFTA in culture because of the cultural exemption negotiated in the FTA, its overall NAFTA objective, which was to protect its access to the U.S. market, would not have been secured by such a decision. Therefore Canada needed strong tactics to be successful in culture. It chose to refuse to negotiate issues relating to culture, relying on the solid backing of the Canadian population, the firm industry consensus in Canada, and a contextual factor – a constitutional debate – to increase its leverage and meet its objectives. As we saw in chapter 3, Canada also withheld its signature at the end of the negotiations, knowing full well that the United States had decided that it wanted a deal before the beginning of the Republican convention, whereas the Mexicans had been in a hurry all along to get an agreement. Once again, this tactic gave Canada more leverage in achieving its objectives. In textiles and apparel, the alliance between the private sector in both the United States and Mexico, which later translated into a common U.S.–Mexican approach on rules of origin, increased their countries' leverage in negotiating with Canada.

In cases where a country does not have issue-specific power, it uses both tactics and resources to produce the best result possible. In textiles and apparel, for example, Canada did not have much issue-specific power but did not lack resources. The Americans had negotiated tariff-rate quotas (TRQs) to compensate the Canadians for textile and apparel goods that did not conform to the FTA rules of origin. Canada wanted a similar deal in NAFTA. As in culture, tactics used by the Canadians included withholding their signature during the end game in order to increase their leverage and secure their preferred outcome. Canada sought compensation from the Americans issue by issue. Although it was not successful on all fronts, it managed to ensure that the access to the U.S. market that it had negotiated under the FTA would not be too much eroded by NAFTA. Tariff preference levels (TPLs) were negotiated to offset the stricter rules of origin, although in wool apparel the quota is barely higher.

Is the Usefulness of Some Tactics Linked to Some Resources?

The cases analysed in this book have also demonstrated that the utility of some tactics can be linked to some resources. A resource that increases a state's dependence may in turn become a strong tactic. For example, both the Canadian and Mexican auto industries are foreign-owned, which increased their dependence vis-à-vis the United States in NAFTA, since General Motors, Ford, and Chrysler all had U.S. headquarters at the time of the negotiations. Canada built an alliance with the Big Three to boost its leverage to keep the Auto Pact intact, whereas Mexico was successful, in part because of the Big Three, in convincing its negotiating partners not to allow new foreign carmakers to enter its market during the phasing out of the auto decree. In textiles and apparel, the concentration of these industries in Quebec increased Canada's dependence. However, this 'weak resource' played in favour of the Canadians when Quebec's minister of international affairs pressed the Canadian government and asked it to pull out of the negotiations in apparel. Although this was not a viable option, since the textile industry would have had to be exempted too, this tactic somewhat increased Canada's leverage. In fact, any domestic constraint – be it a federal system, a constitution, the influence of the private sector, or other factors – can help the state achieve its preferred outcome when that constraint increases its leverage.

The Role of Contextual Factors

A negotiator must be able to use contextual factors to his or her advantage. Such factors or events may alter issue-specific power or may lead to a new set of tactics that will help the state achieve its desired outcome. The Canadian constitutional debate of the summer of 1992 represented such an opportunity in NAFTA. Canada played the unity card in culture and in textiles and apparel. In pharmaceuticals, the GATT package reduced Canada's issue-specific power but then became the formula espoused by the Canadian negotiators in NAFTA.

The Negotiating Team

The negotiating team is one of the key elements in a successful negotiation. A state has to count on highly qualified civil servants, who are able to identify the main objectives of the state, assess its resources, select negotiating tactics, and take advantage of contextual factors. The team's professional expertise and its ability to manage information, to move the negotiation forward, and to anticipate and react quickly to other countries' tactics are crucial to its achieving the state's goals. In the pre-negotiation phase, negotiators must be able to set the agenda and define the issues that will be kept on and off the table. They have to show creative thinking in the formula phase in order to convince the other parties to adopt a common perception of the issues on the table. Finally, in the detail phase, negotiators must demonstrate flexibility and problem-solving skills.

THE FRAMEWORK REVISITED

The application of the framework proposed in chapter 1 to the four NAFTA cases examined in this book suggests that indeed both resources and tactics are the key variables explaining negotiation outcome. Other variables may indirectly influence either issue-specific power or tactics. As we saw above, contextual factors may affect tactics, and so can factors not analysed specifically in this book, such as the ideology of the state and the personality of the negotiators. Contextual factors may also alter issue-specific power during the negotiation process. In fact, the pharmaceutical case has shown that the state's objectives may change, should issue-specific power shift during the negotiations. Although resources are more static in the short run than tactics, they may vary during the negotiations.

The issue of linkages among the different working groups was raised in interviews with the negotiators. As we saw in chapter 2 and also in chapter 4, negotiators denied that there were explicit linkages in NAFTA. But they did acknowledge that there were packages. At the end of the negotiations, as explained in chapter 2, the chief negotiators and the ministers made the final decisions on the issues that were still outstanding. Their goal was to obtain a balanced agreement. The ministers and their chief negotiators relied on issue-specific power and tactics but had to 'prioritize' their objectives. As was clear in chapter 2, commitment to a particular issue played a significant role in explaining outcome at that stage.

This book has attempted to show that frameworks are helpful in analysing trade negotiations. They organize our understanding of these complex processes, by which countries aim to reach a balanced and 'positive-sum' agreement. But the case-study method has its limitations. It does not lend itself to broad generalizations on how a particular framework captures reality in all circumstances. It only suggests that the evidence found in the different cases analysed here supports the usefulness of the framework.

Notes

1. Explaining Negotiation Outcomes

1 Gilbert Winham, 'Multilateral Economic Negotiations,' *Negotiation Journal* 3 (April 1987): 176.
2 Frederick W. Frey, 'Comment: On Issues and Nonissues in the Study of Power,' *American Political Science Review* 65 (Dec. 1971): 1086.
3 See Klaus Knorr, *The Power of Nations: The Political Economy of International Relations* (New York: Basic Books, 1975); Robert O. Keohane and Joseph S. Nye, Jr, *Power and Interdependence* (Boston: Little, Brown, 1977); and William Mark Habeeb, *Power and Tactics in International Negotiations: How Weak Nations Bargain with Strong Nations* (Baltimore, MD: Johns Hopkins University Press, 1988).
4 David A. Baldwin, 'Power Analysis and World Politics: New Trends versus Old Tendencies,' *World Politics* 31 (Jan. 1979): 163.
5 Habeeb, *Power and Tactics in International Negotiation*, 23.
6 The quotation is from Robert Bierstedt, 'An Analysis of Social Power,' *American Sociological Review* 15 (Dec. 1950): 730; quoted in Jack H. Nagel, *The Descriptive Analysis of Power* (New Haven, CT: Yale University Press, 1975), 3.
7 Baldwin, 'Power Analysis and World Politics,' 161. Nagel mentions that Thomas Hobbes may have originated the idea that power is a type of causal relation. See Nagel, *The Descriptive Analysis of Power*, 9; Herbert A. Simon, 'Notes on the Observation and Measurement of Political Power,' *Journal of Politics* 15 (Nov. 1953): 500–16, and see also his *Models of Man* (New York: John Wiley, 1957); James G. March, 'An Introduction to the Theory and Measurement of Influence,' *American Political Science Review* 49 (June 1955): 431–51; Robert A. Dahl, 'The Concept of Power,' *Behavioral*

Science 2 (July 1957): 201–15, and see also his 'Power,' in *International Encyclopedia of the Social Sciences* 12 (New York: Free Press, 1968), 405–15. Other writers have focused on the causal nature of power. See, for example, David Easton, *The Political System* (New York: Knopf, 1953); and William Riker, 'Some Ambiguities in the Notion of Power,' *American Political Science Review* 58 (June 1964): 341–9.

8 Nagel, *The Descriptive Analysis of Power*, 29. Habeeb, *Power and Tactics in International Negotiation*, 15.

9 I. William Zartman, 'The Analysis of Negotiation,' in *The 50% Solution* (Garden City, NY: Anchor Press/Doubleday, 1976), 17.

10 Nagel, *The Descriptive Analysis of Power*, 9–10.

11 The quote is from Baldwin, 'Power Analysis and World Politics,' 163. See Harold D. Lasswell and Abraham Kaplan, *Power and Society* (New Haven, Conn.: Yale University Press, 1950); Harold and Margaret Sprout, *Man–Milieu Relationship Hypotheses in the Context of International Politics*, Center of International Studies, Research Monograph (Princeton, NJ: Princeton University, 1956); Robert A. Dahl, *Modern Political Analysis*, 3rd ed. (Englewood Cliffs, NJ: Prentice-Hall, 1976), and see also his 'Power,' 408; and Nagel, *The Descriptive Analysis of Power*, 14.

12 Dahl, 'Power,' 409.

13 Hans J. Morgenthau, *Politics among Nations* (New York: Knopf, 1960).

14 James E. Dougherty and Robert L. Pfaltzgraff, Jr, *Contending Theories of International Relations: A Comprehensive Survey*, 3rd ed. (New York: Harper & Row, 1990), 82.

15 Habeeb, *Power and Tactics in International Negotiation*, 1.

16 Fred Charles Iklé, *How Nations Negotiate* (New York: Harper & Row, 1964).

17 Arthur Lall, *Modern International Negotiations* (New York: Columbia University Press, 1966).

18 Quoted in Keohane and Nye, *Power and Interdependence*, 42. See also Thucydides, *The Peloponnesian War*, Book V (New York: Modern Library, 1951), 331.

19 Keohane and Nye, *Power and Interdependence*, 49–50, 43.

20 P. Dale Dean, Jr, and John A. Vasquez, 'From Power Politics to Issue Politics: Bipolarity and Multipolarity in Light of a New Paradigm,' *Western Political Quarterly* 29 (March 1976): 17.

21 Ray S. Cline, *World Power Trends and U.S. Foreign Policy for the 1980s* (Boulder, CO: Westview Press, 1980).

22 Baldwin, 'Power Analysis and World Politics,' 163.

23 Habeeb, *Power and Tactics in International Negotiation*, 3.

24 Raymond Aron, *Peace and War: A Theory of International Relations*, Abridged

version (Garden City, NY: Anchor Press/Doubleday, 1973), 62; Annette Baker Fox, *The Power of Small States* (Chicago: University of Chicago Press, 1959), 181, and see also her *The Politics of Attraction* (New York: Columbia University Press, 1977); Erling Bjøl, 'The Small State in International Politics,' in August Schou and Arne Olav Brundtland, ed., *Small States in International Relations* (Stockholm: Almqvist & Wiskell, 1971), 36.

25 I. William Zartman, *The Politics of Trade Negotiations between Africa and the European Economic Community* (Princeton, NJ: Princeton University Press, 1971), 5.

26 Baldwin, 'Power Analysis and World Politics,' 193.

27 Ibid., 192.

28 Charles Lockhart, *Bargaining in International Conflicts* (New York: Columbia University Press, 1979), 93.

29 Lasswell and Kaplan, *Power and Society*; Harold Sprout and Margaret Sprout, *Man-Milieu Relationship Hypotheses,* see also *Toward a Politics of the Planet Earth* (New York: Van Nostrand, 1971).

30 Dahl, 'Power,' 408.

31 Keohane and Nye, *Power and Interdependence*, 50–1.

32 Ibid.

33 Kal J. Holsti and Thomas Allen Levy, 'Bilateral Institutions and Transgovernmental Relations between Canada and the United States,' in Annette Baker Fox, Alfred O. Hero, Jr, and Joseph S. Nye, Jr, eds., *Canada and the United States: Transnational and Transgovernmental Relations* (New York: Columbia University Press, 1976), 283–309; and Allan E. Gotlieb, 'Canada–U.S. Relations: The Rules of the Game,' *SAIS Review* (summer 1982): 177–87.

34 Annette Baker Fox, Alfred O. Hero, Jr, and Joseph S. Nye, Jr, eds., *Canada and the United States: Transnational and Transgovernmental Relations* (New York: Columbia University Press, 1976). This volume first appeared as a special issue of *International Organization* (autumn 1974).

35 Keohane and Nye, *Power and Interdependence*, chap. 7. See also another study, Peter C. Dobell, 'Negotiating with the United States,' *International Journal* 36 (winter 1980–1): 17–69.

36 Keohane and Nye, *Power and Interdependence*, 183.

37 Ibid., 52.

38 Baldwin, 'Power Analysis and World Politics,' 165.

39 Richard Emerson, 'Power-Dependence Relations,' *American Sociological Review* 27 (Feb. 1962): 31–41; John W. Thibault and Harold H. Kelley, *The Social Psychology of Groups* (New York: John Wiley & Sons, 1959); and see also Peter M. Blau, *Exchange and Power in Social Life* (New York: John Wiley

& Sons, 1964), and George Homans, *Social Behavior* (New York: Harcourt, Brace, Jovanovitch, 1961).

40 Habeeb, *Power and Tactics in International Negotiation*, 19.

41 Kenneth Waltz, *Theory of International Politics* (Menlo Park, NJ: Addison Wesley, 1979), 149.

42 Keohane and Nye, *Power and Interdependence*, 11.

43 Habeeb, *Power and Tactics in International Negotiation*, 22.

44 Ibid., 130.

45 Dahl, 'Power,' 409.

46 Glen H. Snyder and Paul Diesing, *Conflict among Nations* (Princeton, NJ: Princeton University Press, 1977), 498.

47 Baldwin, 'Power Analysis and World Politics,' 169.

48 Ibid., 164–6 and 169.

49 Keohane and Nye, *Power and Interdependence*, 19.

50 Bierstedt, 'An Analysis of Social Power'; and Dennis H. Wrong, 'Some Problems in Defining Social Power,' *American Sociological Review* 73 (March 1968): 673–81.

51 For instance, Thomas C. Schelling has emphasized this point in *The Strategy of Conflict* (New York: Oxford University Press, 1960).

52 Samuel B. Bacharach and Edward J. Lawler, *Power and Politics in Organizations*, The Jossey-Bass Social and Behavioral Science Series (San Francisco: Jossey-Bass, 1980), 25. In *Power and Society*, Lasswell and Kaplan also make the distinction between *having* and *exercising* power (see page 71). The rule of anticipated reaction was first described by C.J. Friedrich in *Constitutional Government and Politics* (New York: Harper, 1937). Also, see Nagel, *The Descriptive Analysis of Power*, on anticipated reactions.

53 Dahl, 'The Concept of Power,' 202–3.

54 Ibid., 202; R. Harrison Wagner, 'The Concept of Power and the Study of Politics,' in Roderick Bell, David V. Edwards, and R. Harrison Wagner, eds., *Political Power: A Reader in Theory and Research* (New York: Free Press, 1969), 4; and Henry Mintzberg, *Power in and around Organizations* (Englewood Cliffs, NJ: Prentice-Hall, 1983), 4.

55 Bertand Russell, *Power* (New York: W.W. Norton, 1938), 35.

56 Christer Jönsson, 'Bargaining Power: Notes on an Elusive Concept,' *Cooperation and Conflict* 16 (Dec. 1981), 252, quoted in Habeeb, *Power and Tactics in International Negotiation*, 23. On this point, see also Schelling, *The Strategy of Conflict*.

57 For instance, see R.E. Walton and R.B. McKersie, *A Behavioral Theory of Labor Negotiations* (New York: McGraw-Hill, 1965); and Jeffrey Z. Rubin and Bert R. Brown, *The Social Psychology of Bargaining and Negotiation* (New York: Academic Press, 1975).

58 John S. Odell, 'Latin American Trade Negotiations with the United States,' *International Organization* 34 (Spring 1980): 207–28.

59 François de Callières, *On the Manner of Negotiating with Princes*, trans. A.F. White (Notre Dame, Ind.: University of Notre Dame Press, 1963), originally published in 1716; and Harold Nicolson, *Diplomacy* (New York: Oxford University Press, 1964).

60 Habeeb, *Power and Tactics in International Negotiation*, 13.

61 Jönsson, 'Bargaining Power: Notes on an Elusive Concept,' 250.

62 Dahl, 'Power,' 409.

63 Habeeb, *Power and Tactics in International Negotiation*, 27.

64 Otomar J. Bartos, 'Simple Model of Negotiation: A Sociological Point of View,' *Journal of Conflict Resolution* 21 (Dec. 1977): 565–79.

65 John G. Cross, 'Negotiations as a Learning Process,' in I. William Zartman, ed., *The Negotiation Process* (Beverly Hills, CA: Sage, 1978), 29.

66 I. William Zartman, 'Common Elements in the Analysis of the Negotiation Process,' *Negotiation Journal* 4 (Jan. 1988): 36.

67 Habeeb, *Power and Tactics in International Negotiation*, 12. See also John G. Cross, *The Economics of Bargaining* (New York: Basic Books, 1969); and Bruno Contini, 'The Value of Time in Bargaining Negotiations: Some Experimental Evidence,' *American Economic Review* 48 (June 1958): 374–93.

68 Zartman, 'Common Elements,' 35. Zartman offers a much broader explanation of the negotiation process. See also I. William Zartman, 'Negotiations as a Joint Decision-Making Process,' in Zartman, ed., *The Negotiation Process: Theories and Applications* (Beverly Hills, CA: Sage, 1978), 67–86.

69 I. William Zartman and Maureen R. Berman, *The Practical Negotiator* (New Haven, CT: Yale University Press, 1982).

70 Daniel Druckman, 'Stages, Turning Points, and Crises: Negotiating Military Base Rights, Spain and the United States,' *Journal of Conflict Resolution* 30 (June 1986): 327–60.

71 Brian W. Tomlin, 'The Stages of Prenegotiation: The Decision to Negotiate North American Free Trade,' *International Journal* 44 (spring 1989): 257.

72 Zartman and Berman, *The Practical Negotiator*, 95, 199.

73 Habeeb, *Power and Tactics in International Negotiation*, 136.

74 Zartman, 'Common Elements,' 38–9.

75 Habeeb, *Power and Tactics in International Negotiation*, 24.

76 See the *Concise Oxford Dictionary, Ninth Edition* (Oxford: Oxford University Press, 1995), 1418.

77 Robert D. Putnam, 'Diplomacy and Domestics Politics: The Logic of Two-Level Games,' *International Organization* 42 (summer 1988): 427–60.

78 Winham, 'Multilateral Economic Negotiation,' 177, 179.

79 Roger Fisher, William Ury, and Bruce Patton, *Getting to Yes: Negotiating Agreement without Giving In* (New York: Penguin Books, 1981), 23.
80 David Palmeter lists the series of rulings: U.S. Customs Internal Advice Rulings HQ 000112, 14 Nov. 1991; HQ 000116, 14 Nov. 1991; HQ 544833, 3 Dec. 1991; HQ 000131, 12 Dec. 1991; HQ 000155, 10 Feb. 1992; HQ 000160, 27 Feb. 1992; HQ 000161, 27 Feb. 1992. See David Palmeter, 'The Honda Decision: Rules of Origin Turned Upside Down,' *Free Trade Observer* 32A (June 1992): 514.
81 Keith Bradsher, 'Honda's Nationality Proves Troublesome for Free-Trade Pact,' *New York Times*, 9 Oct. 1992, A1.
82 G. Bruce Doern and Brian W. Tomlin, *The Free Trade Story: Faith and Fear* (Toronto: Stoddart, 1991), 97.
83 Milt Freudenheim, 'Canadians See Rise in Drug Costs,' *New York Times*, 16 Nov. 1992, D1.
84 Fen Osler Hampson with Michael Hart, *Multilateral Negotiations: Lessons from Arms Control, Trade, and the Environment* (Baltimore: MD: Johns Hopkins University Press, 1995), 21.

2. Towards a North American Free Trade Agreement

1 Peter Truell, 'U.S. and Mexico Agree to Seek Free-Trade Pact,' *Wall Street Journal*, 27 March 1990, A3, A22.
2 For more on early Mexican–American relations, see Laurence Whitehead, 'Mexico and the Hegemony of the United States: Past, Present, and Future,' in Riordan Roett, ed., *Mexico's External Relations in the 1990s* (Boulder, CO: Lynne Rienner, 1991), 243–62; Alan Riding, *Distant Neighbors: A Portrait of the Mexicans* (New York: Alfred A. Knopf, 1985); Sidney Weintraub, *Free Trade between Mexico and the United States?* (Washington, DC: Brookings Institution, 1984).
3 Weintraub, *Free Trade between Mexico and the United States?*, 16.
4 Nora Lustig, 'Mexico's Integration Strategy with North America,' in Colin I. Bradford, Jr, ed., *Strategic Options for Latin America in the 1990s* (Paris: Organization for Economic and Co-operation and Development, 1992), 155.
5 Weintraub, *Free Trade between Mexico and the United States?*, 16.
6 See Ronald Reagan, 'Official Announcement,' New York Hilton, New York, 13 Nov. 1979, 11–13.
7 Spencer Rich, 'Governors Flay Changes in Revenue-Sharing Plan,' *Washington Post*, 27 Feb. 1980, A3.
8 Alan Riding, 'Good Neighbor Policy Isn't Good Enough.' *New York Times*, 6 July 1980, sec. 4, p. 3.

9 Anthony Westell, 'Après Quebec, Canada Looks South,' *Christian Science Monitor*, 9 July 1980, 23.

10 Richard G. Lipsey, Daniel Schwanen, and Ronald J. Wonnacott, *The NAFTA: What's In, What's Out, What's Next* (Toronto: C.D. Howe Institute, 1994), 20, mention that 'any truly effective bilateral or multilateral accord to liberalize Canada's trade with third countries would have come at the expense of the United States, and no third country was prepared to jeopardize its trade relationship with the United States for the sake of liberalizing its relatively unimportant trade with Canada.'

11 This paragraph draws from Doern and Tomlin, *Faith and Fear: The Free Trade Story*, 16–30.

12 Ibid., 30.

13 Ibid.

14 In 1867, Sir John A. Macdonald had attempted without success to revive the 1854 Reciprocity Agreement, a limited bilateral free trade agreement abrogated by the United States in 1866. In 1896, the Liberal government of Sir Wilfrid Laurier approached the United States to discuss free trade between the two neighbours. Fifteen years later, in 1911, Laurier was defeated after negotiating a new Reciprocity Agreement with the United States.

15 For an excellent book on the FTA negotiations, see Michael Hart with Bill Dymond and Colin Robertson, *Decision at Midnight: Inside the Canada–US Free-Trade Negotiations* (Vancouver, BC: UBC Press, 1994).

16 For more details on Mexico's economic recovery, see Nora Lustig, *Mexico: The Remaking of an Economy* (Washington: DC: Brookings Institution, 1992).

17 See Gary Clyde Hufbauer and Jeffrey J. Schott, *North American Free Trade: Issues and Recommendations* (Washington, DC: Institute for International Economics, 1992), 18.

18 Linda Diebel, 'Kissinger's Truly New World Order,' *Toronto Star*, 7 Feb. 1993, B1.

19 Javier Garciadiego, *El TLC Día a Día: Crónica de una negociación* (Mexico City, DF: Miguel Angel Porrua, 1994), 13–39.

20 U.S. Congress, Senate, Committee on Banking, Housing, and Urban Affairs, *The Impact of Third World Debt on U.S. Trade*, 101st Cong., 1st sess., 18 Oct. 1989, 36.

21 Hermann von Bertrab, *Negotiating NAFTA: A Mexican Envoy's Account* (Westport, CT.: Praeger/CSIS, 1997), 2.

22 Robert A. Mosbacher, 'Don't Push NAFTA off Fast Track, Mr. Clinton,' *Houston Chronicle*, 7 Jan. 1993, B11.

23 The Canada–Mexico Joint Ministerial Committee was established in 1968.

It is made of cabinet ministers who address bilateral issues. It is chaired by foreign ministers but includes a number of other ministers such as trade, environment, and transport. It meets every two or three years.

24 Glenda Hersh, 'Mulroney Open to Idea of North American Common Market,' UPI, 17 March 1990.

25 Maxwell A. Cameron and Brian W. Tomlin, 'Canada and Latin America in the Shadow of U.S. Power: Toward an Expanding Hemispheric Agreement,' mimeo, Dec. 1993, 10.

26 Federal News Service, 'Joint Statement by Mexico and the United States on Negotiation of a Free Trade Agreement,' 11 June 1990.

27 Cameron and Tomlin, 'Canada and Latin America,' 10–11.

28 Richard G. Lipsey, *Canada at the U.S.–Mexico Free Trade Dance: Wallflower or Partner?* (Toronto: C.D. Howe Institute, Aug. 1990), 2.

29 Ronald J. Wonnacott, 'Canada's Role in the US–Mexican Free Trade Negotiations,' *World Economy* (March 1991), 81.

30 Julius Katz, 'The NAFTA Treaty and the Question of Expansion: Views of the Negotiators (I),' in *Indianapolis Summit: Hemispheric Trade and Economic Integration after NAFTA* (Vancouver, BC: Fraser Institute, 1995), 25.

31 Michael Wilson was minister responsible for industry, trade, and investment. This was an important policy decision. It helped these departments resolve contentious issues among themselves, since there was only one minister involved.

32 George W. Grayson, *The North American Free Trade Agreement: Regional Community and the New World Order* (Lanham, MD: University Press of America, 1995), 86.

33 Rod McQueen, 'Free Trade Talks Remain Stalled: Ministers Play Down Session,' *Financial Post*, 11 Feb. 1992, 3.

34 Quoted in Grayson, *The North American Free Trade Agreement*, 90.

35 Ibid., 91.

36 'NAFTA Negotiator Says Mexico May Expand Foreign Access to Petrochemicals,' *Inside U.S. Trade*, 8 May 1992, 13.

37 'Canada Opposes Changes to FTA Dispute Settlement Procedures in NAFTA,' *Inside U.S. Trade*, 17 July 1992, 3.

38 Ibid.

39 Ibid.

40 Quoted in Grayson, *The North American Free Trade Agreement*, 96.

41 Hermann von Bertrab, *El redescubrimiento de América: Historia del TLC* (Mexico City: Fondo de Cultura Económica, 1996), 139–40.

42 Bernard Simon, 'Canada Ponders Separate Deals with Mexico,' *Financial Times*, 15 Nov. 1993, 4.

43 'Canada Ready to Proclaim NAFTA after Joint Statements Are Issued,'
   Inside U.S. Trade, 3 Dec. 1993, 1. Under the FTA, a working group had been
   established to deal with the same issues. The deadline of this group was
   31 December 1993, with the possibility of a two-year extension.
44 Ibid., 17.
45 Ibid., 17–18.

3. Culture: Preserving the Status Quo

1 Quoted in Allan Smith, 'Canadian Culture, the Canadian State, and the
   New Continentalism,' *Canadian-American Public Policy* 3 (Oct. 1990): 8.
2 Ibid., 10.
3 Canada. Department of Communications, *Vital Links: Canadian Cultural
   Industries* (Ottawa: Supply and Services Canada, April 1987), 21, 23.
4 See Keith Acheson and Christopher Maule, 'Canada's Cultural Policies:
   You Can't Have It Both Ways,' *Canadian Foreign Policy* (winter 1997): 65–81,
   and Daniel Schwanen, *A Matter of Choice: Toward a More Creative Canadian
   Policy on Culture* (Toronto: C.D. Howe Institute, April 1997).
5 *Report of the Royal Commission on the Economic Union and Development
   Prospects for Canada* (Ottawa: Minister of Supply and Services, 1985), vol. 1,
   310.
6 As in the FTA, performing arts (such as theatre, opera, dance), visual arts,
   museums, and so on, are not included and are thus not exempted from the
   NAFTA agreement. Newspapers, though covered by NAFTA, are not
   analysed in this book.
7 United States General Accounting Office, *Report to Congress; North American Free Trade Agreement: Assessment of Major Issues*, vol. 2, GAO/GGD-93-
   137B (Washington, DC: Government Printing Office, Sept. 1993), 100.
8 Jon R. Johnson and Joel A. Schachter, *The Free Trade Agreement: A Comprehensive Guide* (Aurora, ON: Canada Law Book, 1988), 147.
9 Jon R. Johnson, *The North American Free Trade Agreement: A Comprehensive
   Guide* (Aurora, ON: Canada Law Book, 1994), 473.
10 Richard E. Neff and Fran Smallson, *NAFTA: Protecting and Enforcing
   Intellectual Property Rights in North America* (Colorado Springs, CO:
   Shepard's/McGraw-Hill, 1994), 16.
11 Ibid., 23.
12 Charles Levy and Stuart Weiser, 'Intellectual Property,' in Judith H. Bello,
   Alan F. Holmer, and Joseph J. Norton, eds., *The North American Free Trade
   Agreement: A New Frontier in International Trade and Investment in the Ameri-
   cas* (Washington, DC: American Bar Association, 1994), 285.

13 Neff and Smallson, *NAFTA: Protecting and Enforcing Intellectual Property Rights in North America*, 38–9.

14 Dorothy Schrader, 'Intellectual Property Provisions in NAFTA,' in James R. Holbein and Donald J. Musch, eds., *North American Free Trade Agreements* (Dobbs Ferry, NY: Oceana Publications, March 1995), 10.

15 NAFTA annex I, I-M-10, I-M-11.

16 Ibid., I-M-14, I-M-12, I-M-13.

17 Ibid., I-M-14.

18 Ibid., I-M-15, I-M-16, I-M-17.

19 NAFTA annex II, II-M-2.

20 Ibid., II-U-2, II-U-8, II-U-3.

21 Statistics Canada, *Book Publishing 1991–92*, Cat. No. 87–210, Aug. 1993.

22 Statistics Canada, *Periodical Publishing 1991–92*, Cat. No. 87–203, Aug. 1993.

23 Industry, Science and Technology Canada, *Industry Profile 1990–1991: Periodical Publishing*, 4.

24 Statistics Canada, *Film and Video 1991–92*, Cat. No. 87-204, Feb. 1994.

25 Groupe Secor, *Canadian Government Intervention in the Film Industry: A Document Prepared for the Department of Canadian Heritage* (Ottawa: Department of Canadian Heritage, 1994), 24.

26 Singles are not included.

27 Until 1993, Canadian-content recordings were records that met two of the following conditions: the music was composed by Canadian; the instrumentation or lyrics were performed principally by a Canadian; the live performance was wholly recorded in Canada; and/or the lyrics were written by a Canadian. These conditions were established by the Canadian Radio-television and Telecommunications Commission (CRTC). The criteria were modified in December 1993 to allow the credit of 50 per cent of the contribution to a Canadian when this composer and lyricist is collaborating with a non-Canadian. See Public Notice CRTC 1993–173 (8 Dec. 1993).

28 Statistics Canada, *Sound Recording 1991–92*, Cat. No. 87-202, June 1993.

29 A definition of these industries includes the following products: books, periodicals and newspapers; motion pictures; the music and recording industry; radio, television, and cable; theatre; advertising; and computer software. See Stephen E. Siwek and Gale Mosteller, *Copyright Industries in the U.S. Economies: The 1996 Report* (Washington, DC: International Intellectual Property Alliance, 1996), 16–17.

30 U.S. Department of Commerce, International Trade Administration, *U.S. Industrial Outlook 1994*, 24–11, 24–13.

31 Ibid., 31–2.
32 Ibid., 31–3.
33 John Tebbel, *A History of Book Publishing in the United States: The Creation of an Industry, 1630–1865* (New York: R.R. Bowker, 1972), 2.
34 See Néstor García Canclini, 'Las industrias culturales,' in Gilberto Guevara Niebla and Néstor García Canclini, eds., *La educación y la cultura ante el tratado de libre comercio* (Mexico City: Fundación Nexos/Nueva Imagen, 1992), 211.
35 For a good overview of Mexican book publishing, see Javier Wimer, 'El libro mexicano y el tratado de libre comercio,' *La Jornada*, 13 Sept. 1991, 38.
36 See Carl J. Mora, 'Mexican Cinema: Decline, Renovation, and the Return of Commercialism, 1960–1980,' in Michael T. Martin, ed., *New Latin American Cinema*, Vol. 2, *Studies of National Cinemas* (Detroit: Wayne State University, 1997), 37–75; Charles Ramírez Berg, *Cinema of Solitude: A Critical Study of Mexican Film, 1967–1983* (Austin: University of Texas Press, 1992), 50–1; Federico Dávalos Orozco, 'Notas sobre las condiciones actuales de la industria cinematográfica mexicana,' in Delia Crovi Druetta, ed., *Desarrollo de las industrias audiovisuales en México y Canadá* (Mexico City: Facultad de Ciencias Políticas y Sociales de la UNAM, 1995), 149.
37 John Lannert, 'Market Report '92; Mexico's Music Industry; Viva Mexico!,' *Billboard*, 19 Sept. 1992, M4.
38 Covering the whole cultural spectrum, see for example, the *Report of the Royal Commission on National Development in the Arts, Letters, and Sciences, 1949–51* (Massey Report) (Ottawa: King's Printer, 1951). See also *Report of the Special Senate Committee on Mass Media* (Davey Report), 3 vols. (Ottawa: Queen's Printer, 1970); *Report of the Federal Cultural Policy Review Committee* (Applebaum-Hébert Report) (Ottawa: Minister of Supply and Services, 1982); *Report of the Task Force on Funding of the Arts* (Bovey Report) (Ottawa: Minister of Supply and Services, 1986); and the Report of the Cultural Industries Sectoral Advisory Group on International Trade, *Canadian Culture in a Global World: New Strategies for Culture and Trade* (Ottawa, Feb. 1999). Other commissions, task forces, or committees have focused on one particular aspect of Canadian culture. See, for instance, *Report of the Royal Commission on Radio Broadcasting* (Aird Report) 1929; *Report of the Royal Commission on Publications* (O'Leary Report) (Ottawa: Queen's Printer, 1961); *Report of the Special Task Force on the Film Industry* (Raymond–Roth Report) (Ottawa: Minister of Supply and Services, November 1985); *Report of the Task Force on Broadcasting Policy* (Caplan–Sauvageau Report) (Ottawa: Minister of Supply and Services, 1986); *Report of the Girard–Peters Task Force on the Economic Status of Canadian Television* (1991); *Report of the Task*

Force on the Canadian Magazine Industry (March 1994); and the Report of the Mandate Review Committee, *Making Our Voices Heard: Canadian Broadcasting and Film for the 21st Century* (1996).

39 For an excellent review of the development of Canada's copyright laws, on which this paragraph is based, see William L. Hayhurst, 'Intellectual Property Laws in Canada: The British Tradition, the American Influence and the French Factor,' *Intellectual Property Journal* 10 (May 1996): 265–327.

40 Ibid., 283.

41 It was not until the Statute of Westminster of 1931 that Canada was able to enact legislation without any potential interference from the British Parliament.

42 See 'Copyright Law Enacted; U.S. May Challenge Law in NAFTA or WTO,' *World Intellectual Property Report*, June 1997, 184–6.

43 Industry, Science and Technology Canada, *Industry Profile 1990–1991: Book Publishing*, 5.

44 Paul Audley, *Canada's Cultural Industries* (Toronto: James Lorimer/Canadian Institute for Economic Policy, 1983), 61.

45 The Film and Video Production Tax Credit was introduced in December 1995 to replace the CCA.

46 The first radio broadcasting in Canada was transmitted from Montreal on 20 May 1919, from Station XWA (now CFCF). Under the Wireless Telegraph Act of 1905, a licence from the Department of Marine and Fisheries was required to broadcast. By 1927, there were seventy-five radio stations in Canada. See Marc Raboy, *Missed Opportunities: The Story of Canada's Broadcasting Policy* (Montreal: McGill-Queen's University Press, 1990), 21. For an excellent book on Canada's broadcasting law, see Pierre Trudel and France Abran, *Droit de la radio et de la télévision* (Montreal: Editions Thémis, 1991).

47 Mandate Review Committee, *Making Our Voices Heard*, 32.

48 See 'A Short History of Broadcasting Regulation in Canada and the CRTC,' available on the CRTC home page (http://www.crtc.gc.ca). In addition to broadcasting industries, the CRTC also regulates the telecom sector. The 1991 Broadcasting Act 'splits the CBC's board of directors into English and French boards, and removes the requirement that the crown corporation contribute "to the development of national unity."' See William Walker, 'Senate Adjourns after Clearing Way to Sell PetroCan,' *Toronto Star*, 2 Feb. 1991, A6.

49 For more on the CMT/NCN issue, see Acheson and Maule, 'Canada's Cultural Policies – You Can't Have It Both Ways.'

50 It failed in 1859, 1874, 1879, 1909, 1937, 1938, and 1949.

51 On government intervention, see Milton C. Cummings, Jr, 'Government and the Arts: An Overview,' in Stephen Benedict, ed., *Public Money and the Muse* (New York: W.W. Norton, 1991), 31–79; National Endowment for the Arts, *National Endowment for the Arts 1965–1995: A Brief Chronology of Federal Involvement in the Arts* (Washington, DC: National Endowment for the Arts, 1995); Fannie Taylor and Anthony L. Barresi, *The Arts at a New Frontier: The National Endowment for the Arts* (New York: Plenum Press, 1984); and William J. Baumol and William G. Bowen, *Performing Arts: The Economic Dilemma* (New York: Twentieth Century Fund, 1966). Sectors covered by the NEA include music (instrumental and vocal), motion pictures, radio, television, tape and sound recording, dance, drama, folk arts, creative writing, architecture, painting, and sculpture. The NEA had a budget of U.S.$2.5 million in its first fiscal year. In 1992, the budget rose to U.S.$176 million.

52 Cummings writes that 'the program was initially prompted by a 1933 letter from the painter George Biddle to his former roommate in prep school, the new President Franklin D. Roosevelt. Biddle's letter specifically cited the Mexican mural movement.' See Cummings, 'Government and the Arts: An Overview,' 41. On CETA arts programs, see Steven C. Dubin, *Bureaucratizing the Muse: Public Funds and the Cultural Worker* (Chicago: University of Chicago Press, 1987).

53 See, for instance, Office of the United States Trade Representative, *Results of Special 301 Annual Review* (Washington, DC: USTR, 1 May, 1998).

54 See the Act of 3 March 1891, ch. 565, §3, 26 Stat. 1106, 1107.

55 For an excellent review of the manufacturing clause, see Patrice A. Lyons, 'The Manufacturing Clause: A Legislative History,' *Journal, Copyright Society of the U.S.A.* 29 (Oct. 1981): 8–57; and Annette V. Tucker, 'The Validity of the Manufacturing Clause of the United States Copyright Code as Challenged by Trade Partners and Copyright Owners,' *Vanderbilt Journal of Transnational Law* 18 (summer 1985): 577–624.

56 See Frank Luther Mott, *A History of American Magazines 1741–1850* (Cambridge, Mass.: Harvard University Press, 1938), 119.

57 Dan Steinbock, *Triumph and Erosion in the American Media and Entertainment Industries* (Westport, CT: Quorum Books, 1995), 18–21. See also Alan Citron, 'Bill Seeks to Protect Culture from Overseas,' *Los Angeles Times*, 11 Oct. 1991, D2.

58 William B. Ray, *FCC: The Ups and Downs of Radio–TV Regulation* (Ames: Iowa State University Press, 1990), xvii.

59 Telecommunications Act of 1996, Public Law No. 104-104, 8 Feb. 1996.

60 See Rafael Tovar y de Teresa, *Modernización y política cultural* (Mexico City:

Fondo de Cultura Económica, 1994), 21–50, and 327–52 for a chronology of the cultural institutions in Mexico.

61 On government involvement in the book and periodical industries, see Tovar y de Teresa, *Modernización y política cultural*, 180–220.

62 Luis C. Schmidt, 'Computer Software and the North American Free Trade Agreement: Will Mexican Law Represent a Trade Barrier?' *IDEA* 34 (fall 1993): 39.

63 Ramírez Berg writes that the United States reduced its supply of raw film stock to Argentina during the Second World War. See Berg, *Cinema of Solitude*, 38–9.

64 On the film policies of the López Portillo and de la Madrid administrations,' see David R. Maciel, 'Serpientes y Escaleras: The Contemporary Cinema of Mexico, 1976–1994,' in Michael T. Martin, ed., *New Latin American Cinema*, vol. 2, *Studies of National Cinemas* (Detroit: Wayne State University, 1997), 94–120.

65 See *International Trade Reporter*, 'International Intellectual Property Alliance Targets 22 Countries for "Special 301" Lists,' 20 Feb. 1991, 274; John Lannert, 'Pubs. Anxious about Mexico Copyright Law,' *Billboard*, 12 April 1997; 'Mexico's New IP Law Stiffens Penalties; Falls Short of Berne Criteria, Critics Claim,' *International Trade Reporter*, 8 Jan. 1997, 41.

66 M.S. Nader and J. Cervantes, 'Mexico Liberalizes Foreign Investment Regime,' *Mexico Trade and Law Reporter*, 1 March 1994.

67 For an excellent overview of the legal framework for the Mexican broadcasting industry, see Gabriel Sosa Plata, 'El marco legal,' in *Apuntes para una historia de la televisión mexicana* (Mexico City: Revista mexicana de comunicación, March 1998), 213–82.

68 Neff and Smallson, *NAFTA: Protecting and Enforcing Intellectual Property Rights in North America*, 26.

69 Mexico ratified the Convention for the Protection of Performers, Producers of Phonograms and Broadcasting Organizations of 1961 on 17 Feb. 1963. It entered into force on 18 May 1964.

70 'Culture Exemption Not Favoured in Trade Talks,' *Globe and Mail*, 22 Feb. 1991, C1.

71 Reps. Mel Levine (Dem., Calif.), Raymond McGrath (Rep., NY), Howard Berman (Dem., Calif.), Carlos Moorhead (Rep., Calif.) and Jim Cooper (Dem., Tenn.).

72 'House Letter to Hills on Cultural Exemptions,' *Inside U.S. Trade*, 19 April 1991, 5.

73 Michael H. Wilson, *Notes for a Speech by the Honourable Michael H. Wilson, Minister of International Trade, and Minister of Industry, Science and Technol-*

ogy at The Financial Post Conference on North American Free Trade (Montreal, 25 April 1991), 4.

74 Michael H. Wilson, *Notes for an Address by the Honourable Michael Wilson, P.C., M.P., Minister of Industry, Science and Technology and Minister for International Trade to the Central Canada Broadcasters' Association* (Toronto, 24 June 1991), 9. Wilson had made similar remarks at a press conference held in Washington, DC, on 16 May 1991.

75 Peter C. Newman, 'Defending the Canadian Dream,' *Maclean's*, 8 July 1991, 50.

76 Federal News Service, 'Press Conference, Carla Hills, Office of the USTR,' 14 June 1991.

77 Jonathan Ferguson, 'Culture Stand Grows Confused as Mexico Sides with U.S. View,' *Toronto Star*, 16 June 1991, B4.

78 Jonathan Ferguson, 'Showdown on Culture Looms at Trade Talks,' *Toronto Star*, 12 June 1991, A1.

79 Drew Fagan, 'U.S. Tries to Loosen Canada's Grip on Culture: Canadians Urged to Put it All on the Table in Trilateral Free-Trade Talks,' *Globe and Mail*, 21 Aug. 1991, B4.

80 'Business Council Recommends Goals for NAFTA Intellectual Property Rules,' *Inside U.S. Trade*, 15 Nov. 1991, 5.

81 'U.S. Council IPR Recommendations for NAFTA,' *Inside U.S. Trade*, 15 Nov. 1991, 6.

82 Shawn McCarthy, 'Culture Out of Trade Talks, Official Insists,' *Toronto Star*, 5 March 1992, A1.

83 'IPC Letter to Hills on NAFTA,' *Inside U.S. Trade*, 13 March 1992, 18. The companies were Bristol-Myers Squibb, Dupont, FMC Corporation, General Electric, Hewlett-Packard, IBM, Johnson & Johnson, Merck, Monsanto, Pfizer, Procter & Gamble, Rockwell International, and Time Warner.

84 'Culture Not an Issue in Talks: Wilson,' *Toronto Star*, 22 July 1992, A3.

85 The first phase had taken place in 1988.

86 'Industry Seeks Retaliation if Canada Invokes NAFTA Cultural Exemption,' *Inside U.S. Trade*, 18 Sept. 1992, 2.

87 Richard Siklos, 'Wilson Says Culture Not Negotiable,' *Financial Post*, 6 March 1992, 6.

88 Graham Carr notes that the Department of Commerce had identified Europe 'as the most promising area for future expansion by U.S. cultural industries.' See Graham Carr, 'Culture,' in Duncan Cameron and Mel Watkins, eds., *Canada under Free Trade* (Toronto: James Lorimer, 1993), 205.

89 Industry Functional Advisory Committee on Intellectual Property Rights for Trade Policy Matters (IFAC-3), *Report of IFAC-3 on the Intellectual*

Property Chapter and Other Intellectual Property-Related Elements of the North American Free Trade Agreement (NAFTA), 11 Sept. 1992, 15.

90 See 'Hills Says States Opposed Enforcement of Environmental Standards in NAFTA,' *Inside U.S. Trade,* 11 Sept. 1992, 8. Also see 'Les majors veulent rouvrir l'ALENA,' *Le Devoir,* 12 Sept. 1992, A-14.

91 See Marie Tison, 'Les E.-U. menacent d'exercer des représailles contre le Canada,' *La Presse,* 9 Sept. 1992, C3; and Marie Tison, 'Industries culturelles: le représentant de l'Arkansas craint l'exemple canadien,' *La Presse,* 10 Sept. 1992, C3.

92 'IPC Letter on NAFTA,' *Inside U.S. Trade,* 9 Oct. 1992, 18.

93 See section 513 of Public Law 103-182.

4. Textiles and Apparel: Canada, the Odd Man Out

1 See Eric Barry, 'NAFTA and Textiles: Objectives, Results, and Future Implications,' 1. Speech given on 1 May 1993, at the Cormier Center, Bishop's University, Lennoxville, Quebec.

2 Dawn Keremitsis, *The Cotton Textile Industry in Porfiriato, Mexico 1870–1910* (New York: Garland, 1987), 8.

3 U.S. Department of Commerce, International Trade Administration, *U.S. Industry and Trade Outlook 1998* (Washington, DC: International Trade Administration, 1998), 10-1.

4 William R. Cline, *The Future of World Trade in Textiles and Apparel,* rev. ed. (Washington, DC: Institute for International Economics, 1990), 150.

5 Some have argued that a better term for rules of origin in free trade areas would be 'rules of preference,' because tariff preferences are conferred only on products of members. 'When it is necessary to determine origin for other purposes, different rules generally are used.' See N. David Palmeter, 'Rules of Origin in a Western Hemisphere Free Trade Agreement,' mimeo, 31 March 1993, 1–2.

6 The following goods must be made within the NAFTA region, from fibre to finished good: cotton and knit fabrics; MMF non-woven and specialty fabrics; spun cotton and MMF yarns; and MMF carpeting, made-ups, and sweaters. See United States General Accounting Office, *Report to the Congress: North American Free Trade Agreement: Assessment of Major Issues,* vol. 2, 74. For non-man-made sweaters, the 'fibre forward' rule applies only for trade between the United States and Mexico.

7 For example, coated fabric (exceptions are tire cord, belting, and hose, which fall under a 'fibre forward' rule for man-made fibre and a 'yarn forward' rule for cotton), cotton and man-made fibre luggage, handbags,

and flat goods, and curtains made from fabric composed of high twist, 70 denier, 24 filament yarns.

8 Examples include silk, linen, Harris tweed, velveteen, wide-wale corduroy, and some men's shirt fabrics. See Barry, 'NAFTA and Textiles: Objectives, Results, and Future Implications,' 8; and 'Canada Accepts Three-Way Deal, Fall Short on Wool Apparel Demands,' *Inside U.S. Trade*, 14 Aug. 1992, 5.

9 The 'substantial transformation' rule is the general rule of origin used in the United States. Origin is conferred when manufacturing "substantially transforms" a product into a 'new and different article of commerce' with a new name, a new character, and a new use. See *Anheuser-Busch Assn. v. United States*, 207 US 556 (1907).

10 NAFTA 405(6). It applies to goods under chapters 50 to 63 of the Harmonized System.

11 NAFTA Annex 300-B, section 7, paragraph 3.

12 United States General Accounting Office, *Report to the Congress: North American Free Trade Agreement*, 77. See NAFTA annex 300-B, section 7.

13 Edward Alden, 'Canada May Pull Out of NAFTA Textile Agreement as U.S., Mexico Near Deal,' *Inside U.S. Trade*, 8 May 1992, 2.

14 Senate of Canada, *Proceedings of the Standing Senate Committee on Foreign Affairs*, 2 June 1992, 7–8.

15 For Tables 4.1–3, see NAFTA annex 300-B, schedules 6.B.1, 6.B.2, and 6.B.3. Certain types of fabrics deemed to be 'in ample supply' are excluded from the TPLs between the United States and Mexico. Thus apparel made from blue denim, oxford cloth, and cotton and man-made fibre circular-knit fabric under 100 metric yarn number which does not meet the rules of origin has to pay the MFN duty.

16 This provision applies to U.S. producers importing fabric from non-member countries, which cut and export the fabric to Mexico for re-exportation into the United States. This TPL expires when the quantitative restrictions under the MFA are eliminated.

17 'Wilson Letter to Hills on NAFTA Textiles,' *Inside U.S. Trade*, 7 Aug. 1992, 12.

18 Canadian Apparel Manufacturers Institute, 'An Analysis of the North American Free Trade Agreement,' *Submission to the Sub-Committee on International Trade of the House of Commons Standing Committee on External Affairs* (Ottawa, 10 Dec. 1992), 6.

19 Ibid.

20 Notice to Exporters, Serial No. 70, 15 Dec. 1993. Figures were provided by Canada's Department of Foreign Affairs and International Trade, Import

Controls Division 1 (Textiles and Clothing), Export and Import Permits Bureau, April 1994 (hereafter Permits Bureau, April 1994); and see, for wool apparel, the 1994 allocation by the department was as follows: 79.2 per cent of the TPL was allocated based on individual exporters' performance under the FTA TRQ in 1993; 15.8 per cent for goods that used to qualify under the FTA rules but would not satisfy the NAFTA rules; and 5 per cent was set aside for new exporters on a 'first-come, first-served' basis. For the other two TPLs, the allocation was done on a 'first-come, first-served' basis. For 1995, all TPLs were allocated based on exporters' use of their 1994 quota. There was a pool for new entrants equal to 1 per cent of the 1994 quota plus any unused quota, for up to 5 per cent of the total. Any additional unused portion was available on a 'first-come, first-served' basis.

21 Canadian Apparel Manufacturers Institute, 'An Analysis of the North American Free Trade,' 7.
22 *Sub-Committee on International Trade of the House of Commons Standing Committee on External Affairs* (Ottawa, 10 Dec. 1992), 11.
23 The Canadian exporters used 9 per cent of their quota in 1989, 17 per cent in 1990, 27 per cent in 1991, 38 per cent in 1992, and 54 per cent in 1993. Figures provided by the Permits Bureau, April 1994.
24 Canadian Apparel Manufacturers Institute, 'An Analysis of the North American Free Trade,' 7.
25 NAFTA annex 300-B, appendix 6, section B, paragraph 5.
26 U.S. General Accounting Office, *Report to the Congress: North American Free Trade Agreement*, 75–6.
27 NAFTA appendix 2.1, section C. Eric Barry, 'NAFTA: The Preliminary Details,' *Canadian Textile Journal* (Nov. 1992): 19.
28 U.S. Department of Commerce, International Trade Administration, *NAFTA Opportunities: Textile and Apparel Industries* (Washington, DC: International Trade Administration, 1993), 3–4.
29 Ibid.
30 See Fifth Meeting of the NAFTA Commission Joint Statement, Paris, France, 29 April 1998.
31 NAFTA annex 300-B, section 4.
32 Ibid., section 5.
33 Ibid., NAFTA 303 and annex 303.7.
34 The *maquiladora* program was established in 1965. Components of manufacturing products are imported to Mexico free of duty to be assembled or processed and then re-exported. See Kathryn Kopinak, 'The Maquiladorization of the Mexican Economy,' in Ricardo Grinspun and Maxwell A.

Cameron, eds., *The Political Economy of North American Free Trade* (Montreal: McGill-Queen's University Press, 1993), 141–61.

35 U.S. foreign trade zones are areas designated by the government. They 'allow domestic activity to take place as if it were outside U.S. customs territory.' See http://www.ita.doc.gov

36 U.S. General Accounting Office, *Report to Congress, North American Free Trade Agreement*, 17.

37 See NAFTA 303.

38 This measure was extended to cover quilted cotton piece goods, quilted man-made piece goods, and furniture moving pads. See NAFTA annex 303.6(2).

39 U.S. Department of Commerce, International Trade Administration, *NAFTA Opportunities: Textile and Apparel Industry*, 6.

40 U.S. General Accounting Office, *Report to the Congress: North American Free Trade Agreement*, 78.

41 See NAFTA annex 913.5.a-4.

42 Ibid., annex 300-B, section 9.

43 The industry is defined here as SIC 18 (primary textiles), SIC 19 (textile products), and SIC 3257 (motor vehicle fabrics accessories).

44 Industry, Science and Technology Canada, *Industrial Competitiveness: A Sectoral Perspective* (Ottawa, 1991), 111.

45 Ibid., 112.

46 Canadian Textiles Institute, *NAFTA Negotiations and the Canadian Textile Manufacturing Industry* (Ottawa: Canadian Textiles Institute, 4 Feb. 1993), 13. See also Canadian Textiles Institute, *The Canadian Textile Manufacturing Industry* (Ottawa: Canadian Textiles Institute, 28 Jan. 1998).

47 SIC 24 refers to the clothing industry. Among the products of the industry are women's, men's, and children's wear, knitted apparel, and foundation garments. Two other sub-sectors also produce furs and leather apparel. The activities of these two sectors are not covered here.

48 My short history of the U.S. textile industry is based on American Textile Manufacturers Institute, *The U.S. Textile Industry: Scope and Importance 1997* (Washington, DC: ATMI, 1997), Introduction.

49 Debra S. Grill and Mary F. Sharkey, *The Textile/Apparel Industries* (New York: Fairchild Fashion & Merchandising Group, 1991), 16.

50 Laureen A. Murray, 'Unraveling Employment Trends in Textiles and Apparel,' *Monthly Labor Review* 118 (Aug. 1995): 62.

51 Includes SIC (apparel and other textile products).

52 U.S. Department of Commerce, *NAFTA Opportunities: Textile and Apparel Industries*, 2.

53 On the history of the Mexican textile industry, see Irma Portos, *Pasado y presente de la industria textil en México* (Mexico City: Editorial Nuestro Tiempo, 1992).

54 SECOFI, *Tratado de Libre Comercio en América del Norte: La industria textil,* Monografía 13 (Mexico City: SECOFI, Dec. 1991), 6–7.

55 General Agreement on Tariffs and Trade, *Trade Policy Review – Mexico,* vol. 1 (Geneva: GATT, July 1993), 147.

56 Cámara Nacional de la Industria Textil, *Indicadores económicos de la industria textil mexicana* (Mexico City: Cámara Nacional de la Industria Textil, Feb. 1998).

57 Cámara Nacional de la Industria del Vestido, *Sinopsis estadística de la industria mexicana de manufacturas de prendas* (Mexico City: Cámara Nacional de la Industria del Vestido, Feb. 1998).

58 International Trade Commission, *Study on the Operation and Effects of the North American Free Trade Agreement* (Washington, DC: USITC, July 1997), 85.

59 World Trade Organization, *Trade Policy Review – Mexico 1997,* vol. 1 (Geneva: WTO, 1997).

60 GATT article XIX allows a party to impose safeguard import restrictions with appropriate compensation for exporting countries; article XII provides for a balance-of-payments escape clause; and article XXV permits a waiver, whereas article XXXV allows contracting parties not to apply GATT rules to a new contracting party.

61 United States International Trade Commission, *The History and Current Status of the Multifiber Arrangement,* USITC Publication 850 (Washington, DC: Jan. 1978), 8.

62 General Agreement on Tariffs and Trade, *Textile and Clothing in the World Economy* (Geneva: GATT, 1984), 73.

63 U.S. International Trade Commission, *The History and Current Status of the Multifiber Arrangement,* 12.

64 General Agreement on Tariffs and Trade, *Textiles and Clothing in the World Economy,* 73.

65 Ibid., 75.

66 The MFA was extended in 1977, 1981, 1986, 1991, 1992, and 1993.

67 Article XIX quotas covered cotton yarn (1973–4), acrylic yarn (1976–8), double knit fabrics (1976–9), and shirts (30 November 1971–31 December 1978).

68 *The GATT Uruguay Round: A Negotiating History* (Boston: Kluwer and Taxation Publishers, 1993), vol. 1, 273.

69 General Agreement on Tariffs and Trade, *Trade Policy Review – United States 1994*, vol. 1 (Geneva: GATT, June 1994), 164–5.

70 The discussions failed to produce results in 1869, 1871, and 1874. See Doern and Tomlin, *Faith and Fear: The Free Trade Story*, 58. As mentioned by Doern and Tomlin, the Reciprocity Treaty covered essentially natural resources and several agricultural products. It excluded manufactured goods because tariffs on these products represented a major source of revenue.

71 For an excellent review of the early years of the Canadian textile industry, see Canada, *Report of the Royal Commission on the Textile Industry* (Ottawa: King's Printer, 1938).

72 Canada, Royal Commission on Canada's Economic Prospects, *The Canadian Primary Textile Industry* (Ottawa: National Industrial Conference Board, July 1956), 24.

73 Canada, Textile and Clothing Board, *Textile and Clothing Inquiry: Report to the Minister of Industry, Trade and Commerce* (Ottawa: Textile and Clothing Board, June 1980), 11.

74 Ibid., 12–14.

75 Caroline Pestieau, *The Canadian Textile Policy: A Sectoral Trade Adjustment Strategy?* (Montreal: The Canadian Economic Policy Committee and C.D. Howe Research Institute, 1976), 6.

76 Ibid., 13.

77 The committee had representatives from several departments – Industry, Trade and Commerce; External Affairs; Finance; National Revenue; Manpower and Immigration; Labour; Consumer and Corporate Affairs – and from the Canadian International Development Agency and the Privy Council.

78 Canada, Textile and Clothing Board, *Study of the Impact of Potential Free Trade in Textiles and Clothing between Canada and the United States: Final Report* (Ottawa: Textile and Clothing Board, 1984). See also Rodney de C. Grey, *Legal/Institutional Aspects of a 'Free-Trade Area' for Textiles and Clothing between the U.S. and Canada* (Ottawa: Grey, Clark, Shih & Associates, 15 Nov. 1983).

79 Canadian International Trade Tribunal, *Textile Reference: Annual Status Report, October 1, 1996, to September 30, 1997* (Ottawa: CIIT, 1997).

80 Provinces, especially Quebec, Ontario, and Manitoba, have also been assisting their industries. For instance, a mini-summit on textiles was held in September 1977 in Quebec, while the 1978 Quebec budget eliminated the sales tax on all textile and apparel products for an initial period of one

year. More recently, in 1994, the Quebec government announced a tax credit program to promote fashion design and increase sales of high-value-added quality apparel.

81 There are a few exceptions, such as the Textile Human Resources Council (THRC) and the Apparel Human Resources Council (AHRC), funded by the government and recently established as a national labour-management organization to serve the industries' needs in training and human resource development.

82 Canadian International Trade Tribunal, *An Inquiry into Textile Tariffs*, Volume I: *Report* (Ottawa: Minister of Supply and Services, Feb. 1990), 35.

83 World Trade Organization, *Trade Policy Review – Canada 1996*, vol. 1 (Geneva: World Trade Organization, 1996), 94.

84 From 1872 to 1930, Congress undertook several major revisions to the U.S. tariff structure: the Tariff Act of 1872, the Mongrel Tariff of 1883, the McKinley Tariff of 1890, the Wilson–Gorman Tariff of 1894, the Dingley Tariff of 1897, the Payne–Aldrich Tariff of 1909, the Underwood Tariff of 1913, the Fordney–McCumber Tariff of 1922 and the Smoot–Hawley Tariff of 1930.

85 Alfred E. Eckes, Jr, *Opening America's Market: U.S. Foreign Trade Policy since 1776* (Chapel Hill: University of North Carolina Press, 1995), 149–52. The Reciprocal Trade Agreement Program was extended in 1937, 1940, 1943, and 1945.

86 U.S. International Trade Commission, *The History and Current Status of the Multifiber Arrangement*, 1–2. Two cases (women's and girls' cotton blouses and cotton ginghams) were terminated after announcement of the export restrictions. There was a negative finding in the last case (cotton pillowcases).

87 J. Michael Finger and Ann Harrison, 'The MFA Paradox: More Protection and More Trade?' in Anne O. Krueger, ed., *The Political Economy of American Trade Policy* (Chicago: University of Chicago Press, 1996), 209.

88 Ibid., 210. The administration has always been very reluctant to use section 22 as a source of relief for textile products. Section 22 cannot be applied against a WTO member, while implementation of the ATC is done under section 204 of the Agricultural Act of 1956.

89 Under sections 201–4, the U.S. International Trade Commission determines whether an industry is eligible for relief by investigating whether increased imports constitute a substantial cause of serious injury or threatened serious injury to the domestic industry producing like products.

90 Finger and Harrison, 'The MFA Paradox: More Protection and More Trade?' 214.

91 U.S. International Trade Commission, *The History and Current Status of the Multifiber Arrangement*, 7.

92 For example, the United States, through CITA, was the only country that imposed quotas under the ATC in 1995.

93 For an excellent overview of CITA's functions, see U.S. General Accounting Office, *Textile Trade: Operations of the Committee for the Implementation of Textile Agreements* (Washington, DC: General Accounting Office, Sept. 1996).

94 CBERA was enacted on 5 August 1983 and entered into force on 1 January 1984. It is part of the Caribbean Basin Initiative, which was launched in 1982 'to promote political and social stability' in the Caribbean and Central America. CBERA was made permanent in 1990. As of 1996, twenty-four economies were CBERA beneficiaries: Antigua, Aruba, the Bahamas, Barbados, Belize, British Virgin Islands, Costa Rica, Dominica, Dominican Republic, El Salvador, Grenada, Guatemala, Guyana, Haiti, Honduras, Jamaica, Montserrat, Netherlands Antilles, Nicaragua, Panama, St Kitts and Nevis, St Lucia, St Vincent and the Grenadines, and Trinidad and Tobago.

  ATPA, passed by Congress on 26 November 1991, authorizes the president to grant reduced-duty or duty-free treatment to Bolivia, Colombia, Ecuador, and Peru. These preferential tariffs will remain in effect until 3 December 2001. The WTO renewed the temporary waiver of the United States for this program on 14 October 1996.

  To qualify for CBERA countries must 'afford internationally recognized workers rights under the definition used in the U.S. Generalized System of Preferences (GSP) program and ... provide effective protection of intellectual property rights (IPR), including copyrights for film and television material.' The president may waive either condition if he determines that it would be in the economic or security interests of the United States. ATPA beneficiaries must also meet the same conditions, in addition to the U.S. requirements for narcotics certification. See U.S. International Trade Commission, *Caribbean Basin Economic Recovery Act and Andean Trade Preference Act: Impact on the United States*, USITC Publication No. 3058 (Washington, DC: Sept. 1997), 3, 57–9.

95 For more on tariff protection affecting the Mexican textile industry between 1830 and 1850, see Keremitsis, *The Cotton Textile Industry in Porfiriato, Mexico, 1870–1930*, 7–31.

96 WTO, *Trade Policy Review–Mexico 1997*, chap. 3, section on maquiladoras.

97 See Héctor Zanella, 'Severa reducción en la planta del sector textil,' *El Financiero*, 13 Feb. 1994, 10; and Isabel Becerril, 'Listas en 15 días las reglas para la subasta de 14 cuotas textiles,' *El Financiero*, 14 Feb. 1994, 27.

98 Mary Sutter, 'Nation's Textile Producers Feel Growing Pains,' *Business Mexico,* 1 Sept. 1997.

99 Barry, 'NAFTA and Textiles,' 7, 6.

100 'Textile, Apparel Recommendations on NAFTA,' *Inside U.S. Trade,* 25 Oct. 1991, 9.

101 In their NAFTA position paper on textiles, the Mexicans wrote: 'México se pronunció por la formación de un grupo especial para discutir todo lo relacionado con la industria textil. La propuesta estuvo fundamentada en la importancia económica de esta industria.' (Mexico called for a special working group on textiles. The proposal was based on the economic importance of this industry.) See SECOFI, *La industria textil,* 17.

102 Scott Otteman, 'NAFTA Negotiators Said to Agree on Basic Methods for Rules of Origin,' *Inside U.S. Trade,* 26 July 1991, 3.

103 'Textile, Apparel Recommendations on NAFTA,' *Inside U.S. Trade,* 25 Oct. 1991, 9.

104 The maximum tariff in Mexico was 20 per cent at the time of the NAFTA negotiations. See SECOFI, *La industria textil,* 13, 18. The Mexicans acknowledged that average U.S. tariffs were lower: 6.8 per cent for fibres, 9 per cent for textiles, and 18.5 per cent for clothing.

105 'U.S. Expected to Present Strict Textile Content Proposal in NAFTA Talks,' *Inside U.S. Trade,* 24 Jan. 1992, 1–2. Also see Eric Barry, 'Notes from CTI,' *Canadian Textile Journal* (June 1992): 22.

106 'Hills Letter on NAFTA Textiles,' *Inside U.S. Trade,* 12 June 1992, 15.

107 Alkman Granitsas, 'U.S., Canadian Negotiators Clash over Textile Rule of Origin Proposal,' *Inside U.S. Trade,* 14 Feb. 1992, 22.

108 Hufbauer and Schott, *North American Free Trade: Issues and Recommendations,* 156.

109 'NAFTA Text on Textiles,' *Inside U.S. Trade (Special Report),* 27 March 1992, S-2, S-3. See article X04, section 3, of the Dallas Text on Textiles.

110 Alkman Granitsas, 'Canadian Apparel Makers Claim NAFTA Could Cost Canada 50,000 Jobs,' *Inside U.S. Trade,* 10 April 1992, 1.

111 Ibid., 12.

112 Ibid., 13.

113 'NAFTA Talks Still Sticking on Textiles,' *Women's Wear Daily,* 10 April 1992, 19.

114 'U.S. Seeking Compromise with Canada on Rules of Origin for NAFTA Textiles,' *Inside U.S. Trade,* 17 April 1992, 17.

115 Philippe Dubuisson, 'Libre-échange: plusieurs propositions ne satisfont pas le Québec,' *La Presse* (Montreal), 14 April 1992, B1.

116 Edward Allen, 'Canada May Pull Out of NAFTA Textile Agreement as U.S., Mexico Near Deal,' *Inside U.S. Trade*, 8 May 1992, 2.

117 'Industry Sees NAFTA Textiles Deal Threatened by Canada's Quota Demands,' *Inside U.S. Trade*, 24 April 1992, 17.

118 Jack Kivenko, president of the Canadian Apparel Manufacturers Institute, in an interview with *Le Devoir* (Montreal). See Catherine Leconte, 'Libre-échange à trois: l'industrie du vêtement veut une autre stratégie,' *Le Devoir*, 12 May 1992, A5. See also Barrie McKenna, 'Rag Trade Facing Disaster,' *Globe and Mail*, 12 May 1992, B6.

119 Catherine Leconte, 'Le libre-échange nord-américain "nous tuera,"' *Le Devoir*, 16 May 1992, B2.

120 Michel Venne, 'Libre-échange à trois: Québec appuiera à fond l'industrie québécoise du vêtement,' *Le Devoir*, 29 May 1992, A2. Réal Laberge, 'Québec veut exclure le textile du libre-échange,' *Le Soleil* (Quebec City), 29 May 1992, B1. See also Manon Corneiller, 'Ciaccia ne voit pas de problème au libre-échange à trois sauf pour l'industrie du vêtement,' *Le Devoir*, 4 June 1992, A5.

121 'Canadian Negotiators Informally Propose Exclusion of Apparel from NAFTA,' *Inside U.S. Trade*, 12 June 1992, 1.

122 Interview by the author with a senior Mexican trade official, Mexico City, Feb. 1994.

123 The figure is 99.4 percent in 1992 and 75 percent in 1993. The NAFTA conversion factor was used in 1993, which explains the smaller figure. However, it does not mean that Canada's exports to the United States were smaller. In fact, under the old conversion factor, they probably would have been higher or at the same level. Figures provided by Permits Bureau, April 1994.

124 'U.S., Mexico Resolve Remaining Hurdle on NAFTA Textile Deal, Anger Retailers,' *Inside U.S. Trade*, 29 May 1992, 1.

125 Alkman Granitsas, 'Canadian Apparel Makers Claim NAFTA Could Cost Canada 50,000 Jobs,' *Inside U.S. Trade*, 10 April 1992, 12.

126 'Chief NAFTA Negotiators Meet This Week to Tackle Remaining Thorny Issues,' *Inside U.S. Trade*, 5 June 1992, 2.

127 'Canadian Negotiators Informally Propose Exclusion of Apparel from NAFTA,' *Inside U.S. Trade*, 12 June 1992, 1, 14.

128 Ibid., 15.

129 'Canada Seeks to Block U.S. Market Access in NAFTA Textile Deal,' *Inside U.S. Trade*, 24 July 1992, 3.

130 'Canada Says Hard Issues Remain in North American Trade Deal,' *Reuter Library Report*, 20 July 1992.

131 'Wilson Letter to Hills on NAFTA Textiles,' *Inside U.S. Trade*, 7 Aug. 1992, 12, 13.
132 Drew Fagan, 'Conflict over Clothing Sector Adds to NAFTA Logjam,' *Globe and Mail*, 4 Aug. 1992, B8, B1.
133 Canadian Apparel Manufacturers Institute, 'An Analysis of the North American Free Trade Agreement,' 10.
134 Gilles Lajoie, 'Libre-échange nord-américain: fabricants de textile et de vêtements divergent d'opinion,' *Les Affaires*, 22 Aug. 1992, 4.

5. The Automotive Sector: Working with the Industry

1 See section 202 of the U.S. implementing legislation. 103 PL.182; 1993 HR 3450; 107 Stat. 2057.
2 'Canada May Accept 60 Percent Content in NAFTA Autos, But Seeks Phase-In,' *Inside U.S. Trade*, 3 July 1992, 3.
3 See Palmeter, 'The Honda Decision: Rules of Origin Turned Upside Down,' 513–23; and Frédéric Cantin and Andreas F. Lowenfeld, 'Rules of Origin, the Canada–U.S. FTA, and the Honda Case,' *American Journal of International Law* 87 (July 1993): 375–90.
4 U.S. Customs Internal Advice Ruling HQ 000160, 27 Feb. 1992.
5 'FTA Panel Finds in Favor of Canada over Dispute on Rule of Origin for Autos,' *Inside U.S. Trade*, 12 June 1992, 2.
6 U.S. Customs Internal Advice Ruling HQ 000131, 12 Dec. 1991.
7 Palmeter, 'The Honda Decision,' 515.
8 U.S. Department of Commerce, International Trade Administration, *NAFTA Opportunities: Motor Vehicles and Auto Parts* (Washington, DC: International Trade Administration, 1993), 5.
9 See NAFTA articles 402(3) and 403.
10 To determine the net cost of a good, the producer may use of three methods: calculate the total cost of all goods, subtract all excluded costs, and then reasonably allocate a percentage to the good; calculate the total cost for all goods, reasonably allocate it to the good, then subtract any excluded costs included in the total cost of the good; or reasonably allocate each cost with respect to the good so as not to include any excluded costs. See NAFTA article 402(8). For reasonable allocation of costs, see Revenue Canada, Customs, Excise and Taxation. *Customs Notice N-840: NAFTA Rules of Origin Regulations* (Ottawa, 17 Dec. 1993), schedule VII(3), (4), and (5). 'Total cost' is defined as the total of all product costs, period costs, and other costs incurred in the territory of one or more of the NAFTA countries. 'Product costs' are costs associated with the production of a good; they include the value of materials, direct labour costs and

direct overhead. 'Period costs' are costs, other that product costs, expensed in the period in which they are incurred, while 'other costs' are all costs that are not product costs or period costs. Ibid., Part I, Definitions and Interpretation. 'Non-allowable interest costs' are interest costs incurred by a producer on the producer's debt obligations that are more than 700 basis points above the yield on debt obligations of comparable maturities issued by the federal government of the country in which the producer is located. Ibid. For calculation of the value of non-originating materials (VNM), see section 9 of the Uniform Regulations for light-duty vehicles and section 10 of the Uniform Regulations for heavy-duty automotive goods.

11 House of Commons, *Sub-Committee on International Trade of the Standing Committee on External Affairs and International Trade*, 4 Feb. 1993, 7, 44.

12 U.S. Department of Commerce, International Trade Administration, *NAFTA Opportunities: Motor Vehicles and Auto Parts*, 6.

13 Jon R. Johnson, 'NAFTA and the Trade in Automotive Goods,' in Steven Globerman and Michael Walker, eds., *Assessing NAFTA: A Trinational Analysis* (Vancouver, BC: Fraser Institute, 1993), 108.

14 See NAFTA 511.

15 'Canada May Accept 60 Percent Content in NAFTA Autos, But Seeks Phase-In,' *Inside U.S. Trade*, 3 July 1992, 3.

16 See NAFTA 403(5)(a), 403(5)(b), 403(6)(a), and 403(6)(b).

17 See NAFTA 403(3)(a), (b), and (c).

18 General Motors of Canada, General Motors Corporation, General Motors de México, S.A. de C.V., and any subsidiary directly or indirectly owned by them.

19 See NAFTA annex 403.3. CAMI may choose to average the calculation of its regional value-content requirement over two fiscal years if its plant or the GMC plant with which it is averaging is closed for more than two consecutive months.

20 See NAFTA 403(4).

21 Testimony of Sandy Moroz, Canada's chief negotiator for rules of origin, before the Standing Senate Committee on Foreign Affairs. See Senate of Canada, *Proceedings of the Standing Senate Committee on Foreign Affairs*, 9 June 1993, 17.

22 See NAFTA appendix 300-A.1(1) and (2).

23 See NAFTA appendix 300-A.2(26).

24 See NAFTA appendix 300-A.2(2).

25 See NAFTA appendix 300-A.2(6). Independent *maquiladoras* – i.e., those not owned by the assembler – are now permitted to become national suppliers. See NAFTA appendix 300-A.2(4).

26 See NAFTA appendix 300-A.2(7). General Motors de México, S.A. de C.V., fought very hard for this provision. The company declared that it was the most at disadvantage and therefore pushed for 20 per cent. In fact, Johnson mentions that for the 1992 model only Ford met the requirement of 36 per cent. See Johnson, 'NAFTA and the Trade in Automotive Goods,' 117.
27 For assemblers starting production after model year 1991, only the total national value added is used. See NAFTA appendix 300-A.2(5). For reference value, see NAFTA appendix 300-A.2(5), and for total national value added, see NAFTA appendix 300-A.2(27).
28 See NAFTA appendix 300-A.2(12).
29 See NAFTA appendix 300-A.2(14). For a definition of extended trade balance, see appendix 300-A.2(27). In calculating its extended trade balance, existing manufacturers are allowed to use trade balance surpluses earned before model year 1991, up to U.S.$150 million a year, until the surpluses have been eliminated. See appendix 300-A.2(16). General Motors de México, S.A. de C.V., lobbied for that provision. Having a large number of *maquilas*, General Motors has traditionally been exporting most of its production and has not been able to use more than 20 per cent of its trade surpluses.
30 See NAFTA appendix 300-A.2(17).
31 See NAFTA appendix 300-A.2(22).
32 See NAFTA annex I, I-M-34, 35.
33 See NAFTA appendix 300-A.2(24) and appendix 300-A.1(4).
34 See NAFTA annex 913.5 a-3.
35 See Motor Vehicle Manufacturers' Association, *Member Company Profiles of the Motor Vehicle Manufacturers's Association, 1993 Edition* (Toronto: Motor Vehicle Manufacturers' Association, 1993), 5–16; James M. Rubenstein, *The Changing of the US Auto Industry: A Geographical Analysis* (New York: Routledge, 1992), 32; and Canada, *Royal Commission on the Automotive Industry* (Ottawa: Queen's Printer, 1961), 5–6.
36 U.S. Department of Commerce, International Trade Commission, *U.S. Industry and Trade Outlook '99*, 36–12, 37–6.
37 For a good overview of the Mexican auto industry, see Isabel Studer, 'The Impact of NAFTA on the Mexican Auto Industry,' *North American Outlook* 5 (Nov. 1994): 20–55; and Rogelio Ramírez de la O, 'The Impact of NAFTA on the Auto Industry in Mexico,' in Sidney Weintraub and Christopher Sands, eds., *The North American Auto Industry Under NAFTA* (Washington, DC: Center for Strategic and International Studies, 1998), 48–91.
38 Rámirez de la O, 'The Impact of NAFTA on the Auto Industry in Mexico.'
39 See *Report of the Royal Commission on the Automotive Industry* (Bladen Report), and *Canadian Automotive Industry, Performance and Proposals for*

Progress: Inquiry into the Automotive Industry (Reisman Report) (Ottawa: Minister of Supply and Services Canada, 1978).

40 James G. Dykes, *Background on the Canada–U.S. Automotive Products Trade Agreement* (Toronto: Motor Vehicle Manufacturers' Association, Sept. 1975), 8.

41 See Bladen Report and Reisman Report.

42 As note 41.

43 Reisman Report, 18–20.

44 Ibid., 19.

45 Simon Reich, 'NAFTA, Foreign Investment and the Auto Industry: A Comparative Advantage,' in Maureen Appel Molot, ed., *Driving Continentally: National Policies and the North American Auto Industry* (Ottawa: Carleton University Press, 1993), 80–1. See also Mira Wilkins and Frank Hill, *American Business Abroad: Ford on Six Continents* (Detroit: Wayne State University Press, 1964), 37.

46 U.S. Public Advisory Board for Mutual Security, *A Trade and Tariff Policy in the National Interest* (Washington, DC: GPO, 1953), quoted in Eckes, *Opening America's Market*, 158.

47 See Douglas R. Nelson, 'The Political Economy of U.S. Automobile Protection,' in Anne O. Krueger, ed., *The Political Economy of American Trade Policy* (Chicago: University of Chicago Press, 1996), 133–91.

48 The Super 301 provisions of the Omnibus Trade and Competitiveness Act of 1988 requires the USTR to review U.S. trade expansion priorities, identify priority foreign-country practices whose elimination will most likely increase U.S. exports, report to Congress, and initiate section-301 investigations on any priority foreign-country practices that were not solved within twenty-one days of publication of the report. Super 301 expired in 1997 but was reinstituted on 26 January 1999, with a ninety-day deadline instead of twenty-one days.

49 See Douglas C. Bennett and Kenneth E. Sharpe, *Transnational Corporations versus the State: The Political Economy of the Mexican Auto Industry* (Princeton, NJ: Princeton University Press, 1985), 94–129.

50 See Florencio López-de-Silanes, 'Automobiles: Mexican Perspective,' in Sidney Weintraub with Luis Rubio F. and Alan D. Jones, eds., *U.S.–Mexican Industrial Integration: The Road to Free Trade* (Boulder, CO.: Westview Press, 1991), 100; and Glen Taylor, 'Strategic Manpower Policies and International Competitiveness: The Case of Mexico,' in Maureen Appel Molot, ed., *Driving Continentally: National Policies and the North American Auto Industry* (Ottawa: Carleton University Press, 1993), 239.

51 Robert Pear, 'U.S. Says Honda Skirted Customs Fees,' *New York Times*, 17 June 1991, D1.

52 'Lawmakers Call for Multiple Inquiries into Auto "Transplant" Business,' *Inside U.S. Trade*, 21 June 1991, 11.

53 Paul McKeague, 'Climate of Uncertainty: Ruling Raises Fears Investment Will Be Scared Off,' *Ottawa Citizen*, 8 March 1992, E5.

54 Chrysler Corporation, Ford Motor Company, and General Motors Corporation, *Proposed Policy Positions for the Automotive Provisions of a North American Free Trade Agreement*, 9 Sept. 1991, 3.

55 Peter Morton, 'Trilateral Free Trade Hinges on U.S., Mexico Resolving Differences,' *Financial Post*, 30 Dec. 1991, 29.

56 'U.S., Canada Auto Negotiators Seek to Clarify Mexican Offer on Auto Decree,' *Inside U.S. Trade*, 17 April 1992, 3.

57 'Mexico Offers to Phase out Auto Restrictions over 12 Years as Part of NAFTA, 8 May 1992, 5–6.

58 Francisco Gómez Maza, 'Ablandan los representantes estadounidenses su posición en la mesa del sector automotriz,' *El Financiero*, 7 May 1992, 14.

59 The NAFTA provisions on these issues are similar to what was agreed on at that time. See Darío Celis and Socorro López, 'Acuerdo trilateral sobre el capítulo automotriz; se establece un plazo de 10 años de transición,' *El Financiero*, 8 July 1992, 17.

60 'Administration Sends out Conflicting Signals on Concluding NAFTA Negotiations,' *Inside U.S. Trade*, 10 July 1992, 8–9.

61 'NAFTA Negotiators Grapple with New Auto Proposals before Ministerial,' *Inside U.S. Trade*, 24 July 1992, 14.

62 Darío Celis, 'Listo, el capítulo automotriz: A salvo, la industria nacional de autopartes dentro del tratado,' *El Financiero*, 29 July 1992, 1.

63 Joe Burey, 'Auditor: Memo Accusing Honda of Misstating North American Content Still Valid,' *Inside U.S. Trade*, 2 Aug. 1991, 8.

64 Jonathan Ferguson, 'Free Trade Delay Spells Bad News for Mulroney,' *Toronto Star*, 25 Aug. 1991, B4.

65 Chrysler, Ford, and General Motors, *Proposed Policy Positions*, 9 Sept. 1991, 7–8.

66 House Majority Leader Richard Gephardt (Dem., Mo.), Sander Levin (Dem., Mich.), Ron Wyden (Dem., Ore.), Donald Pease (Dem., Ohio), and Jim Moody (Dem., Wisc.).

67 'Canadian Parts Industry Pushes Increase in Car Content under NAFTA,' *Inside U.S. Trade (Special Report)*, 18 Oct. 1991, S-3.

68 'U.S., Canada, and Mexico to Kick off NAFTA Negotiations Next Week,' *Inside U.S. Trade*, 17 Jan. 1992, 15.

69 'Rules of Origin Provision Included in Draft NAFTA Agreement,' *International Trade Reporter*, 25 March 1992, 562–7.

70 'Inventoriable costs' were defined as direct cost of labour and overhead or manufacturing costs, while 'period costs' meant R&D-related costs that can be allocated to a part, an operation, or a process.
71 'U.S. Expected to Push Streamlined Rules of Origin for Autos in NAFTA,' *Inside U.S. Trade*, 24 January 1992, 14.
72 *North American Report on Free Trade*, 9 March 1992.
73 'U.S., Canada Auto Negotiators Seek to Clarify Mexican Offer on Auto Decree,' *Inside U.S. Trade*, 17 April 1992, 3.
74 Ibid.
75 'U.S. Accepts New Approach for Auto Rules of Origin, Expects Higher Threshold,' *Inside U.S. Trade*, 29 May 1992, 2.
76 Ibid., 1.
77 'Ottawa May Hike Car Rule to 60%,' *Toronto Star*, 4 June 1992, D1.
78 'Canada May Accept 60 Percent Content in NAFTA Autos, But Seeks Phase-In,' *Inside U.S. Trade*, 3 July 1992, 3.
79 'U.S. Accepts New Approach for Auto Rules of Origin, Expects Higher Threshold,' *Inside U.S. Trade*, 29 May 1992, 2.

6. The Pharmaceutical Industry: Ending Canada's Compulsory Licensing Regime

1 A compulsory licensing system requires the patentee to grant a licence to those willing to pay a royalty.
2 United States General Accounting Office, *Report to the Congress: North American Free Trade Agreement: Assessment of Major Issues*, 92.
3 Article 1709(11) also requires that, in any infringing proceeding relating to a patent process, the burden of establishing that the allegedly infringing product was made by a process other than the patented process be placed on the defendant when the product is new and when there is a substantial likelihood that the allegedly infringing product was made by the process and the patent owner has been unable, through reasonable efforts, to determine the process actually used.
4 Article 1720(6) provides that this requirement in article 1709(7) does not have to be imposed for use without the authorization of the right holder, where authorization for such use was granted before the text of the Draft Final Act Embodying the Results of the Uruguay Round of Multilateral Trade Negotiations 'became known.'
5 Neff and Smallson, *NAFTA: Protecting and Enforcing Intellectual Property Rights*, 82.
6 Ibid., 83.

7 U.S. Department of Commerce, International Trade Administration, *NAFTA Opportunities: Pharmaceuticals* (Washington, DC: International Trade Administration, 1993), 2–3.

8 Standards are approved by a recognized body and are not mandatory, whereas compliance with technical regulations is mandatory.

9 Myron J. Gordon and David J. Fowler, *The Drug Industry: A Case Study of the Effects of Foreign Control on the Canadian Economy* (Ottawa: Canadian Institute for Economic Policy, 1981), 34.

10 Jonathan Liebenau, *Medical Science and Medical Industry: The Formation of the American Pharmaceutical Industry* (Baltimore, MD: Johns Hopkins University Press, 1987), 11–29.

11 Peter Temin, *Taking Your Medicine: Drug Regulation in the United States* (Cambridge, MA: Harvard University Press, 1980).

12 U.S. Department of Commerce, International Trade Administration, *U.S. Industry & Trade Outlook '99* (Washington, DC: ITA, 1998), 11–10 – 11–13.

13 Ibid.

14 For more on the Mexican pharmaceutical industry, see Enrique Gruner Kronheim, 'Pharmaceuticals: Mexican Perspective,' in Sidney Weintraub with Luis Rubio F. and Alan D. Jones, eds., *U.S.–Mexican Industrial Integration: The Road to Free Trade* (Boulder, Col.: Westview Press, 1991), 180–9; Alfredo Salómon, 'La industria farmacéutica en tiempos de competencia,' *Comercio Exterior* 47 (March 1997): 203–7; and Yamilia Orozco Herrera and Luis E. Montelongo Comas, 'La industria farmacéutica mexicana: Apertura comercial y nueva ley de patentes,' *El Mercado de Valores* (Sept. 1998): 22–33.

15 This section draws on Robert Goyer, *Regulatory Aspects and Their Influence on Pharmaceutical Research and on the Introduction of Drugs in Canada* (Ottawa: Minister of Supply and Services, 1986).

16 Hayhurst, 'Intellectual Property Laws in Canada: The British Tradition, the American Influence and the French Factor,' 265–327.

17 Canada, Royal Commission of Inquiry on the Pharmaceutical Industry, *Report of the Royal Commission of Inquiry on the Pharmaceutical Industry* (Ottawa: Minister of Supply and Services, 1985), 14–15.

18 Canada, Royal Commission on Patents, Copyright and Industrial Design, *Report on Patents of Invention* (Ottawa: Queen's Printer, 1960); Canada, Department of Justice, Restrictive Trade Practices Commission, *Report Concerning the Manufacture, Distribution and Sale of Drugs* (Ottawa: Queen's Printer, 1963); Canada, Royal Commission on Health Services, *Report of the Royal Commission on Health Services* (Ottawa: Queen's Printer, 1964); and

Canada, House of Commons, Special Committee on Drug Costs and Prices, *Second Report of the Special Committee of the House of Commons on Drug Costs and Prices* (Ottawa: Queen's Printer, 1966–67).

19 *Report of the Royal Commission of Inquiry on the Pharmaceutical Industry,* 425–6.

20 Ibid., 363.

21 For an excellent overview of Bill C-22, see Robert M. Campbell and Leslie A. Pal, *The Real World of Canadian Politics: Cases in Process and Policy* (Peterborough, ON: Broadview Press, 1989), 53–106.

22 World Trade Organization, *Trade Policy Review – Canada 1998* (Geneva: WTO, March 1999), 78.

23 Patented Medicine Prices Review Board, *Tenth Annual Report for the Year Ended December 31, 1997* (Ottawa: PMPRB, 1997).

24 Ibid., 8.

25 World Trade Organization, *Trade Policy Review – Canada 1998,* 78.

26 James Harvey Young, *Securing the Federal Food and Drugs Act of 1906* (Princeton, NJ: Princeton University Press, 1989).

27 Food and Drug Administration, 'Milestones in U.S. Food and Drug Law History,' *FDA Backgrounder* (3 May 1999).

28 Ibid.

29 Temin, *Taking Your Medicine,* 18–37.

30 Ibid.

31 The FDA had been under the Federal Security Agency since 1940.

32 Temin, *Taking Your Medicine,* 18–37.

33 See PhRMA, *Pharmaceutical Industry Profile* (Washington, DC: PhRMA, 1999), available at http://www.phrma.org.

34 Ibid.

35 Ibid.

36 England had adopted the Statute of Monopolies in 1623.

37 For an excellent review of the history of industrial property law in Mexico, see David Rangel Medina, *Derecho intelectual* (Mexico City: McGraw-Hill, 1998), 3–5.

38 General Agreement on Tariffs and Trade, *Trade Policy Review – Mexico* (Geneva: GATT, 1993), 159–60.

39 Fela Viso Gurovitch and Carmen Giral Barnes, 'Mexico,' in Richard N. Spivey, Albert I. Wertheimer, and T. Donald Rucker, eds., *International Pharmaceutical Services: The Drug Industry and Pharmacy Practice in Twenty-three Major Countries of the World* (New York: Pharmaceutical Products Press, 1992), 335.

40 See FTA 2004.

41 Canada, Interdepartmental Working Group, *1991 Pharmaceutical Review* (Ottawa, Oct. 1991), 52.

42 Ibid., 54.

43 Nicolas Y.J. Crowley, *Pill Pirating or Drug Heist? Canadian Regulation of the Pharmaceutical Industry* (New Orleans: Association of Canadian Studies in the United States, 19 Nov. 1993), 31.

44 'International Trade, Talks Unlikely to Produce Reductions in Non-Tariff Barriers, Experts Say,' *Daily Report for Executives*, 31 July 1991, A-14.

45 David Crane, 'Trade Talks Jeopardizing Drug Prices,' *Toronto Star*, 20 November 1991, C9.

46 Ross Duncan and Dave Blaker, *Trends in the Pharmaceutical Industry in Canada in the Post-1987 Environment* (Ottawa: Interdepartmental Working Group, 1991), 60.

47 Shawn McCarthy, 'Canadian Manufacturers Warn Ottawa,' *Toronto Star*, 5 Dec. 1991, B1.

48 Milt Freudenheim, 'Canadians See Rise in Drug Costs,' *New York Times*, 16 Nov. 1992, D1.

49 'Negotiators Close on NAFTA Intellectual Property, But Obstacles Remain,' *Inside U.S. Trade*, 8 May 1992, 11.

50 'IPC Letter to Hills on NAFTA, *Inside U.S. Trade*,13 March 1992, 18. In November 1991, the United States Council for International Business had also called for the elimination of compulsory licensing by the Canadians. See 'U.S. Council IPR Recommendations for NAFTA,' *Inside U.S. Trade*, 15 Nov. 1991, 6.

51 See the Dallas Composite Text, Intellectual Property, article 2210(11).

52 'Negotiators Close on NAFTA Intellectual Property, But Obstacles Remain,' *Inside U.S. Trade*, 8 May 1992, 10.

53 NAFTA 1709 and article 31 of TRIPS.

54 'Negotiators Close on NAFTA Intellectual Property, But Obstacles Remain,' *Inside U.S. Trade*, 8 May 1992, 10.

Index